PRE-PĀṆINIAN GRAMMAR

By the same author

(Marathi)

Bhāratīya Sāhityaśāstra

Rukmiṇī Svayaṁvara

Alaṁkārapradīpa

Sāṅkhyakārikā

Spandakārikā of Rāmakaṇṭha

Bhāratīya Sāhityaśāstrātīla Saundaryakalpanā

Rāṣṭrīya Utthānāt Sāhityāce Sthāna

Varhāḍacā Kūḷakāyadā (Berar Tenancy Act)

Madhyapradesh Public Trusts Act

Sanskrit Puṣpāñjali (Ed.)

(English)

Indological Papers

(Dr. Deshpande's writings/essays on Indology published from time to time)

Abhinavagupta

PRE-PĀṆINIAN GRAMMAR

G. T. DESHPANDE

Popular Prakashan
www.popularprakashan.com

POPULAR PRAKASHAN PVT. LTD.
301, Mahalaxmi Chambers
22, Bhulabhai Desai Road
Mumbai-400026

ISBN: 978-81-7154-893-4

First Printed 2011

Typesetting
Santosh Gaikwad

Printed in India
by Rama Printers
4743/23, Ansari Road, Darya Ganj
New Delhi-110 002

Published by Ramdas Bhatkal for
Popular Prakashan Pvt. Ltd.,
301, Mahalaxmi Chambers
22, Bhulabhai Desai Road
Mumbai 400026

FOREWORD

The traditional Indian science of language forms an important chapter in the history of the development of Indian thought. It is, in fact, one of the major contributions to the world tradition of knowledge and learning. It has a long history of over three thousand years which begins with the beginning of civilization in this country. Some of the eminent scholars of the West have recognised the Indian science of language as the foremost science to have evolved in India. The book entitled *Pre-Pāṇinian Grammar* by late Dr. G. T. Deshpande needs, therefore, no justification for the students of Indology.

Not only is this book an analysis of the linguistic material gleaned from the Pre-Pāṇinian works, it epitomizes the vast grammatical data spread over centuries from the Vedic period down to the time of Pāṇini covering more than a millennium of ancient Indian thought. Grammatical facts reflected in the *Padapāṭhas*, the *Prātiśākhyas* and the *Nirukta*, the three milestones in Indian linguistics, are discussed threadbare. The systematic arrangement of the data with an awareness of the significance of every single detail is very impressive. Exhaustive lists of the Pre-Pāṇinian grammarians as well as the statistical data concerning the contents of the *Nirukta* and many other minute details speak for the painstaking and thorough study of the whole literature by the author. The first impression a reader gets about the book is, therefore, that of exhaustive treatment of the material.

This is, however, not a mere compilation of the Pre-Pāṇinian grammatical material. Nor is it just a survey. Both the beginning and the concluding chapters appear to point at the thesis the learned author of this book wants to put forth; the thesis that the whole linguistic tradition in India regards Sanskrit as a single, indivisible language. On a number of occasions the reader comes across discussions about the artificial division of Sanskrit into *Vaidika* and *Laukika.* And every discussion ends with the conclusion that the tradition looks at this division as unreal. The author is not merely satisfied with this thesis of the indivisibility of Sanskrit as a major presupposition of the Indian linguistic tradition. The whole exercise of the elaborate arguments through all the chapters boils down to Pāṇini's affiliation with the Pre-Pāṇinian, rather, the Vedic linguistic tradition. Despite its title the book is aimed at offering new directions to the Pāṇinian studies in the light of the Pre-Pāṇinian material. A corollary to the thesis of the indivisibility of Sanskrit is the thesis, the confirmation of the traditional view, that Pāṇinian grammar is primarily a *Vedāṅga.*

This claim put forth by the author in this book may be challenged, since recent studies have convincingly proved that Pāṇinian grammar is not a *Vedāṅga;* it is primarily a grammar of Sanskrit spoken in his time and only secondarily is it a Vedic grammar. However, the observation made here, namely, that we cannot demarcate between *Vaidika* and *Laukika* Sanskrit in Pāṇini's grammar, except when there is a specific mention, is absolutely correct. The excellent exposition in the last chapter of the four rules in the *Aṣṭādhyāyī* which are shorn of their Vedic context and included in the *Laukika* section in the *Siddhāntakaumudī* establishes the point beyond doubt. Here is an implicit warning to the students of Pāṇini not to look at the *Aṣṭādhyāyī* through the window of the *Siddhāntakaumudī* alone. It is shown with illustrations how a Pāṇinian student is misguided by Bhaṭṭoji Dīkṣita. It is here that we see the critical thinking and deep insight of the author. Though we are fortunate to be benefited by his profound scholarship reflected in this book, we are indeed unfortunate that his dream of writing another book, a fresh study of Pāṇini in the light of the observations in this book, remains unrealised.

Even the incidental observations made by the author testify to his all-round scholarship. The discussion on the usage of the word *paśu,* on the *mantra* part *yavanānām pataye namaḥ,* on the change of meaning of the word *yajatrāḥ* are a few examples.

A serious student of the Indian Intellectual tradition will find this book useful both as a lesson in theorization and as a summary of some noteworthy theoretical points. The progressive march of the *Prātiśākhyas* is, for instance, summed up simply as proceeding from *padasandhi* to *varṇasandhi.* Similarly, the evolution of Indian grammatical thought is described as proceeding from nomenclatory to prescriptive. The question *kasmāt* in the *Nirukta* is described as a question with reference to the *pravṛttinimitta.* The contrast between the earlier and the later linguistic traditions is made clear by pointing out that the earlier tradition aimed at splitting *saṁhitā* into *padas* and *padyas* while the later tradition aimed at building the *padas.* A modern student may not agree with the description of the *Nirukta* as *sāmānyaśāstra* and of *Vyākaraṇa* as *viśeṣaśāstra* or with the meaning of the word *vṛtti* in this book. But every reader will, I am sure, be impressed by the upright personality of the veteran Indologist committed to the search for truth and leaving no stone unturned in his endeavour to achieve the goal. It is reflected on every page of this book which contains the cream of his lifelong pursuit of knowledge.

Pune, 2011 **Saroja Bhate**

Dr. Ganesh Tryambak Deshpande

Someone who has not known Dr. Ganesh Tryambak Deshpande (1910-1989) either personally or through his works might consider even factual statements made about him as exaggerations, but those who knew him would consider them as understatements. Indeed, words fail to portray his personality and to bring out the true value of his contribution to under-standing, interpretation and appreciation of Indian Poetics. Fortunate are those who knew him in person and through his writings, and I am one such person.

Dr. Deshpande was the Head of the Department of Sanskrit, Nagpur University when I joined for my final M. A. in Marathi in 1958-59. Earlier we had been introduced by Prof. P. S. Rege (then Principal, Ismail Yusuf College, Mumbai), a well-known Marathi poet. However it was only a nodding acquaintance and it continued to be so. It was only when I had an opportunity of studying his Marathi book *Bhāratīya Sāhityaśāstra* (Indian Poetics) that I had the revelation of the unfathomable depth of his study and his scholarship embellished with utmost humility of the person. That work of his retains even to this day in the 21st century its towering status.

P. S. Rege, W. L Kulkarni and R. B. Joshi, all well known names from Mumbai in the field of Marathi literature, were great admirers of Dr. Deshpande. They were stunned to see the profundity of his diligent studies, thinking and perception which spoke of his singular devotion and dedication to the subject of his studies. They organised his lectures in Mumbai Marathi Sahitya Sangh (मुंबई मराठी साहित्य संघ), Mumbai, on the subject Bhāratīya Sāhityaśāstra. An unabridged version of that lecture-series is his book *Bhāratīya Sāhityaśāstra* (Popular Prakashan, Mumbai 1958). This book no doubt won for him the degree of Doctor of Letters from Nagpur University, an award from Maharashtra State

Government and also the Sahitya Akademi Award. But above all that, the real value of contribution of this book was the new direction, the new vision it lent to the studies in literary criticism. Its impact on the thinking and perception of subsequent literary critics cannot be overstated. *Saundarya Āṇi Sāhitya* (सौंदर्य आणि साहित्य, Mouj Prakashan, 1955) by B. S. Mardhekar is the only work that could be considered com-parable to Dr. Deshpande's *Bhāratīya Sāhityaśāstra.* Mardhekar's *Saundarya Āṇi Sāhitya* rendered all earlier works on Aesthetics obsolete. *Bhāratīya Sāhityaśāstra* did precisely the same in respect of earlier works on Literary Criticism. These two books are the beacon lights in the field of Aesthetics and Literary Criticism respectively. This apart, *Bhāratīya Sāhityaśāstra* is a guiding force in appreciating the study of Poetics. The four principles enunciated in it to approach a critique are :

1) Lakṣyānusārī lakṣaṇam;

2) Prādhānyena vyapadeśā bhavanti;

3) Yathottaram munīnām prāmāṇyam;

4) Siddha-paramatānuvāda.

Unfortunately, this has not received due attention of the students of Literary Criticism. Following this four-fold principle, Dr. Deshpande has clearly brought out the dividing line between *Laukika-Alaukikavāda* and explained the *Alaukikavāda* of Bharata Muni and Abhinavagupta. This unique contribution of Dr. Deshpande is of significance to scholars from all over the world.

Born in a middle-class family of agriculturists in a remote village, Wadnergangai, Amaravati District (Maharashtra), Ganesh Tryambak Deshpande studied Law after his graduation with Sanskrit as one of the subjects for B. A. He did practise as a lawyer for a few days, but the sudden demise of his father compelled him to take to teaching in Amaravati. A decade after his graduation, he completed his post-graduation in Sanskrit and topped the list in Nagpur University. He taught Sanskrit and Law in Shivaji College, Amaravati until 1958 when he joined the Post Graduate Teaching Department (PGTD) at Nagpur University. He was a born teacher and a good orator. During his tenure as Head of the Department of Sanskrit at PGTD, he introduced the disciplines of Grammar and Vedas for Post-Graduate studies. The research work was at its highest pitch during his association with the Department and it is to his credit that the maximum number of doctoral dissertations were completed in the Department during his tenure. This would also vouch for his commitment to students and the studies. No wonder he was granted Emeritus Professorship by the University Grants Commission. He was Visiting Professor at Benaras Hindu University, Benaras, and Kalidasa Sanskrit University at Ujjain.

Dr. Deshpande's other works in chronological order are:

1) *Sanskrit Puṣpāñjali* (Ed.)
(Thakur & Co., Amaravati - 1950)

2) *Rukmiṇī-svayaṁvara* (Ed.)
(G. V. Joshi, Amaravati - 1951)

3) *Berar Tenancy Act*
(Thakur & Co., Amaravati - 1952)

4) *Madhya Pradesh Public Trusts Act*
(Thakur & Co., Amaravati - 1953)

5) *Alaṁkārapradīpa*
(Thakur & Co., Amaravati - 1954)

6) *Sāṅkhyakārikā*
(Navayug Book Depot - Amaravati - 1955)

7) *Spandakārikā*
(Series of Essays)
(Chhanda, Mumbai - 1957-58)

8) *Indological Papers*
(Dr. Deshpande's writings/essays on Indology published from time to time)
(Vidarbha Sanshodhan Mandal, Nagpur -1961)

9) *Bhāratīya Sāhityaśāstrātīla Saundaryakalpanā*
(Lecture Series)
(Publication Divn., Delhi -1962)

10) *Rāṣṭrīya Utthānāta Sāhityāce Sthāna*
(Information & Broadcasting Ministry, Delhi - 1964)

11) *Abhinavagupta*
(Sahitya Akademi, Delhi - 1989)

In addition to this, Dr. Deshpande wrote and published a large number of articles on Sanskrit Grammar, Linguistics, Vedas and Literary Criticism. It is possible that some of his earlier books could have been prompted by the pressures of worldly necessities. Yet looking at the quality of these works even the pressure of circumstances could be considered a blessing in disguise. His inborn intellect was honed with his studies of Sanskrit Literature and Criticism, Indian Philosophy, Kashmir Shaivism, Law, Grammar and Vedas. Ordinarily it is natural that an author's quality of literary appreciation pervades his writings in literary criticism. However, in the writings of Dr. Deshpande, one cannot miss his sharp and incisive intellect and literary acumen in dealing with various topics and intricate issues.

From 1964 I lived in the vicinity of Dr. Deshpande's residence and even in the PGTD, Nagpur, the Marathi Department where I worked was adjacent to the Sanskrit Department. As such I was the beneficiary of his intellectual and scholarly association to my heart's content. I have been teaching his book *Bhāratīya Sāhityaśāstra* for years and it has positively influenced my views and writings on Poetics. I am grateful to him for that.

His book *Pre-Pāṇinian Grammar* is being published after his death and after a considerable lapse of time. Whenever I uttered a word of praise for his *Bhāratīya Sāhityaśāstra* he would feel embarrassed and once he mentioned in all humility, 'I am now writing on Pre-Pāṇinian Grammar and hope that book will turn out to be as good.' While this work was to be in several volumes, the project remained incomplete due to his ill-health. Even this first volume, which was to serve more as an introduction to the whole project, will motivate many of the students and scholars to undertake further research in the topic. I am sure, like *Bhāratīya Sāhityaśāstra,* this book will generate fresh perspectives in the study of Sanskrit Grammar.

It is more as exception that works of such stature are produced and fortunate are those who get an opportunity to partake of the joy of studying such works and learning from such scholarly authors. I have been such a fortunate one.

My grateful respects to his memories.

Dr. Da. Bhi. Kulkarni
(Retd.) Professor and Head of Department,
Marathi (PGTD), Nagpur University.

Publisher's Note

Sometime before 1980, Prof. G. T. Deshpande handed over to us the manuscript of *Pre-Pāṇinian Grammar*. This was the first part of a series which, to the extent we remember, was meant to be in six parts. Two decades earlier Prof. Deshpande had written a comprehensive work on Indian Poetics, *Bhāratīya Sāhityaśāstra*. In the first part of that work, he had traced the evolution of Aesthetic theory as developed by Sanskrit Aesthetists. In the second part he had tried to reinterpret the positions taken by various philosophers in the light of this evolutionary approach. In a similar manner, this project on Grammar would have tried to interpret how the Grammarians evolved the seemingly rigid Sanskrit Grammar and tried to interpret *Vyākaraṇa* from a similar evolutionary viewpoint.

On the one hand, with advancing age, he was unable to complete this project; on the other hand, the limitations of letter-press composing made the setting of this manuscript a hazardous job. As publishers, we plead guilty to not finding the right technical solutions while the author was in a position to see the book through the press. It was only after the computer-setting was sufficiently advanced to take care of all the intricacies required for a subject of this nature, that we were able to undertake the production of this manuscript.

Fortunately, the author's daughter-in-law Dr. Manjushree Deshpande had in the meantime pursued the study of Sanskrit with great zeal. She had not only completed her Doctorate in Alaṁkāraśāstra but was also working as a Research Fellow in the Centre for Advanced Studies in Sanskrit, Pune University. She is presently working as visiting faculty in the Department of Sanskrit, University of Pune. We could therefore depend upon her to go through the book on behalf of her late father-in-law. For proofs she also received help from her brother-in-law Shri

Vinaykumar Deshpande who is a keen student of languages. Thanks are also due to Dr. Siddharth Wakankar for his erudite suggestions and for meticulously going through the proofs. We are also grateful to Mrudula Joshi and Jyotsna Borde for their assistance.

Mumbai, 2011 **Ramdas Bhatkal**

Acknowledgement

A little over two decades have passed since Prof. G. T. Deshpande deserted his kith and kin, academic associates and social acquaintances. Yet his scholarship and love continue to be remembered and cherished by one and all who knew him as a scholar or in a personal capacity. He was variously known as G. T., Nanasaheb or as Prof. Deshpande.

We, the members of Deshpande family, do bow in gratitude and respect to all such associates.

This work, fondly published by Ramdas Bhatkal for Popular Prakashan, is a very singular salute to Nanasaheb. It is significant that in 1958 *Bharatiya Sahityashastra* was published by him in Marathi and was followed by a Hindi translation in 1962 and an English translation in 2009. Now this major work is being published posthumously by the same publisher.

Mention of Dr. Mrs. Saroja Bhate and Dr. D. B. Kulkarni who have penned the Foreword and the Biographical Note respectively must be made. Being a posthumous publication, many other fans of Nanasaheb like Prof. K. R. Joshi stood by us. Sincere thanks to all such friends, associates and wellwishers.

Such scholarly works need meticulous care as well as devotion and dedication. In this respect the unfailing efforts of Mrudula Joshi and her expertise need to be acknowledged. Jyotsna Borde with her special skills and vast experience in checking the references and the proofs and Santosh Gaikwad of Pune, who is experienced in typesetting challenging and complicated books with enthusiasm, have helped immensely.

Members of the Author's family

Contents

Chapter One

DAIVĪ VĀK and MĀNUṢĪ VĀK

संस्कृतं नाम दैवी वागन्वाख्याता महर्षिभिः (Kāvyādarśa, 1.33)

Sanskrit is termed *Devavāṇī*. Daṇḍin equates these two terms in the above statement and further says that Sanskrit is the *Daivī vāk* as explained by the great sages. Evidently, the three sages referred to here are the three famous *munis* of *grammar*, viz., Pāṇini, Kātyāyana and Patañjali. These three sages have explained to us the words in the *Devavāṇī* in respect of their form, meaning and relation. The words they have explained are of two types: the *Vaidika* and the *Laukika*.[1] These three sages are not the makers of these words. The words, meanings and their relations are, for them, already established facts based on the *Veda* and the *Loka*. They only explained them to us and, as Kātyāyana tells us,[2] gave a science for our guidance as a matter of *Dharmaniyama* resulting in the *abhyudaya*.

The earliest extant effort in this direction in its complete form is available to us in the form of the famous *Aṣṭādhyāyī* of Pāṇini. Pāṇini, however, is not the first *muni* to do this work for us. He himself refers to ten predecessors of his by name, and to the *Ācāryāḥ*, who might be his teachers (referred to respectfully), or the term may indicate those ancient teachers referred to by the *Prātiśākhyas* by using the same term.[3]

---

1. अथ शब्दानुशासनम्... केषां शब्दानाम् ?
लौकिकानां वैदिकानां च । - *Mbh., Paspaśā*, Vol. I, P. 1

2. प्रसिद्धे शब्दार्थसम्बन्धे, लोकतोऽर्थप्रयुक्ते
शब्दप्रयोगे शास्त्रेण धर्मनियमः । - also *Ibid*, pp. 6-8.
न तद्वच्छब्दान्प्रयोक्ष्यमाणो वैयाकरणकुलं गत्वाह -
'कुरु शब्दान्, प्रयोक्ष्ये' इति । - *Ibid*, p. 7.

3. Yudhiṣṭhira Mīmāṁsaka has given an extensive list of the pre-Pāṇinian Grammarians. See संस्कृत व्याकरणशास्त्र का इतिहास, भाग १ pp. 51-56.

Yāska's *Nirukta*, the *Ṛk-Prātiśākhya* and the *Taittirīya Prātiśākhya* are generally treated to be earlier than Pāṇini's work. The authors of these treatises also mention their predecessors, who, taken together, number fifty-seven. Even though the *Prātiśākhyas* are not treated as strictly grammatical works of the nature of *Aṣṭādhyāyī*, still so far as they deal with the topics of *saṁhitā, lopa, āgama, svara* and the like, and in so far as Pāṇini also has dealt with these topics in his work and has also used the terms from the *Prātiśākhyas* [4] at many places, we may say that those also are grammatical activities relating of course to the Vedic *pada* and the Vedic *saṁhitā*. They do not deal with the *laukika* words except the word *'iti'* used in the *Padapātha* called *'anārṣa iti.'*[5] The case of *Nirukta* is somewhat different. It deals with the etymology of Vedic words; but while deriving the Vedic words it resorts, at times, to the *bhāṣika dhātus.*[6] We have in *Nirukta* a division of *dhātus* as *naigama* and *bhāṣika.*[7] *Nirukta* further refers to *Vaiyākaraṇas* as a school, and calls itself an appendix of grammar [8] leading the grammar to perfection. In the *Prātiśākhyas* we get such terms as *ārṣa iti* and *anārṣa iti* [9] and also the term *Chandobhāṣā*.[10] This indicates that the words were divided into *ārṣa* and *anārṣa*, as also the speech into *Chandobhāṣā* and the *Bhāṣā* that was not *Chāndasaḥ*. If we start from Patañjali and go

---

4. For example : 'अप्लुतवदुपस्थिते.' P. 6.1.29.

5. प्राक् चानार्षादितिकरणात् पदान्तान् तद्युक्तानाम् - *Ṛk-Pr.* I.58.

6. अथापि भाषिकेभ्यो धातुभ्यो नैगमाःकृतो भाष्यन्ते - *Nir.* II.2.

7. न सर्वाणीति गार्ग्यः, वैयाकरणानां चैके । - *Ibid* I.12.

8. तदिदं विद्यास्थानं व्याकरणस्य कार्त्स्न्यम् । - *Ibid* I.15.

9. प्रकृत्या इति करणादौ प्रगृह्याः स्वरेषु चार्ष्यां प्रथमो यथोक्तम् । *Ṛk. Pr.* II.51.

10. गुरुत्वं लघुता साम्यं ह्रस्वदीर्घप्लुतानि च ।
लोपागमविकाराश्च प्रकृतिर्विक्रमः क्रमः ॥
स्वरितोदात्तनीचत्व श्वासो नादोऽङ्गमेव च ।
एतत् सर्वं तु विज्ञेयं छन्दोभाषामधीयता ॥ - *T. Pr.* XXIV. 5.

back to the Veda we come across the following notions: the *laukika* and the *Vaidika* words in the *Mahābhāṣya*, the *Chāndasaḥ* and the *bhāṣā* in Pāṇini, the *bhāṣika* and the *naigama dhātus* in the *Nirukta* and the *ārṣa* and *anārṣa* words in the *Prātiśākhya*. The basis of the *Prātiśākhya* is the *Padapāṭha*. The *Padapāṭha* is the first *pauruṣeya* effort to analyse and explain the *apauruṣeya* speech of the *Veda*.[11]

What does his distinction indicate? Does it mean that the *laukika* words are in any way different from the *Vaidika* ones in form, sense and relation? The reply is that they are not. But this is the *siddhānta*. There is a *pūrvapakṣa* in the *Pūrvamīmāṁsā* which indicates that there were thinkers who held that the *laukika* and the *Vaidika* words were not the same in form, sense and relation. *Śabara* on I. iii. 30. states the *pūrvapakṣa* as follows:

'किं य एव लौकिकाः शब्दास्त एव वैदिका उतान्ये ।
यदा त एव, किं त एव तेषामर्था ये लोके, उतान्ये इति
संशयः । तत्र अन्ये लौकिकाः शब्दाः, अन्ये वैदिका,
अन्ये च तेषामर्था इति ब्रूमः । कुतः, व्यपदेशभेदात्
रूपभेदाच्च । ...शब्दान्यत्वाच्च न त एव अर्थाः ।
... तस्मादमीषामन्ये अर्थाः।'

The *pūrvapakṣin* here says that the words in the *Veda* are not the same as *laukika* words because of different name (व्यपदेश) and form (रूप). Thus being different in form they are different in meaning. On this the *siddhāntin* says as follows:

प्रयोगचोदनाभावादर्थैकत्वमविभागात् (पू. मी. I. iii.30)
एवं प्राप्ते-ब्रूमः । य एव लौकिकाः शब्दास्त एव वैदिकाः ।
त एव तेषामर्था इति । कुतः । प्रयोगचोदनाभावात् ।
एवं प्रयोगचोदना संभवति यदि त एव शब्दाः त एवार्थाः ।
इतस्था शब्दान्यत्वेऽर्थो न प्रतीयेत । तस्माद् एकशब्दत्वम् ।
उच्यते । प्रयोजनमिदम् । हेतुर्व्यपदिश्यतामिति ।
ततो हेतुरुच्यते - अविभागादिति । न तेषामेषां च विभागमुपलभामहे ।

11. पदानां पौरुषेयत्वात् । पौरुषेयत्वादवग्रह करणस्य यथालक्षणं पदानि कर्तव्यानि - *Pradīpa* on P. VIII.1.16.

अत एवैकशब्दत्वम् । तांश्च तांश्चार्थानवगच्छामः ।
अतो नान्यत्वं च वदामः । तस्मात् त एव शब्दा अर्थाश्च ।

That is, the words that are *laukika* are the same that are *Vaidika*, for, on hearing the *Vaidika* word we understand what the *Veda* asks us to do. If the *laukika* and the *Vaidika* words are the same in form and also in meaning, then only, we can have the grasp of the Vedic command. If the words were different, the command would not have been understood. Then again, in the actual use of the words, we do not find any difference as the *laukika* and the *Vaidika*. Hence, the words are the same. From those words we understand respective meanings. Hence, the meanings also are the same in both the *laukika* and the *Vaidika* use. Hence, we hold that both in the *loka* and the *Veda* the words and their meanings are non-different.

Dealing with the topic in different context, *Nirukta* also comes to the same conclusion. The following statement of Yāska may be noted in this connection :

(१) इन्द्रियनित्यं वचनमौदुम्बरायणः । तत्र चतुष्ट्वं नोपपद्यते । अयुगपदुत्पन्नानां वा शब्दानामितरेतरोपदेशः । शास्त्रकृतो योगश्च । व्याप्तिमत्त्वाच्च शब्दस्य । अणीयस्त्वाच्च शब्देन संज्ञाकरणं व्यवहारार्थं लोके । तेषां मनुष्यवद् देवताभिधानम्। पुरुषविद्याऽनित्यत्वात् कर्मसंपत्तिर्मन्त्रो वेदे । (*Nir.* I.2)

(२) अनर्थका हि मन्त्राः (इति कौत्सः) (*Ibid* I. 15)
अर्थवन्तः शब्दसामान्यात् । (*Ibid* I. 16)

Yāska classifies the Vedic words into four categories: *nāma*, *ākhyāta*, *upasarga* and *nipāta*. Audumbarāyaṇa objects to this very attempt of the *Nairuktas*. He says that the classification of the words, the determination of the mutual relationship of the words, the effort at their derivation - all this is useless; for the words are *'anitya'*; they last only for the moment in which they are uttered. To this Yāska replies: The word is universal though the sound of the utterance is momentary (hence our attempt at *nirukti* is justified). If so, where is the necessity of uttering words? The reply is that by uttering words, we convey the meaning in minimum effort, and that facilitates our worldly affairs. The opponent has to admit this position. Then Yāska says: The meaning of the words used in our ordinary life is the same even when those words are used in the divine language, i.e., *Veda*. Then why use the Vedic *mantras* at the rituals, if the common language can carry the same import? The reply is that the knowledge of the man is very fickle; he may forget; he may commit mistakes. Hence to conduct ritual faultlessly *mantras* have been given in the *Veda*. At another place the opponent Kautsa says that the Vedic *mantras* have no meaning. To this Yāska replies that the Vedic *mantras* have meaning for, the words used in the *Veda* are the same as the *laukika* words and the meaning is also the same. In both these arguments Yāska maintains that the *laukika* and the *Vaidika* words are non-different and their meaning is also non-different.

The *Prātiśākhyas* also maintain the same view in their respective fields. In the *Vājasaneyi-Prātiśākhya*, Kātyāyana says :

स्वरसंस्कारयोः छन्दसि नियमः । लौकिकानामर्थपूर्वकत्वात् ।
न, समत्वात् (*Vāj. Pr.* I. 1-3)

The *Prātiśākhya* teaches the rules of *svara* and *saṁskāra* like *lopa, āgama,* etc. The *pūrvapakṣin* says that these are meant only for the *Vedic* words and not for the *laukika* ones; for, as the *laukika* words are used according to the motive of the speaker, no rules may be made for them. To this the author replies that these are not meant only for *Vaidika* words; they are equally applicable to the *laukika* words also; for, both these words are alike in form and sense. Uvaṭa says :

न चैतद् यद् वैदिकानां स्वरसंस्कारनियमोऽभ्युदयहेतुः । किं तर्हि । लौकिकानामपि नियमोऽभ्युदयहेतुरेव । कुतः ? समत्वात् तुल्यत्वात् शब्दानाम् । य एव लौकिकास्त एव वैदिकाः, त एव तेषामर्थाः । (*Ibid*)

So the final position is this. Whether we look at the problem from the view of the *Mīmāṁsaka* or the *Nairuktas* or the *Prātiśākhya*, the conclusion is that the *laukika* and the *Vaidika* words are non-different in form, sense and relation. The rules discovered in respect of *Vaidika* words, therefore, will equally apply to *laukika* words also.

If this is the position in respect of *laukika* and *Vaidika* words, then, what is the justification for this division? What follows is an attempt to answer this question.

Patañjali speaks of *laukika* and *Vaidika* words. This division corresponds to the *bhāṣā* and *chāndasaḥ* of Pāṇini. In the *Prātiśākhya* we have *'ārṣa'* and *'anārṣa'* division. What does the *Nirukta* say about words? We have, in the *Nirukta, bhāṣika* and *naigama* division, but that pertains to the roots, not words. Here we are reminded of the reply Yāska has given to Audumbarāyaṇa.[12] There he says तेषां मनुष्यवद्देवताभिधानम्. We at once catch an idea. There is देवताभिधान and there is मनुष्याभिधान, and both are alike. The four categories of words, viz, *nāma, ākhyāta, upasarga* and *nipāta*, are the same both in human speech (मनुष्याभिधान) and divine speech (देवताभिधान). The import of these four kinds of words is also the same in both. These four categories of words are used in the human speech for conveying the intent of man to man, and that in divine speech for conveying the intent of man to god, or of god to god.[13] There is however, one fundamental difference. While conveying our thoughts to man we may use these words in any order we like, but while conveying our intent to god we must maintain the fixed order of words (आनुपूर्वी). This order is given to us in the form of the Vedic *mantras*. Yāska says : पुरुषविद्याऽनित्यत्वात् कर्मसम्पत्तिर्मन्त्रो वेदे (*Nir.* I. 2.7) Thus, Yāska equates देवताभिधान to the *mantra* in the Veda.

The *Mīmāṁsakas* tell us that the *Veda* consists of two portions: the *Mantra* and the *Brāhmaṇa*. *Mantra* is again of three types:

12. *Vide, Supra,* page 4, quotation.

13. यथैव हि मनुष्याः प्रयोजनेषु नामाख्यातोपसर्गनिपातैः यथार्थमभिदधाति, एवमेव देवा अपि। ...तेषामेव शब्दानामियमेव व्यवस्था देवेष्वपि देवानपि प्रति । Durga on 'मनुष्यवद्देवताभिधानम्' - *Nir.* I.1.2.6.

Ṛk, Yajus, and Sāman.[14] *Mantra* is देवताभिधान or divine speech as Yāska tells us, and that it is like human speech in respect of form, sense, and relation. We thus get four types of speech *(Vāk).* They are:

वाक् (अभिधान)

दैवी वाक् (देवताभिधान) मानुषी वाक् (मनुष्याभिधान)

ऋक् यजुस् सामन्

While explaining the verse चत्वारि वाक्परिमिता पदानि । (*Rg.* I. 164-45) Yāska refers to these four types of speech as the opinion of the *Nairuktas.* He says: ऋचो यजूंषि सामानि, चतुर्थी व्यावहारिकी इति नैरुक्ता: Out of these the first three types are the *mantras.* This is not Yāska's own imagination. He supports his statement by a *Brāhmaṇa* passage which runs thus: "अथापि ब्राह्मणं भवति । सा वै वाक् सृष्टा चतुर्धा व्यभवत् । एष्वेव लोकेषु त्रीणि पशुषु तुरीयम् । या पृथिव्यां साग्नौ सा रथन्तरे । यान्तरिक्षे सा वायौ सा वामदेव्ये । या दिवि सादित्ये सा बृहति सा स्तनयित्नौ । अथ पशुषु । ततो या वागत्यरिच्यत तां ब्राह्मणे न्यदधुः । तस्मात् ब्राह्मणा उभयीं वाचं वदन्ति । या च देवानां या च मनुष्याणाम्" - (*Nir.* XIII. 9)

It has not been possible to trace the origin of this passage. But there are similar passages in the *Kāṭhaka* and the *Maitrāyaṇī* versions of *Yajurveda.* They are:

(१) सा वाक् चतुर्धा व्यभवत् । एषु लोकेषु त्रीणि तुरीयाणि, पशुषु तुरीयम्, या पृथिव्यां साग्नौ सा रथन्तरे, यान्तरिक्षे सा वाते सा वामदेव्ये, या दिवि सा बृहतौ सा स्तनयित्नौ, अथ पशुषु, ततो या वागत्यरिच्यत तां ब्राह्मणे न्यदधुः, तस्मात् ब्राह्मणः उभयीं वाचं वदति यश्च वेद यश्च न, या बृहद्रथंतरयोः यज्ञादेनं तया गच्छति, या पशुषु तया ऋते यज्ञम् । (*Maitrāyaṇī Saṁhitā,* I. II.5)

(२) वाग् दृष्टा चतुर्धा व्यभवत् । एषु लोकेषु त्रीणि तुरीयाणि, पशुषु तुरीयम्, या दिवि सा बृहति सा स्तनयित्नौ, यान्तरिक्षे सा वाते सा वामदेव्ये, या पृथिव्यां साग्नौ सा रथन्तरे, या पशुषु, तस्या यदत्यरिच्यत तां ब्राह्मणे न्यदधुः । तस्माद् ब्राह्मणः उभे

---

14. तच्चोदकेषु मन्त्राख्या । तेषामृग्यत्रार्थवशेन पादव्यवस्था । गीतिषु सामाख्या । शेषे यजुः शब्दः । पू.मी. II. 1.32, 35-37.

वाचौ वदति । दैवीं च मानुषीं च करोति ... या बृहद्रथन्तरयोः तया एवं यज्ञमागच्छति, या पशुषु तया ऋते यज्ञमाह । (*Kāṭhaka Saṁ.* XIV. 5)

If we put these three passages together for comparison we get the following points:

(i) The speech (*Vāk*) is divided in two main divisions, one consisting of three sections (त्रीणि तुरीयाणि) and the other consisting of one section (तुरीयम्);

(ii) The first section has its perfect form in the *sāman*,[15] the second division is found in the *paśus*;

(iii) Both these divisions are found present in the *Brāhmaṇa*;

(iv) Hence, the *Brāhmaṇa* speaks both these speeches, the 'daivī' and the *mānuṣī vāk*. *Maitrāyaṇī* uses the word *ubhayī* only, without mentioning what those 'two' are; the *Kāṭhaka* mentions them as *daivī* and *mānuṣī*; the *Brāhmaṇa* quoted by Yāska makes it still further clear and says: या च देवानां या च मनुष्याणाम्।

(v) The *saṁhitās* here equate *paśu* and *mānuṣa*. We need not be surprised at that. There is hardly any difference between the human child and *paśu*, both expressing their intents by cries. The *Atharvaveda* uses the word *paśu* to mean human child, in the *mantra* वितिष्ठन्ता मातुरस्या उपस्थात् नानारूपाः पशवो जायमानाः । (XIV.ii.25).[16] It is interesting to note that the *mantra* comes from the *Vivāha Sūkta* and confers the blessing on the bride that she should have children (*paśavaḥ*) playing on her lap;

(vi) The Brāhmaṇa uses *daivī vāk* in the sacrifice and he uses the *mānuṣī vāk* in the field other than sacrifice.

---

15. पुरुषस्य वाग् रसः । ऋचः साम रसः । *Chāndogya*, I.1.2.

16. See also देवीं वाचमजनयन्त देवास्तां विश्वरूपा पशवो वदन्ति (*Ṛg.* VII 100. 11). The words विश्वरूपाः पशवः have been interpreted as 'व्यक्तवाचः and अव्यक्तवाचः प्राणिनः' Here व्यक्तवाचः are human beings. See also Yudhiṣthira Mīmāṁsaka, *op. cit.* p. 3.

It will be clear now that the term *daivī vāk* is used to denote the *mantras* used in the sacrifice, i.e., the *Vedic mantras* of the type of *Ṛk, Yajus* and *Sāman*. 'This *vāk* in the form of loose words (*pada*) is *mānuṣī vāk*. Even the *Vedic padas* are *mānuṣī*.[17] The very *padas* in the form of *mantra* are *daivī*. The essence of the *mantra* lies in the fixed order (आनुपूर्वी), of *padas* used in them. We cannot substitute a synonym in the place of any word in the *mantra*, nor can we change the order in which they appear in the *mantra*. We cannot say वह्निमीळे पुरोहितम् in place of अग्निमीळे पुरोहितम्[18] or आयाहि वीतये वायो in place of वाय आयाहि वीतये ।[19] The words and their order must be maintained in the *mantras* in the same form as we received them. It is not so with *mānuṣī vāk*. There we may substitute a synonym or we may use the words in the order we like.

We may now be in a position to appreciate the opening statement of Patañjali in his *Bhāṣya*. He says:

अथ शब्दानुशासनम्... केषां शब्दानाम् । लौकिकानां वैदिकानां च । तत्र लौकिकास्तावत्- गौरश्वः पुरुषो हस्ती शकुनिर्मृगो ब्राह्मण इति । वैदिकाः खल्वपि- शन्नो देवीरभिष्टये । इषे त्वोर्जे त्वा । अग्निमीळे पुरोहितम् । अग्न आयाहि वीतये । इति।

Mbh,, Paspaśāhnika, Vol. I, P. 11.

Here Patañjali gives instances of the *laukika* and *the vaidika* words. Gauḥ, aśvaḥ, puruṣaḥ, etc. are the instances of *laukika*, but the examples of *vaidika* are given in the form of the mantras as they are recited.[20] He cannot give *Vaidika* examples as शम् । नः । देवीः । अभिष्टये । or इषे । त्वा । उर्जे । त्वा । or अग्निम् । ईळे । पुरःऽहितम् । for, that would not be in the mantra form and hence will not be an instance of the *daivī vāk* or the *vaidika* speech. The *padas* as such, even though taken from the *mantra*, will be as good as the *laukika*

---

17. See note No. 11, *Supra*.
18. *Ṛg.* I. 1.1.
19. *Ṛg.* I. 2. 1.
20. See *Pradīpa* on these examples in the *Mahābhāṣya* - तत्र लोके पदानुपूर्वीनियमाभावात् पदान्येव दर्शयति - गौरश्व इति । वेदे तु आनुपूर्वी नियमात् वाक्यानि उदाहरति - शन्न इति ।

words, though both will be of the same form, meaning and relation.

The *saṁhitās* quoted above say that the *brāhmaṇas* use both the *daivī* and the *mānuṣī vāk*. The first they use in the *yajña* and the second they use outside *yajña*. Patañjali explains this by giving an instance of the sages Yarvāṇa and Tarvāṇa.[21]

It is for this reason that great care has to be taken while uttering the words of the *daivī vāk*. Slight change in the pronunciation would change the meaning. Even the changed *svara* would make a different sense, and the meaning intended by the original seer would not be conveyed. Such a mistaken utterance may, on the other hand, even carry altogether an opposite sense. Yāska has quoted a verse to show how a wrong pronunciation resulted in the total frustration of Tvaṣṭṛ, Vṛtra's father. It is important to note the wording of the verse:

मन्त्रो हीनः स्वरतो वर्णतो वा मिथ्या प्रयुक्तो न तमर्थमाह ।
स वाग्वज्रो यजमानं हिनस्ति यथेन्द्रशत्रुः स्वरतोऽपराधात् ॥[22]

The pronoun 'तम्' is very important here. It means 'that meaning', i.e., the meaning intended by the author. It depended on the correct pronouncing of the *svara* and the *varṇa*. Hence it is that the *Prātiśākhyas* deal with them in such details. The rule 'स्वरसंस्कारयोश्छन्दसि नियमः' indicates the importance of *svara* and *Saṁskāra* in the recitation of the *mantras*.

But this gave rise to a controversy. There were some who held that while it was necessary to observe the rules of *svara* and *saṁskāra* in uttering the words of the *daivī vāk*, it was not so with the *laukika* words; for, in reciting the *mantra* the reciter

---

21. cf. एवं हि श्रूयते - यर्वाणस्तर्वाणो नाम ऋषयो बभूवुः प्रत्यक्षधर्माणः परावरज्ञाः विदितवेदितव्याः अधिगतयाथातथ्याः । तत्रभवन्तः 'यद्वानः, तद्वानः' इति प्रयोक्तव्ये 'यर्वाणः, तर्वाणः' इति प्रयुञ्जते । याज्ञे पुनः कर्मणि नापभाषन्ते - *Mbh,, Paspaśāhnika,* Vol. I, P. 11.

22. *Pāṇinīya Śikṣā,* 52.

tried to convey the intent of the original seer, but, in the *laukika* speech, he used the words according to his own intent. The *Prātiśākhyas,* however, did not agree with this position. They said the words in both the speeches being the same in form, sense and relation, would convey the same sense both in the *daivī* and *laukika* speech. It was, therefore, proper to maintain the uniformity in *svara* and *saṁskāra* in both these speeches; that alone would lead to *abhyudaya.*[23] Patañjali refers to this controversy when he says,

वेदमधीत्य त्वरिता वक्तारो भवन्ति वेदान्नो वैदिकाः
शब्दाः सिद्धा लोकाच्च लौकिकाः, अनर्थकं व्याकरणम्

and replies saying, "समानायामर्थगतौ शब्देनापशब्देन च धर्मनियमः क्रियते 'शब्देनैवार्थोऽभिधेयो, नापशब्देन इति । एवं क्रियमाणमभ्युदयकारि भवतीति ।"[24]

While the *Prātiśākhyas* attempted to explain and teach the *svara* and *saṁskāra* of the *mantras* and the words (पद) used in them, the *Nirukta* emphasised the other apsect of them. It tried to explain the meaning of the words in the *mantra* (and thereby the *mantrārtha* also) by tracing them to *ākhyāta.* There were certain reciters of the *mantra* who held that this was not necessary, perhaps it was useless, to attempt finding out the meaning of the *mantras* and the words used in them; for according to them *mantras* had no meaning.[25] Yāska replied them saying that the words of the *mantra* being the same as those in the *laukika* where they had meaning, the attempt to find out the meaning of the *mantras* and the words in them, was not at all useless. It was on the other hand, necessary for the reciter of the *mantra* that he knew its meaning. A mere reciter without knowledge of the

23. न चैतद् यद् वैदिकानां शब्दानां स्वरसंस्कारनियमोऽभ्युदयहेतुः । किं तर्हि लौकिकानामपि शब्दानां नियमोऽभ्युदयहेतुरेव - Uvaṭa on *Yaj. Pra.* I-3.

24. *Mbh. Paspaśā,* Vol. I, p. 5 & 8.

25. 'अनर्थका हि मन्त्राः' opinion of Kautsa, quoted in *Nirukta,* I. 15.

mantra was as good as *sthāṇu* standing only to bear the weight on his head. It was as dull as the fuel not having the touch of fire, which therefore did not shine.[26] Yāska supported his opinion by quoting a *mantra* itself.[27] Then again he said that if a person knowing the *mantras* is treated as superior to those who do not know them, then a person knowing their meaning will still be more praised.[28] Patañjali also maintains the same position when he says:

अनर्थकं मा अधिगीष्महि इति अध्येयं व्याकरणम् । and शास्त्रपूर्वकं यः शब्दान् प्रयुङ्क्ते सोऽभ्युदयेन युज्यते । *Mbh. Paspaśā,* Vol. I, p. 2 & 10.

The *Prātiśākhyas* explained the *svara* and *saṁskāra* of the words as they appeared in the *mantra* and outside *mantra,* i.e., as *pada.* The *Nirukta* tried to explain the meaning of the *padas* by referring them to *ākhyātas.* Both these currents ultimately got merged into grammar and got unified in the concept of *prakṛti* and the *pratyaya.* There was, for example, the *pada 'yajñaḥ'.* The *Prātiśākhya* said that it was to be uttered 'end-acute' (अन्तोदात्त) as यज्ञः. The *Nirukta* said that it has its origin in the यजतिक्रिया i.e., the action denoted by यजति. Now the grammarian analysed the word form as यज्ञः = यज् + ञः (ञ+स्) = यज् + न + स्. The *Nirukta* says 'यज्ञः कस्मात् । प्रख्यातं यजति कर्म इति नैरुक्ताः' = (3.16) While Pāṇini says 'यजयाचयतविच्छप्रच्छरक्षो नङ्' (3.3.90).

Here the *ākhyāta* denoting यजतिक्रिया is given to us by the *Nairuktas* and the rules of *ścutva* etc. and those of *svara* are given by the *Prātiśākhyas* while teaching *svara* and *saṁskāra* of the *pada* as it appeared in the *mantra* and outside the

26. यद् गृहीतमविज्ञातं निगदेनैव शब्द्यते । अनग्नाविव शुष्कैधो न तत् ज्वलति कर्हिचित् (*Nirukta,* I. 18 also quoted in *Mahābhāṣya, Paspaśā*) स्थाणुरयं भारहारः किलाभूत्, अधीत्य वेदं न विजानाति योऽर्थम् *Nirukta* I.18)

27. *Ṛg.* X. 71.4 quoted by Yāska in I. 19.

28. यथा जानपदीषु विद्यातः पुरुषविशेषो भवति । पारोवर्यवित्सु खलु भूयोविद्यः प्रशस्यो भवति । - *Nirukta,* I. 16.

mantra.[29] Even the concepts of *nāma, ākhyāta, upasarga* and *nipāta* were given to the grammarians by their predecessors. Grammar, thus, was directly connected with the analysis of the *padas* as they appeared in the *mantra* and outside *mantra*. It is an *anvākhyāna* of the *daivī vāk* in so far as it explains the *svara-saṁskāra* of the *padas* contained in the *mantras*. The purpose of this *anvākhyāna* is to protect this *daivī vāk* in respect of the *svara-saṁskāra* and to hand it over to the next generation and from it to the next in *continuum*, in the form in which it was received. This is the import of the term *Vedarakṣā*. Patañjali says: रक्षार्थं वेदानामध्येयं व्याकरणम्.[30] It is to be noted that this *Vedarakṣā* is the first and the foremost purpose of grammar. It stands as the first *prayojana* in the statement रक्षोहागमलघ्वसंदेहाः प्रयोजनम्.[31] *Ūha* and others are subsidiary and depend on this *Vedarakṣā* for their fulfilment. The nature of this *Vedarakṣā* is stated by the *Prātiśākhyas* as पदाध्ययनमन्तादिशब्दस्वरार्थज्ञानार्थम्,[32] ऋषिप्रोक्तमन्त्रादि-शब्दस्वरज्ञानार्थम् and आम्नायदार्ढ्यार्थम्.[33]

---

29. यजेः नङ् । Here न is changed to ञ by 'स्तोश्चुना श्चुः' which joined with ज् becomes ज्ञ. This *Sandhi* rule is already given to us by the *Prātiśākhya* (See *Ṛk. Pr.* IV.). Regarding स्वर, यज् is उदात्त by धातोः (6.1.162) and नङ् is उदात्त by आद्युदात्तश्च (3.1.3). When joined together into यज्ञः the उदात्त of the root disappears and the प्रत्ययस्वर prevails by सतिशिष्टस्वर maxim. Hence य becomes अनुदात्त by अनुदात्तं पदमेकवर्जम् (6.1.158). The rules of accents and their modifications were already determined by the *Prātiśākhyas* (See *Ṛk. Pr. Paṭala* III). This shows how concepts of *Prātiśākhya* and *Nirukta* formed the basis of rules in grammar.
30. *Mahābhāṣya : Paspaśā*.
31. *Ibid.*
32. *Atharvaveda Prātiśākhya (Caturadhyāyī)*, 4.107.
33. *Atharva Prātiśākhya* (Ed. Surya Kanta), I.3. Both these *Prātiśākhyas* of the *Atharva Veda* give the purposes as to why the *Mantra*-text was reduced to *pada*-text. They are: to know (i) the ends + the beginnings of *padas*; (ii) The *Svara* of *padas*; (iii) to know the meaning. *A.P.* adds one more viz. (iv) आम्नायदार्ढ्य i.e. fixing the text of a particular *Śākhā*.

The *daivī vāk* thus explained and taught in respect of *svara-saṁskāra* is known as Sanskrit. Hence, Sanskrit = *anvākhyātā daivī vāk*.

When did this *'anvākhyāna'* start ? It is important to ask this question here because that would give us the point of time in the course of the flow of this speech when the Vedic was changed into Sanskrit. We are told that there is an important difference between the Vedic language and the Sanskrit language. While Vedic is the language of the *Vedas*, Sanskrit is the language of the grammarians, that it came after the Vedic at a certain point of time, and in the end it died (as an advent of grammarians.)[34] It is therefore necessary to find out when this *anvākhyāna* started.

Now, let us start from Pāṇini. Pāṇini presupposes the *Nirukta* and the *Prātiśākhya*. The *Nirukta* also presupposes the *Prātiśākhya*, for it refers to the *svara-saṁskāra* which is the subject-matter of the latter.[35] The *Prātiśākhya* presupposes the *Padapāṭha*. So *Padapāṭha* is the earliest available attempt in the direction of the *anvākhyāna*. But *Padapāṭha* also presupposes a system. The division of *saṁhitā* into *padas*, the breaking of the *padas* into *padyas*, the *avagraha* of *upasarga* and the *ākhyāta* and that of case affixes and the *taddhita* affixes from nouns, and the adding of *'iti'* to certain *padas* all this is so uniformly done

34. It is interesting to note a few observations of scholars in this respect. According to Taraporevala, "Sanskrit died as a result of Pāṇini's grammar" (*Elements of the Science of Language*, p.152). He further says, "Sanskrit got rigid at the very core and it *died*" (p. 267)." S. K. Chatterji says, "Sanskrit could not remain bound to the standard of Pāṇini's age for ever. There is an evolution of Sanskrit all through." (*Indo-Aryan and Hindi*, p. 68). Govind Sastri Pardesi observes, "Sanskrit would become spoken language of India, if all the editions of Pāṇini's grammar were drowned", and Taraporevala adds, "If every Pandit who remembered Pāṇini's grammar were exiled." (*op.cit.*, p. 429 N.2).

35. पदप्रकृतीनि सर्वचरणानां पार्षदानि (*Nir.* I. 17).

in the *Padapāṭha* that it is not possible to explain this fact except by assuming a system behind it. We do not know from whom the first author of the *Padapāṭha* received this system.

However, *Taittirīya Saṁhitā* tells us that it was Indra who broke the *padas* into two parts. This was the act of *vyākṛti*, i.e., the breaking of the *pada* into *prakṛti* and *pratyaya*. Before that the speech was *avyākṛta*, not being divided into *prakṛti* and *pratyaya*. So we may say that Indra was the first grammarian of the *divyā vāk*.[36] Bṛhaspati, under whom Indra studied, gave his pupil *pratipadapāṭha*, i.e. enumeration of full words only.[37] We may, therefore, assume that the *mantras* were first reduced to *padas* by Bṛhaspati. Now, there is a statement in the *Ṛk-Tantra*: ब्रह्मा बृहस्पतये प्रोवाच, बृहस्पतिरिन्द्राय, इन्द्रो भरद्वाजाय, भरद्वाज ऋषिभ्यः, ऋषयो ब्राह्मणेभ्यः । (*Paṭala - I*)

If this is accepted then we have to assume that Brahmā gave Bṛhaspati the full *mantra*-sentences, i.e. *vākya* consisting of inter-related *padas*. We have to assume that when Brahmā transferred through his *upadeśa* the *mantra* sentences, the understanding of the inter-relatedness (*sāmarthya*) of the *padas* also must have been given to him. Thus the basis of *pada* division which is of the nature of *sāmarthya* (inter-relatedness)[38] must have been brought home to Bṛhaspati by Brahmā; or else the meaning of the *mantras* would never have been understood by his pupil, i.e., Bṛhaspati. So the seed of the *anvākhyāna* has to be assumed to lie with Brahmā, though the act of *anvākhyāna* goes to the credit of Bṛhaspati.

---

36. वाग्वै पराच्यव्याकृतावदत् । ते देवा इन्द्रमब्रुवन् इमां नो वाचं व्याकुरु इति । तामिन्द्रो मध्यतोऽवक्रम्य व्याकरोत् (T.S. VI. 4.7). Sāyaṇa explains: "ताम् अखण्डां वाचं मध्ये विच्छिद्य प्रकृतिप्रत्ययविभागं सर्वत्राकरोत् ।

37. एवं हि श्रूयते - बृहस्पतिरिन्द्राय दिव्यं वर्षसहस्रं प्रतिपदोक्तानां शब्दानां शब्दपारायणं प्रोवाच नान्तं जगाम (*Mahābhāṣya: Paspaśā*).

38. How *Pada* division is based on *Sāmarthya* will be made fully clear in the II chapter dealing with *Padapāṭha*.

We may therefore say that the concept of *sāmarthya* which is at the basis of *pada*-division goes to the credit of Brahmā, the act of breaking the *mantra* into *padas* goes to Bṛhaspati and the concept of breaking the *pada* into *prakṛti* and *pratyaya* goes to Indra, who is the first grammarian.

Now, we are told that Brahmā is the first to receive this *Divyā Vāk*.[39] If so then the first receiver of the *mantras* is also the first to conceive the idea of *sāmarthya*, the basis of the *pada*-division. He received the *mantras* in the revealed form and he conceived the idea of handing them to Bṛhaspati in the form of speech consisting of inter-related *padas*, i.e. *vākya*. Splitting of the *padas* and the *pāṭha* thereof was done by Bṛhaspati. The moment the *mantra* is reduced to *padas*, the *padas* become *laukika*. This act necessarily demands *svara-saṁskāra*, with which starts the grammatical activity. This means that Brahmā is the one to whom the *mantras* are revealed and he is also the one who reduces them to a speech of inter-related *padas* which is *vākya*. Brahmā receives the speech as *Divyā-Vāk* and he hands it over to Bṛhaspati in the form which subjected to analysis becomes *Mānuṣī Vāk*. This speech now being accompanied by *svara-saṁskāra* is *saṁskṛta*; for it is *anvākhyāta*. If this be the position, we are hardly justified in saying that there was a period of Vedic language followed by a period of *Sanskrit* language, or that there is a Vedic grammar and the other is Sanskrit grammar. It only means that *mantra* as revealed speech is *Divyā Vāk* and as subjected to analysis it is Sanskrit. (*Saṁskṛtam nāma daivī vāg anvyākhyātā maharṣibhiḥ*). There is no difference in them either in point of time or in point of grammar.

We may feel like dubbing this as an *arthavāda*. But we should think a while before we do so. The grammatical activities of the later *munis* appear to have their germ in the *mantras* themselves. Let us have a few examples:

---

39. यो वै ब्रह्माणं विदधाति पूर्वं । यो वै वेदांश्च प्रहिणोति तस्मै ।

- *Śvetāśvatara*, VI. 18

(1) Pāṇini derives the word *nadī* as णद अव्यक्ते शब्दे, पचाद्यच् (नदट्), टित्त्वात् ङीप् - नदी. This is a grammatical activity. The *Nirukta* says : नद्यः कस्मात् । नदना इमा भवन्ति शब्दवत्यः (2.24). This is also a grammatical activity and might have formed the basis of Pāṇinian derivation. But what is the basis of Yāska's idea? Let us put the following *mantra* from *Atharva Veda* by Yāska's side यददः संप्रतीयतीरहावनदता हते । तस्मादा नद्यो नाम स्थ ॥ (II.13.1)

Can this *mantra* not be the basis of Yāska's derivation?

(2) The word पवित्र is derived as पूञ्+ष्ट्रन् (*Un.* III. 185). Yāska says पवित्रं पुनातेः (*Nir.* V. 6). Now compare: येन देवाः पवित्रेणात्मानं पुनते सदा । (*Sāma, Uttara,* V.1.8.1)

(3) *Mahābhāṣya* says: धिनोतेर्धान्यम् (5.1.4). This is grammarian's derivation. Compare: धान्यमसि धिनुहि देवान् (*Yajurveda,* I. 20).

(4) The *Nirukta* derives the word मघ from मंह्; see मघमिति धननामधेयम् मंहतेर्दानकर्मणः (I. 7.).

Compare: स्तोतृभ्यो मंहते मघम् (*Ṛg.* I. 11.3).

(5) The *Nirukta* derives the word अश्विनौ from अश्. It says: अश्विनौ व्याश्नुवाते सर्वम् (12.1). Compare: पूर्वीरश्नन्ता अश्विना (Ṛg. VIII. 5.31)

All these comparisons clearly point out that the later sages found the basis of derivations in the *mantras.*[40] I have selected here one instance from each *Saṁhitā* to show how the germ of *'anvākhyāna'* is found in them. I have selected one proper name to show that even in that case the *anvākhyāna* is found in the *mantras.* Many such instances can be collected from the *Vedic mantras.* This clearly points to the fact that the grammatical activity started with the first teaching of the Vedic *mantra* by Brahmā to Bṛhaspati. The *Mantras* were revealed to Brahmā, who expressed

40. Durga on *Nir.* 1.14 says : अपि च रूढिशब्दव्युत्पत्तिः मन्त्रेष्वपि विद्यते । यदसर्पत तत् सर्पिरिति म । यन्नवमेव नवनीतमभवदिति मन्त्रः। अपि च ब्राह्मणान्यपि अनेकधातुजान्येव कृत्वा निरुच्यन्ते । So, according to *Nairuktas,* the basis of their *niruktis* is the *mantras.* Yudhisthira Mīmāṁsaka has given a few more such examples *op. cit.* pp. 40.

them in full sentences. This was the stage of *Vākya*. Bṛhaspati was the first to analyse them into names and their significances.[41] This was the stage of *pada*-s. They were received by Indra who broke them into *varṇas* in the form of *prakṛti* and *pratyaya*. This was the stage of *prakṛti-pratyaya-vibhāga*. This whole knowledge was handed down to Bhāradvāja. From Bhāradvāja it came to *ṛṣis* and from them to *Brāhmaṇas*. Here we find the glimpse of *vākya-sphoṭa*. *Vākya* is always a revealed expression.[42] When analysed, it gives rise to *pada-sphoṭa* and that in turn to *varṇa-sphoṭa* (conceived as *prakṛti* and *pratyaya*). If thus we find the nucleus of grammatical activity (*anvākhyāna*) immediately after the first handing down of the *mantra* by Brahmā, it is for us to judge whether Brahmā's being treated as the first grammarian is only an *arthavāda*, or whether it points to the fact that the *anvākhyāna* began with the first teaching (*upadeśa*) of the *mantras*.

The *Nirukta* tells us that the name of a thing is related to the *kriyā* denoted by आख्यात which expresses the action of that thing. Hence, the name would have the action as its meaning, as well as the *nimitta* for using that name for that thing, e.g. नदी कस्मात्, नदते: । पवित्रमिति कस्मात्, पुनाते: ।

We may therefore say that there are names, the actions as the meaning of those names, and the *vācya-vācaka* relation on which they stand. This perhaps is hinted at by Manu when he says:

सर्वेषां स तु नामानि कर्माणि च पृथक् पृथक् ।
वेदशब्देभ्य एवादौ पृथक्-संस्थाश्च निर्ममे ॥ (1.21)[43]

---

41. बृहस्पते प्रथमं वाचो अग्रं यत् प्रैरत नामधेयं दधाना: (*Ṛg.* 10.71.1).
42. तत्र अखण्डपक्षे प्रतिभा वाक्यार्थ: (Puṇyarāja on *Vākya-padīya*, II.1). Also Durga: संहिताया: प्रकृतित्वं ज्याय: । मन्त्रो हि अभिव्यज्यमान: पूर्वम् ऋषे: मन्त्रदृश: संहितया एव अभिव्यज्यते, न पदै: । - *Nir.* 1.17.
43. The meaning of this verse, suggested here, is different from that given by either Kullūka or Medhātithi. It is however submitted that the basis of the meaning is found in Medhātithi's commentary itself after giving another meaning stating केचिदाहु:. This other meaning is perhaps better suited to the context in which the verse appears in Manu. See also Yudhiṣṭhira Mīmāṁsaka, *op. cit.* p. 2.

The word *'kasmāt'* used by the *Nairuktas* enquires about the *pravṛtti-nimitta*. The *pravṛtti* though logically prior to the utterance of the word, is known only after the word is uttered. This is hinted at by Vyāsa when he says:

अनादिनिधना नित्या वागुत्सृष्टा स्वयंभुवा ।
आदौ वेदमयी नित्या ततः सर्वाः प्रवृत्तयः ॥[44]

Brahmā uttered the Veda (*Vedamayī Vāk*) first and then only the *pravṛttis* were known.

The *nāma*, the *karman* (sense and *pravṛtti*), and their relation are given to us by the Veda. They are therefore *siddha*. They cannot be created for us by the grammarian. This reminds us of the *vārtika*: सिद्धे शब्दार्थसंबन्धे लोकतोऽर्थप्रयुक्ते शब्दप्रयोगे, शास्त्रेण धर्मनियमः ।[45]

But while for Vyāsa the *pravṛtti* starts from the Veda, for Kātyāyana it starts from the *loka*. How do we reconcile these two positions?

As a matter of fact there is no conflict in these two positions. The words which form the subject matter of grammatical study are the same whether they come from the *Veda* or from the *Loka*. They have the same form, meaning and relation. The difference is only in the starting point of study. One may start the study of words by picking them up from the *Veda*; the other may pick them up from the *laukika* use and study them. The *Prātiśākhyas* for example, study the *Vaidika* words and say, "यथैव वैदिकास्तथैव लौकिकास्त एव तेषामर्थाः ।"[46]

The *Mīmāṁsakas* and the Grammarians take the *laukika* words and say:

"यथैव लौकिकास्तथैव वैदिकास्त एव तेषामर्थाः ।[47]
and "केषां शब्दानाम्, लौकिकानां वैदिकानां च"[48]

---

44. *Mahābhārata, Śānti,* 231.56.
45. *Mbh., Paspaśā,* Vol. I, pp 6-8.
46. Uvaṭa on *Yajus Pr.* I.3.
47. Śābara on *Pūrva Mīmāṁsā,* I. iii.30.
48. *Mbh., Paspaśā,* Vol. I, p 1.

But the process of study is the same, being of the nature of going from the known to the unknown. The *Prātiśākhyas* would say: such are the *svara-saṁskāras* of the Vaidika words, follow them in the *laukika* use also; that would lead to *abhyudaya*; the Grammarians would say: the meaning can be expressed both by *śabda* and *apaśabda*, use the *śabda*, however, for that would lead to *abhyudaya*.[49] This is the import of the *Dharmaniyama*. And what is the nature of this *abhyudaya*? *Abhyudaya* consists in being recognised as the *śiṣṭa* (authority) in society.[50] Secondly, the term *loka* does not mean anybody and everybody in society. It means the *śiṣṭa* as described by Patañjali in:

एतस्मिन् आर्यावर्ते आर्यनिवासे ये ब्राह्मणाः कुम्भीधान्या अलोलुपा अगृह्यमाणकारणाः किंचिदन्तरेण कस्याश्चिद् विद्यायाः पारं गताः तत्रभवन्तः शिष्टाः ।

(*Mahābhāṣya* VI.3.109)

Such *śiṣṭas* only are consequently gifted with उभयी वाक्. Hence शिष्टाः शब्देषु प्रमाणम्. Being grounded in their learning and experience and having developed the faculty of insight and inspiration, they are the proper authorities in respect of the use of words. The *Vākyapadīya* -(I.37-38) says:

आविर्भूतप्रकाशानामनुपप्लुतचेतसाम् ।
अतीतानागतज्ञानं प्रत्यक्षान्न विशिष्यते ॥
अतीन्द्रियानसंवेद्यान् पश्यत्यार्षेण चक्षुषा ।
ये भावान् वचनं तेषां नानुमानेन बाध्यते ॥

■■

49. *Ibid.*

50. Commenting on पू. मी. I.39. Śabara says के शास्त्रज्ञाः । शिष्टाः । तेषामविच्छिन्ना स्मृतिः शब्देषु वेदेषु च । तेन शिष्टाः प्रमाणं श्रुतिस्मृत्यवधारणे. Also Patañjali 'शिष्टाः शब्देषु प्रमाणम् ।: *Mbh.,* on VI. 3, 109, Vol. III. p. 174.

Chapter Two

PADAPĀṬHA : THE FIRST STEP TOWARDS ANVĀKHYĀNA

It has been shown in the first chapter that the term *Daivī Vāk* primarily applies to the Vedic *mantras*, even though in common parlance we apply it to the Sanskrit language in general. These Vedic *mantras* appear before us in the form of *Saṁhitā*. The first attempt to reduce it to *padas* was an act of *Vyākaraṇa*. For example, the *mantra*: अग्निमीळे पुरोहितम् यज्ञस्य देवमृत्विजम् । होतारं रत्नधातमम् ॥ (Ṛg. I. 1.1) is an instance of *Daivī Vāk*, but अग्निम् । ईळे पुरःऽहितम् । यज्ञस्य । देवम् । ऋत्विजम् । होतारम् । रत्नऽधातमम् । is an attempt at explaining the nature of the above instance of the *Daivī Vāk*. Hence the words in the *Padapāṭha* are instances of *Mānuṣī Vāk*, and as these words are subjected to the modifications of *Svara* and *Saṁskāra*, they are the *Saṁskṛta* words.

Where was the necessity of reducing the *Daivī Vāk* into the *padas*? The reply is found in one statement of *Caturadhyāyī*, which states: पदाध्ययनमन्तादिशब्दस्वरार्थज्ञानार्थम् (4.107). The study of the *padas* is done in order to know the end and beginning of the words (i.e. the extent of a word), the proper form of words, and of their accent and meaning. The *Atharva Prātiśākhya* also has a similar statement ऋषिप्रोक्तमन्त्रादि - शब्दस्वरज्ञानार्थः पदविभागः (1.3)...." The division of the *Saṁhitā* into *padas* is done in order to know the beginning of words, accent and thereby meaning of stanzas uttered by the sages. The following examples will make the point clear:

(1) स देवाँ एह वक्षति (ऋ. 1.1.2) = सः । देवान् । आ । इह । वक्षति । (प.पा.) It is only from the *Padapāṭha* that we know that the *pada* ends in 'n' and not in nasalised 'ā' (ending of *pada*); that the next *pada* begins with आ and not ए (beginning of *pada*); that the proper form of words is आ । इह । and not एह् । (*Śabda*); and that व॒क्ष॒ति॒ is *anudātta* (*Svara*).

(2) How the meaning is known from the *Padapāṭha*, will be clear from the following example: The *Saṁhitā* अवसाय पद्वते रुद्र मृळ (ऋ. 10-109-1) has the following *padas* अवसाय । पत्ऽवते । रुद्र । मृळ । and the *Saṁhitā* विमुच्या वयोऽवसायाश्वान् (ऋ. 1.104-1) has the following *padas* विऽमुच्य । वय: । अवऽसाय । अश्वान् । The word अवसाय in the first example is the dative of अवस i.e. grass, while in the second example it is a ल्यबन्त from अव + √ सो. This difference of the meaning of the word अवसाय can be known from the *Padapāṭha* only.

The *Padapāṭha* of each *Saṁhitā* has uniformity in so far as that particular *Saṁhitā* is concerned. But *Padapāṭhas* of different *Saṁhitās* point to different methods of reading *padas* as will be seen from the following examples. Moreover, different scholars read *padas* differently at times. Thus:

(i) The *padas* of तन्नस्तपउत सत्यं च वेत्तु (अ.वे.) are read by Śaunaka as तत् । न: । तप: । उत । सत्यम् । च । वेत्तु । but according to *Atharva Prātiśākhya* the *padas* should be read as तम् । न: । तप: । etc.

(ii) The *Padakāras* of the *Ṛgveda* and the *Taittirīya Saṁhitā* read the second member of a compound with a different accent. e.g. पुरोहितम् is read by Śākalya as पुर:ऽहितम्। while by Ātreya as पुर: - हि त म् ।

(iii) *Yajurveda* repeats the *pada* in all cases of *avagraha*. e.g. अस्मे इत्य स्मे । ऊँ इत्यूँ । But in the Śākala Śākhā these *padas* are read as अस्मे इति । ऊँ इति ।

(iv) The *padas* of वने न वाय: (ऋ .10.29.1) are read by Śākalya as वने । न । वा । य:। but they are not approved by Yāska who reads them as वने । न । वाय: । supporting his reading by saying: वा इति च य इति च चकार शाकल्य: । उदात्तं तु आख्यातमभविष्यत् । असुसमाप्तश्च अर्थ: (*Nir.* 6.19). Likewise in the *mantra* यदिन्द्र चित्रमेहनाऽस्ति (ऋ. 5.39.1) Yāska refers to two types of *padapāṭha* - मेहना according to Sākalya, but मे । ह । ना (three *padas*) according to गार्ग्य (4.4).

However, the peculiarities of each *Śākhā* were uniformly observed in that particular *Śākhā* both in respect of the *Saṁhitā* and the *padas*. Thus the *Śākhā* represented by *Atharva Prātiśākhya* uniformly reads दीर्घमायुः कृणोतु मे । while that represented by *Caturadhyāyī* reads दीर्घमायुस्कृणोतु मे ।. These readings peculiar to each *Śākhā* were determined by the *Pārṣadas*. The *Prātiśākhyas* give us the idea as to how the *Saṁhitā* and the *padas* were read in that particular *Śākhā*. The *Atharva Prātiśākhya* has the following statement in this respect:

तदिदं व्याकरणं पुरस्तादध्येयम् अलं विज्ञानाय ।
आम्नायदार्ढ्यार्थम् । शाखान्तरेषु अन्यथा निगदत्वात् ।
समानशब्दानां स्वरान्यत्वात् वर्णान्यत्वाच्च । (I.3.)

The extant *Padapāṭha* of the *Ṛgveda Saṁhitā* goes in the name of Śākalya; that of the *Taittirīya Saṁhitā* is credited to Ātreya; Gārgya is said to be the author of the *Sāmapadapāṭha*; and the *Padapāṭha* of *Vājasaneyi Saṁhitā* is said to have been prepared by Mādhyandina (or Kātyāyana). We do not know who reduced the *Atharvaveda* to the *padas*. (Can he be Śaunaka)?

The point to be considered at this stage is: How were the *padas* formed and what was the principle behind them? The extant *Prātiśākhyas* take the *Saṁhitā* and the *padas* for granted and state the rules of reducing the *padas* to *Saṁhitā*. We have no direct access to any work which would give us the idea as to how the *Saṁhitā* was reduced to *padas*.

However, we have some material in the *Prātiśākhyas* which may guide us to frame a hypothesis in this respect. The fourth chapter of the *Caturadhyāyī* deals with the rules of reading *padas* and the *Atharva Prātiśākhya* is mainly concerned with it though the material is at places mixed with the rules of preparing the *Saṁhitā* from the *padas*. It is very likely that we may get some clue from them in respect of how the *padas* were constructed out of the *Saṁhitā*.

Before we do that it would be well for us to study the structure of the *Prātiśākhyas*. The extant *Prātiśākhyas* are:

(1) the *Ṛgveda Prātiśākhya* ascribed to Śaunaka,

(2) the *Vājasaneyi Prātiśākhya*,

(3) the *Taittirīya Prātiśākhya*,

(4) the *Ṛk-tantra*, the *Prātiśākhya* of the *Sāmaveda*,

(5) *Śaunakīya Caturadhyāyī*, the *Prātiśākhya* of one *Śākhā* of the *Atharvaveda* and

(6) the *Atharva Prātiśākhya* belonging to another (unknown) *Śākhā* of the *Atharvaveda*.

The rules in all these *Prātiśākhyas* are prescriptive and except the last mentioned work and the last chapter of the *Caturadhyāyī*, all the works deal with the *Saṁhitā* rules and not the rules of the *pada*. This being the general nature of the *Prātiśākhya* works, scholars suppose that the fourth chapter of the *Caturadhyāyī* is out of the scope of the *Prātiśākhya*, e.g. Whitney introduces the fourth chapter of the *Caturadhyāyī* in these words: "Our three preceding chapters have covered the whole ground which a comparison of other treatises shows it to have been the bounden duty of a *Prātiśākhya* to occupy, and in this final chapter are brought up matters which might have been left out unhandled without detriment to the character of the work as a complete and comprehensive phonetic manual for the school to which it belonged. Its first three chapters teach the construction of the *pada*-text; whereas we have hitherto assumed this text as established, and have been taught how to construct the *Saṁhitā* upon its basis, we now look upon the body of the traditional scripture from just the opposite point of view and receive directions for forming the *pada*-text from it. No other of the kindred treatises thus includes the plan of constructing the *pada*-text; the *Vājasaneyi Prātiśākhya* is the only one which takes up the matter at all" (p.183). On the basis of this material and the *Atharva Prātiśākhya*, it may be possible for us to build up a tentative hypothesis regarding the stages in the growth of *Prātiśākhya* literature.

It has been held by all scholars that *pada* is later than *Saṁhitā*. Durga, for example, stating the two interpretations of the terms पदप्रकृतीनि पार्षदानि ultimately states his view as संहितायाः प्रकृतित्वं ज्यायः । मंत्रो हि अभिव्यज्यमानः पूर्वमृषेः मंत्रदृशः संहितया एव अभिव्यज्यते न पदैः । (*Nir.* I. 17.4)

The first step that was taken in the matter of understanding the import of *mantras* was to divide it into the *padas*. The *Padapāṭha* formed as it were the running commentary on the *Saṁhitā*. The formation of the *pada*-text must have proceeded on certain principles, which must have been laid down in certain manuals. The manuals might have contained guiding lines for *'iti-karaṇa'*, for *'avagraha'*, and *'vigraha'*, for *'pragṛhya'* etc., which are the peculiarities of the *padapātha*. The existence of such manuals can be inferred from a statement of Durga, which states the nature of *Pārṣada* or the *Prātiśākhya*, thus: स्वचरणपरिषद्येव यैः प्रतिशाखानियतमेव पदावग्रहप्रगृह्याक्रमसंहितास्वरलक्षणमुच्यते, तानि इमानि पार्षदानि प्रातिशाख्यानि इत्यर्थः । (*Nir.*1.17.4)

The *Pārṣadas* or the *Prātiśākhyas* are the works which guide you in respect of the *avagraha, pragṛhyatva,* peculiarities of *krama-saṁhitā* and the *svara*. It will be readily seen that this description applies only to that type of *Pārṣada* which constructs the *pada*, for *avagraha* and *pragṛhyatva* are related to the reading of *pada* and not of *Saṁhitā*.

Yāska says, पदप्रकृतीनि सर्वचरणानां पार्षदानि (I.17). It can be interpreted in two ways. It can mean that the *Pārṣadas* are *'padarūpa'*; It can also mean that the *Pārṣadas* are those the source of which are *padas* - पदानि प्रकृतिः - मूलम् - यस्याः (सा पर्षत्) । This ambiguous expression probably refers, according to Dr. Sūryakānta, to the types or stages of *Prātiśākhya*. In his introduction to *Atharva Prātiśākhya*, (pp. 24-32) he has discussed this question and arrived at certain conclusions in regard to the stages in the development of *Prātiśākhya* literature. It will be useful for our study to get acquainted with his argument. I give here the gist of his argument, as far as possible, in his own words. "Suppose", he says, "in ten passages of the *Atharvaveda Saṁhitā* आ represents the *pada* ending in ऐ, or the *saṁhitā* अ represents the *pada* ending in ए. Now, the first step towards the grammatical analysis would be to pick up those ten passages and say that in these ten passages and in *these only,* the *saṁhitā* आ is equal to *pada* ऐ and *saṁhitā* अ is equal to *pada* ए. The same principle can be extended to the cases of *avagraha* and accentuation. These statements will, of course, be nomenclatory and vary with different *Śākhās* of the *Saṁhitā,* because with variation of interpretation, the variation in the *pada* arose. This is one stage of *Prātiśākhya* and naturally earlier too, because it directly follows the *pada*-formation. Yāska's पदप्रकृति meaning पदरूपम् refers to this stage.

The *padas* being thus codified, the second stage naturally was to devise rules in order to turn *padas* into *Saṁhitā* and the manuals embodying these rules are represented by the present *Prātiśākhyas.* The formation of this type was not at all difficult. The material in the form of nomenclatory statements was already there. What the followers of each *Śākhā* had to do was simply to revert the nature of the statement, viz., to turn that from nomenclatory to prescriptive, e.g. a nomenclatory rule existed in the *Ṛgveda* tradition to the effect that such and such words which show ष् in the *Saṁhitā* have स् in the *Pada.* It was just reversed to the form that such and such words which show स् in the *pada* should exhibit ष् in the *Saṁhitā.* All the rules in the *Prātiśākhyas* at the second stage should have been of this type, and so they are found to a great extent in the *Ṛgveda Prātiśākhya, Taittirīya Prātiśākhya,* and *Vājasaneyi Prātiśākhya.* The process of the abbreviation was yet to come.

While the first stage was nomenclatory, this second stage was descriptive (*lakṣaṇa*). Naturally, this second type must have thrown aside the first one. Again this stage being of *lakṣaṇa*-type, it could be easily reduced to the form of abstract rules, e.g. उकारोदय ओकारम्. This is what we find in the majority of the rules in the present *Prātiśākhyas*. Yāska's पदप्रकृति in the sense of पदानि प्रकृतिर्यस्या: refers to this second stage.

It is noteworthy in this context that the nature of Bṛhaspati's grammar was that of *'pratipadapāṭha'*. It tried to enumerate the *padas* in the *Deva-vāṇī*. Pāṇini's grammar is that of *lakṣaṇa*-type (न हि पाणिनिना शब्दाः प्रोक्ताः । किं तर्हि । सूत्रम् । - *Mbh. Paspaśā*, Vol. I., p. 12.). This shows that the grammar at one stage was nomenclatory which gradually was substituted by the prescriptive one. The *Prātiśākhyas* represent the intermediate stage in which both these types are present, one type more in one and less in the other. The *Ṛk-prātiśākhya*, the *T. Prātiśākhya*, the *V. Prātiśākhya*, the *Ṛk-tantra*, and the *Caturadhyāyī* are more of prescriptive nature, while the *Atharvaprātiśākhya* shows more of the nomenclatory type. If we study this material of nomenclatory nature from the extant *Prātiśākhyas*, we may be able to get at the logic of the *pada* construction.

Let us study the following statement from the *Atharva Prātiśākhya* :

कानि पुनरस्य प्रातिशाख्यस्य प्रयोजनानि ।
वक्ष्यति - एतावत्त्वमपवाद आबाधश्चार्थशब्दतः ।
सांवेदनं न्यायमुखं पञ्चस्वर्थेषु वर्तते ॥ (I.3)

This passage states the purposes of the *Atharva Prātiśākhya*. They are five, viz. (i) एतावत्त्वम् (limitation), (ii) अपवाद : (exception), (iii) अर्थत: शब्दत:च आबाध: (similarity in respect of sense and sound), (iv) सांवेदनम् (suffering), and (v) न्यायमुखम् - (rules of the *pada*). The import of these terms and the illustrations given are as follows:-

(i) एतावत्त्वम् (limitation) :- यत्र एतानि पदानि एवमादिषु भवन्ति, अतो न अन्यथा- i.e. where such and such words followed by such and such, are such and not otherwise. For example :

(1) पूषा त्वेतश्च्यावयतु प्रविद्वान् (Ṛg. X. 17.3)
पूषा । त्वा । इतः । च्यावयतु । प्र । विद्वान् । - पदपाठ.

(2) उत वायः सहस्य प्रविद्वान् (Ṛg. I. 147.5)
उत । वा । यः । सहस्य । प्रऽविद्वान् । - पदपाठ.

In the first case the *upasarga* प्र is separated as an independent *pada*, while in the second it is shown as a member of the compound by an *avagraha*. (In the *Saṁhitā* both are read as प्रविद्वान्). Why? The reply is:

अत्र च ' प्र । विद्वान् ' विगृह्यते, समासोऽन्यत्र ।
किं कारणम् । प्र इत्यस्य च्यवतिना सामर्थ्यम् ।
पूषा त्वेतः प्र च्यावयतु विद्वानिति ।

In the first example प्र and विद्वान् are separated as independent *padas* because प्र is related in sense with च्यवति but in the second case प्र is related with विद्वान् and hence it is shown as a compound. Thus the *pada* construction here is based on *sāmarthya*.

(1) कर्मन् कर्मन् आभगम् (A.V. 4.23.3).
कर्मन्ऽकर्मन् । आऽभगम् । - पदपाठ

(२) उदीरय पितरा जारमाभगम् (A.V. 18-1-23)
उत्ऽईरय । पितरा । जारम् । आ । भगम् । - पदपाठ.

The *Saṁhitā* reads आभगम्. In the first case आऽभगम् is a compound, but in the second case आ and भगम् are separated as independent *padas*, for here आ is related in sense (समर्थ) with जारम्.

(1) अधिश्रिते अग्निहोत्रे (A.V. 15-12-1)
अधिऽश्रिते । अग्निऽहोत्रे । - पदपाठ.

(2) यदन्यस्यामधिश्रितम् । - (A.V. I.32.4)
यत् । अन्यस्याम् । अधि । श्रितम् । - पदपाठ.

In the first case अधिऽश्रित is a compound, but in the second अधि is separated from श्रित as an independent *pada* because it (अधि), being *karmapravacanīya*, is not related in sense with श्रित.

These examples show that the construction of *padas* in एतावत्त्व depends on the *sāmarthya* of words in the *mantra*.

(ii) Keeping अपवाद aside for the present, for it will be discussed along with न्यायमुख at a later stage, we shall take आबाध first. आबाध is explained as यत्रैतत् शब्दार्थतः तुल्या संहिता भवति - i.e. where the combination is alike in respect of the particular word or sense. Thus we have such words as गर्भादम् (A.V. 1.15.3), अन्नादम् (A.V.5.14.1), अन्नादीः (A.V.15.14.3). Now the question is whether the combination here is that of अ + अ (अन्न + अदीः) or अ + आ (अन्न + आदीः). Here we can get a clue from such words as हविरदान् (4 अ) where we clearly see that the word is हविः + अदान्. On the basis of this we can say that the above words are compounds of गर्भऽअदम् । अन्नऽअदम् । अन्नऽअदीः Likewise we find आबाध in respect of sense. For example the line तन्नस्तप उत सत्यं च वेत्तु we may have the combination of तत् + नः or तम् + नः. In one case we shall have the *pada* तत् as taken by Śaunaka; in the second case as तम् as is taken by *Atharva Prātiśākhya*. Another example of आबाध may be given as प्रजाया अरतिं तरामसि (A.V. 1.15.7) where the *pada* may be प्रजायै or प्रजायाः. It is to be taken as प्रजायै । अरतिम् and not प्रजायाः on the strength of sense (*sāmarthya*). Likewise in the line वशा हि सत्या वरुणस्य राज्ञः (1.10.1) the *padas* are वशाः and सत्याः, not वशा and सत्या. Here also *pada* is to be determined by सामर्थ्य i.e. sense.

(iii) सांवेदनम् (suffering): There are some words which though similar in form denote different meaning if the accent is changed. For example,

ज्येष्ठं । = best; ज्ये॒ष्ठ = eldest (पूर्वजात)
कृष्णं । = मृग; कृ॒ष्ण = black

Such words are to be particularly noted in the *pada* construction in respect of their accent.

(iv) न्यायमुख (general rules) and (v) अपवाद (exception). After the above peculiarities have been noted what remains are the general types of *sandhi* and the exceptions i.e., एकोदात्तं पदम् न्याय - that a word has one *udātta* is a general rule (न्याय) but the words like बृ॒हस्पतिं । and others are exceptions. (अपवाद).

The purposes enumerated above point to two things - (i) Even though the *padas* can generally be constructed without difficulty, still there are occasions when they are to be determined on the strength of the sense. In such cases the principle of *sāmarthya* has to be followed. This becomes all the more clear in the case of एतावत्त्व. Thus whether a *nipāta* is to be treated as an *upsarga* and attached to the verb form, or it has to be treated as *karmapravacanīya* and should be treated as a seperate *pada*, depends on the *sāmarthya* of that word. In all such cases the rule समर्थः पदविधिः । meaning that the rules of the *pada* apply to those that are related in sense, is the governing principle. In case of *'ābādha'* the form of the *pada* is to be determined both by referring to the meaning as well as to the form. Where the cases of *'ābādha'* are to be resolved by form, it is *'varṇavidhi'*. Then there is a third type of *pada* in which certain affixes are seen separated from the *prātipadikas*. e.g. ऋषिऽभिः । Such cases are noted by the *Caturadhyāyī* and *Vājasaneyi Prātiśākhya*. They may be termed as *pratyayavidhi*s in respect of the *padas* which are thus *avagṛhita*. Then there is a fourth type of *padas* which are not shown with *avagraha*, the reason being that the *Padakāra* himself was, perhaps, in doubt as to how it should be read. See for example, the *Sūtra*s उत्तम्भनादीनि संशयात् (वा. प्रा. 5-39); 'षोडशी सन्देहात् (चतु. 4.57). In case of many *pada*s it is difficult to determine as to where the अवग्रह be placed. Such words are treated as निपातनs and are noted in वा. प्रा. 5-37 and चतुरध्यायी 4. 47 to 71.

That in the matter of *pada* construction, meaning of the *mantra* was a criterion has been hinted at by Yāska also. He says:

अथापि इदमन्तरेण पदविभागो न विद्यते ।
'अवसाय पद्वते रुद्र मृळ' (X.169.1) ।
पद्वत् अवसं गावः पथ्यदनम् । अवतेः गत्यर्थस्य असः नामकरणः ।
तस्मान्न अवगृह्णन्ति । 'अवसायाश्वान्'
इति स्यतिरुपसृष्टः मोचने तस्मादवगृह्णन्ति ।

Here Yāska has taken two examples to drive home his point, अवसाय पद्वते रुद्र मृळ and अवसायाश्वान्. In the first case अवसाय is the dative case of the base अवस hence it is not *avagṛhīta*, but in the second case अवसाय is an infinitive from अव + √ सो and hence it is shown as अवऽसाय. This is an example of एतावत्त्व. Second example given by Yāska is that of *'ābādha'* He says:-

दूतो निर्ऋत्या इदमाजगाम (10.165.1) - आकारान्तं पदम्
परो निर्ऋत्या आचक्ष्व (10.164.1) - ऐकारान्तं पदम् ।

The *pada* in the first example is either the ablative or the genitive of the base निर्ऋति; hence आकारान्त; while in the second example, it is dative according to the sense and hence ऐकारान्त. That the accent in the words coming under सांवेदन was entirely dependent on meaning requires no exposition.

We may, therefore, conclude that the main principle behind the *pada* construction was that of *sāmarthya* as indicated by Pāṇini in the rule 'समर्थः पदविधिः' (P. 2.1.1) - which would mean in this context as follows : 'the *vidhi* i.e. the rules regarding the *pada*s i.e. the construction of *pada* is based on the *sāmarthya* i.e. their inter-relatedness in the sentences of the *Saṁhitā* text.' This is how the rule has been understood by the *Atharva Prātiśākhya*.

This rule as quoted and understood by the author of the *Atharva Prātiśākhya* equates with the rule 2.1.1 in Pāṇini's *Aṣṭādhyāyī* and is used as a *paribhāṣā*. The import of that rule will be explained later on, when we come to Pāṇini's *Aṣṭādhyāyī*.

The methods adopted by the *padakāra*s in reducing *Saṁhitā* to *pada* are as follows :-

(i) to remove all the *sandhis* which have appeared in the *Saṁhitā* text and show the beginnings and the endings of the *padas* clearly and separately,

(ii) to show separately the *nipātas* and the *upasargas* which are not related to *dhātu*s and are of the nature of *karmapravacanīya* or which is *anarthaka*,

(iii) to point out by *avagraha* the members of compound and certain affixes affixed to *prakṛtis*,

(iv) *Samāpatti*:- to exhibit the *pada* in its natural form by removing all the *Saṁhitā* modifications such as *ṣatva, ṇatva, ṣṭutva* and so on, and to show the *pada* as it would appear when standing independently e.g. प्रणइन्दो (संहिता) = प्र / न:/ इन्दो मोष्टुव: (सं) = मो इति । सु । न: । where णत्व + षत्व is removed.

(v) *Itikaraṇa*:- to add the word *'iti'* to the *padas* of certain type such as *pragṛhya*, the particle *'u'* and *riphita visarga* and so on, e.g. ऊँ इति । वायो इति etc.

(vi) *Carcā*:- to repeat the *pada* to which *'iti'* is added and to give the better understanding of the same. e.g. ऋषिभिरिति ऋषिऽभि: । अकरित्यक: । etc.

These are the general methods of reducing the *saṁhitā* to *padas* and they have been generally followed by the *padakāras* of all the *Śākhās*. In respect of *itikaraṇa* and *carcā*, we find differences in different *Śākhās*, yet the general form of the *Padapāṭha* is the same.

The *Padapāṭha* has helped us a great deal in understanding the meaning of the *mantras* and the authors of the *Padapāṭhas* have, in various ways, tried to bring out the hidden meaning of the *mantras*. We may note here the work done by them.

The extant *Padapāṭha* of the *Ṛgveda Saṁhitā* is attributed to Śākalya. There was one *Śākalya* who according to *Bṛhadāraṇyaka Upaniṣad* was present in the assembly of King Janaka and he had philosophical discussion with Yājñavalkya. According to the *Purāṇas*, this Śākalya was the author of the *Padapāṭha*. The *Brahmāṇḍa Purāṇa* (1.2.34:32) says:

शाकल्यः प्रथमस्तेषां तस्मादन्यो रथीतरः ।
बाष्कलिश्च भरद्वाजः इति शाखाप्रवर्तकाः ॥
देवमित्रश्च शाकल्यः ज्ञानाहंकारगर्वितः ।
जनकस्य च यज्ञे वै विनाशमगमद् द्विजः ॥

This *Padapāṭha* of Śākalya has been the basis of the *Ṛkprātiśākhya*. Yāska has referred to this *Padapāṭha*. e.g. *Nirukta* 5.21. Yāska quotes the *mantra* अरुणो मासकृत् वृकः (10.5.19). He takes the *pada* as मासकृत् while Śākalya takes as मा । सकृत् । He also controverts with Śākalya in respect of the *padas* in वनेनवायः। There was also another *padapāṭha* of *Ṛgveda* which goes in the name of Rāvaṇa. From whatever portions of the *Rāvaṇa Bhāṣya* have come to light, it appears that Rāvaṇa did not follow Śākalya's *Padapāṭha* in many places.

The *Padapāṭha* of *Vājasaneyi Saṁhitā* of *Yajurveda* goes in the name of Mādhyandina (Pt. Bhagavaddatta says its author was Kātyāyana). The *Padapāṭha* of *Taittirīya Saṁhitā* goes in the name of Ātreya. This is stated by Bhaṭṭa Bhāskara in his *Bhāṣya* as उखश्चात्रेयाय ददौ येन पदविभागश्चक्रे । The *Kāṇḍānukramaṇī* refers to Ātreya as *padakāra* यस्याः पदकृदात्रेयो वृत्तिकारस्तु कुण्डिनः । *Baudhāyana Gṛhyasūtra* also says आत्रेयाय पदकाराय in the section of Ṛṣitarpaṇa.

Gārgya is the author of *Padapāṭha* of *Sāmaveda*. This we know from the commentary on *Nirukta*. Durga says on *Nirukta* 4.3.4.–:

बह्वृचानां 'मेहना' इत्येकं पदम् । छन्दोगानां त्रीण्येतानि पदानि, मे, ह, ना इति। तदुभयं पश्यता भाष्यकारेण शाकल्यगार्ग्ययोः अभिप्रायौ अत्रानुविहितौ ।

Skandasvāmī also says: एकमिति शाकल्यः, त्रीणि इति गार्ग्यः ।

Gārgya's *Padapāṭha* had some peculiarities. He has divided a *pada* which is considered normally as indivisible e.g. सम्-उद्रः। Yāska appears to have based his derivations, many times, on Gārgya's *Padapāṭha* e.g. मि-त्रम् । प्रमीतेस्त्रायते इति प्रमित्रः (10-21) सम् + उद्रः । समुद्रवन्ति अस्मादापः इति समुद्रः । The author of the *Atharva Padapāṭha* has followed the *Padapāṭha* of *Ṛgveda*. We do not know the name of this author. (Can we say that he might be Śaunaka?).

In many places the authors of the different *Padapāṭhas* do not agree with one another. But each one of them has followed his own tradition. This has been expressly brought out by Skandasvāmī in his *Nirukta Bhāṣya* on the word Āditya. He says:

शाकल्यात्रेयप्रभृतिभिः नावगृहीतम् । पूर्वनिर्वचनाभिप्रायेण गार्ग्यप्रभृतिभिः अवगृहीतम् । विचित्राः पदकारणामभिप्रायाः । क्वचिदुपसर्गविषयेऽपि नावगृह्णन्ति । यथा शाकल्येन 'अधिवासम्' इति नावगृहीतम् । आत्रेयेण तु 'अधि-वासम्' इत्यवगृहीतम् । (नि. 2.1.13).

This clearly shows that the attempt of the *Padakāras* was towards the analysis of the *mantras* into *padas,* to understand their imports and as such it was the first as well as the most important step in the study of the *Devabhāṣā*.

The following peculiarities of the various *Padapāṭhas* should be noted to appreciate the difference in them.

1. *The use of avagraha* :- When an *avagraha* is to be shown in the *Padapāṭha* of *Ṛgveda* and *Atharvaveda,* the *pada* is not repeated, but, only one *avagraha* is used, e .g. पुरःऽहितम्। त्रिऽ सप्ताः । But in the *Yajurveda* and *Sāmaveda,* the *pada* is first shown as it is and then repeated to show the *avagraha* e.g. श्रेष्ठतमायेति श्रेष्ठऽतमाय (वा.सं.), श्रेष्ठतमायेति श्रेष्ठऽतमाय (सा.सं). Secondly, in the *Ṛgveda-padapāṭha,* even though there is an

avagraha between the two *padas* still, the accent is kept as it was in the *pada* without *avagraha*. Same is the case with *Vājasaneyi Padapāṭha*. But in the *Taittirīya* and *Maitrāyaṇī*, the parts separated are treated as independent segments for the purpose of accentuation. e.g. श्रेष्ठतमायेति श्रेष्ठ ऽतमाय (*वा.सं.*) but श्रेष्ठतमायेति श्रेष्ठ-तमाय (*तै.मै.*सं.)

2. In respect of the words followed by 'iva':- *Ṛgveda, Śukla-Yajurveda* and *Maitrāyaṇī* show the word with इव as a compound e.g. पिताऽइव (*ऋ.* 35); राजेवेति राजाऽइव (*यजु.* 63.9) राजेवेति राजाऽइव (*मै.*). But in *Taittirīya* and *Sāmaveda* they are not so treated, but, shown as independent words, e.g. राजा। इव । (*तै.*); क्षो³णी ²। इ³व (सा). Both these concepts have come down to the *Bhāṣā* also e.g. in वागर्थाविव, we find a compound, but, in कचाचितौ विश्वगिवाराजौ गजौ, इव is not compounded. The rule is इवेन समासो विभक्त्यलोपः पूर्वपदप्रकृतिस्वरत्वं च । (*Vārtika* on P. 2.1.4.)

3. *Peculiarities of accent*:- In the *padapāṭha* of *Ṛgveda, Yajurveda* and *Atharvaveda,* if there is *Udātta* at the end of the first part of the *avagṛhita pada*, it has influence on the accent of the second part i.e. even though the parts are separated for other purposes, still, for determining the accent, they are treated as one word. But this is not the case with the *Taittirīya padapāṭha* e.g.

   वीरवत्ऽ तमम् । घृतऽप्रतीका । (ऋ.) श्रेष्ठतमायेति श्रेष्ठऽतमाय (*यजु.*); प्रजावतीरिति प्रजाऽवती (*यजु.*); अग्निऽस्वाता; अग्निऽतेजाः (*अथर्व*). But see the तैत्तिरीयपदपाठ which shows: श्रेष्ठतमायेति श्रेष्ठ-तमाय, and प्रजावतीरिति प्रजाऽवती । The *Maitrāyaṇī Saṁhitā* in this respect shows an option, while one *padapāṭha* follows the *Taittirīya* system, the other *padapāṭha* follows *Ṛgvedic* system e.g. श्रेष्ठतमायेति श्रेष्ठऽतमाय or श्रेष्ठतमायेति श्रेष्ठ-तमाय; अघशंस इत्यघऽशंसः or अघशंस इत्यघऽशंसः ।

4. *Iti-karaṇa:-* In the *Ṛgveda* and the *Atharva, 'iti'* is used after the *pragṛhya* vowels and the *Riphita visarga* if that is not seen in the *Saṁhitā.* e.g. वायो इति (प्रगृह्य); अकरित्यकः; प्रातरिति (रिफित विसर्ग).

But in the *Yajurveda 'iti'* is also used in the case of *avagṛhīta pada* in addition, e.g. विष्णो इति (प्रगृह्य); अकरित्यकः (रिफित विसर्ग); श्रेष्ठतमायेति श्रेष्ठऽतमाय (अवग्रह).

In the *Taittirīya* and *Maitrāyaṇī Padapāṭha 'iti'* is used in all the above cases and in the case of *Upasarga* also e.g. प्रेति. If there are two *Upasargas* coming together 'iti' is used with the second *Upasarga* e.g. संप्रयच्छति = सम् । प्रेति । यच्छति। In *Sāmaveda 'iti'* is used with the *Pragṛhya* vowel e.g. त्वे[1] । इति[2]

5. *Padapāṭha and Sāmarthya* - The peculiarities shown above in respect of the *padapāṭha* are mostly formal, i.e., they are meant to show whether the *padas* are of the nature of a compound or whether the ending vowel of a *pada* is *pragṛhya,* or whether the *visarga* is a *riphita visarga* and so on. But, there are a few cases where the *pada* has been determined on the basis of the relation in meaning, i.e. *Sāmarthya.* The two cases in respect of which there was a controversy between Śākalya and Yāska have been shown before. It is also shown that the cases of *'Etāvattva'* and *'Ābādha'* are also the cases where the *pada* has to be determined on the basis of *Sāmarthya.* The following two examples are still more illuminating in this respect.

(a) The *mantra* भद्रं कर्णेभिः शृणुयाम देवाः भद्रं पश्येमाक्षभिर्यजत्राः is found in *Ṛgveda* 1.89.8; *Yajurveda* 25.21; *Maitrāyaṇī* 4.16.2; *Kāṇva* 35.1, and *Taittirīya Āraṇyaka* 1.1.1. In all the *Saṁhitās* except *Maitrāyaṇī* and the *Taittirīya Āraṇyaka* the word *'Yajatrāḥ',* has been shown (or recited) as *sarvānudātta* (य_ज_ त्रा_:) and has been taken to qualify the word *devāḥ* (दे_ वा_:) which is also *sarvānudātta* being a vocative form.

The meaning in that case will be हे यजत्राः देवाः, वयं कर्णेभिः भद्रं श्रृणुयाम. But in one recension of *Maitrāyaṇī Saṁhitā* it is shown as *'Ādyudātta'* (यजत्राः). The meaning in that case will be हे देवाः, यजत्राः वयं भद्रं शृणुयाम. This difference in reading of the *pada* यजत्राः has been pointed out by Bhaṭṭa Bhāskara in his *Bhāṣya* on the *Taittirīya Āraṇyaka* 1.1.1.

(b) The second example is ' एष्टाराय: from *Yajurveda*. This *mantra* occurs in *Vājasaneyi Saṁhitā* 5.7.; *Śatapatha* 3.4.3. 21; *Aitareya Brāhmaṇa* 1.26; and *Taittirīya Saṁhitā* 1.2.11. The notes of the *Bhāṣyakāras* in respect of this *mantra* are as follows:

(i) एष्टा रायः । यजतेः कृतसंप्रसारणस्य एतद्रूपं निष्ठाप्रत्यये परतो दानार्थस्य । आ इष्टा रायः मर्यादया इष्टानि धनानि । - Uvaṭa.

(ii) हे इष्टः । तृजन्तस्य संबुद्धिः । - Sāyaṇa.

(iii) हे एष्टः । ...यद्वा एष्टा इति प्रथमान्तम् । Sāyaṇa.

(iv) हे एष्टः एषणशील । केचिन्निष्ठायां वर्णव्यत्ययेन इकारस्य एकारमाहुः, आमन्त्रितत्वं च मन्यन्ते । तदा आद्युदात्तत्वं च दुर्लभम् । शाखान्तरे तु " आ इष्टः एष्टः " इति मत्वा अवग्रहं कुर्वन्ति - Bhaṭṭa Bhāskara.

From the above remarks of the *Bhāṣyakāras*, it is clear that in the *Taittirīya Padapāṭha*, the word एष्टः has been understood as one word, while, in the *Mādhyandina Padapāṭha* it is taken as an *avagṛhīta pada* and is recited as आऽ इष्टः. Again, it is taken as vocative by the *Taittirīya Padakāra*, while by the *Mādhyandina Padakāra* it is treated as an adjective of 'Rāyaḥ.'

This is a clear indication of the fact that the *Saṁhitā* was reduced into *pada*s on the basis of *sāmarthya* and the meaning of the *mantra* as was understood by the authors of the various *Padapāṭhas*. It is true that when we study the *mantras* today our best and the principal guide is the *Padapāṭha*. But it is also equally true that the guiding principle for the author of the *Padapāṭha* was the meaning and the *sāmarthya* as he understood it in reducing a particular *mantra* to *padas*. For the author of the *Padapāṭha* the main rule to follow was समर्थः पदविधिः as understood by the unknown author of the *Atharvaveda Prātiśākhya*.

This much discussion should give us an idea of the *Padapāṭha*, its purpose, and the method of the *pada*-construction.

Before we close this chapter, we shall try to get an idea of another *pāṭha* of the *Veda* known as *Kramapāṭha*. *Ṛk-Prātiśākhya* has dealt with this subject in detail along with the argument to establish the necessity of it (see *Ṛk. Pr.* - *Paṭalas* X and XI).

Kramapāṭha is based on the combination of the *Saṁhitāpāṭha* and the *Padapāṭha* together in respect of two *padas* of a verse each time in succession. This will be clear by an example :

(1) संहिता पाठ - पर्जन्याय प्रगायत दिवस्पुत्राय मीळ्हुषे ।

(२) पदपाठ - पर्जन्याय । प्र । गायत । दिवः । पुत्राय । मीळ्हुषे

(३) क्रमपाठ -पर्जन्याय प्र । प्रगायत ।
गायत दिवः । दिवस्पुत्राय ।
पुत्राय मीळ्हुषे । मीळ्हुष इति मीळ्हुषे ।

In the *Saṁhitāpāṭha*, the unit is half a verse; in the *Padapāṭha* the unit is a *pada*; in the *Kramapāṭha* the unit is two *padas* at a time coming in succession. The method of reading *Krama* is that you start reading the first two *padas* of a *mantra* in the *Saṁhitā* form; then you leave the first *pada* and add the third *pada* to second in succession and read them again in the *Saṁhitā* form, then leave the second and add the fourth, and in this way go to the end of half the verse. It is like a chain - 1-2; 2-3; 3-4; 4-5 and so on. Thus the unit of *Krama* each time is two *padas* read together in *Saṁhitā* form. The peculiarity of

Krama lies in the fact that when you read a *Krama* unit (*Krama-varga*) you exhibit the *'Ārṣī Saṁhitā'* as it stands between these two *padas,* and at the same time, you exhibit the beginning of the first *pada* and the end of the second *pada* in that unit.

At one stage the *Kramapāṭha* had been a matter of controversy as is evidenced by the *Ṛk-Prātiśākhya.* Śaunaka has very ably defended its necessity. Gradually it was picked up and absorbed by all the other *Śākhās* of different Vedas.

The *Saṁhitāpāṭha* is the original form of the *Veda.* The *Padapāṭha* is the first attempt on the part of the Vedic scholar in understanding its meaning. The *Kramapāṭha* is later than the *Padapāṭha* and depends on both the *Saṁhitā* and the *pada* for its existence. Yet it is very old. Traditionally Bābhravya Pāñcāla is said to have introduced it for the *Ṛgveda.* This Bābhravya is mentioned in the *Ṛṣi-Tarpaṇa* portion of the *Āśvalāyana* (3.4.4) and *Śāṅkhyāyana Gṛhya Sūtra.* (4.10.2) Secondly, all the three *pāṭha*s have been referred to in the *Aitareya Āraṇyaka* in the Chapter of *Saṁhitopāsanā* by the terms *Śauddhākṣara, Pratṛṇṇa,* and *Ubhayamantareṇa.*

The following are some of the purposes for which *Kramapāṭha* was introduced :-

The main purpose of all these attempts was *'Vedarakṣā'.* The *Veda* was to be saved both from being wrongly pronounced as well as from being wrongly interpreted. The first was the saving of the *Veda* from formal decay and the second was the saving of it from semantic one. While the *Prātiśākhya* was an attempt in the first direction, the *Nirukta* was that in the second. The *Kramapāṭha* is also an attempt to save the *Veda* from formal decay and stands as a joining link between the *Saṁhitā* and the *Pada.*

Now, to save the *Veda* from formal decay it was necessary to recite the *Saṁhitā* exactly in the form in which it was handed down by the teacher to the pupil in the long and continuous tradition (*Sampradāya*); and to save the *Veda* from wrong interpretation it was necessary to reduce the *Saṁhitā* to *padas* in pure form. This work was done by Śākalya and others in respect of their own *Saṁhitās*. But while reducing the *mantras* to *pada* form, at many places, the original form of the *pada* as a member of the *Saṁhitā* was many times lost e.g. the *Saṁhitā* मोषुण: when reduced to *padas* was read as मो इति । सु । न: । where the *Nata Sandhi* appearing in *Saṁhitā* recital was lost. It was necessary that the reciter should know the pure form of the *padas* and at the same time the original *Saṁhitā* form be not damaged. For this purpose the *Kramapāṭha* was introduced. How was this achieved by the *Kramapāṭha*?

(1) In the *Saṁhitāpātha* all the *padas* in a half *Ṛk* are recited in *Saṁhitā*. In the *padapāṭha* every *pada* is recited in its pure form. In the *Kramapāṭha* each time two *padas* are recited in *Saṁhitā*. The result is that the *Ārṣī Saṁhitā* in respect of these two *padas* is maintained and at the same time the beginning of the first and the end of the second *pada* are exhibited in the pure form. The example of *Krama* given above (viz., पर्जन्याय प्र । प्र गायत । गायत दिव: । दिवस्पुत्राय etc.) will show that in the *Kramapāṭha* each *pada* (except the first one) is repeated twice and while in its first appearance it exhibits its ending letter in its pure form, in its second appearance it exhibits the beginning letter in pure form. Thus the knowledge of the *pada* in its pure form as well as its modification in the *Saṁhitā* form are known at the same time in *Kramapāṭha*.

(2) The purpose of the *Kramapāṭha* is quite different from that of the *Padapāṭha*. While the *padapāṭha* shows each *pada* in its original form, the *Kramapāṭha* shows how the two *padas* standing in the *Saṁhitā*-relation affect each other. This will be clear from the following examples:-

(i) संहिता - अग्ने अच्छा वद ।
पद - अग्ने । अच्छ । वद ।
क्रम - अग्ने अच्छ । अच्छा वद ।

Here in the first *Krama* unit the *pada* अच्छ appears in pure form as it is found in the *padapāṭha*, but, in the second *Krama* unit, it is in *Saṁhitā* with वद and hence is modified as अच्छा वद ।

(ii) संहिता - यच्छक्वरीषु बृहता ।
पद - यत् । शक्वरीषु । बृहता ।
क्रम - यच्छक्वरीषु । शक्वरीषु बृहता ।

Here in the first *Krama* unit the *pada* शक्वरीषु stands in Saṁhitā relation with यत् and hence appears in the modified form but in the second *krama* unit it is shown in the pure form as in *padapāṭha*.

(iii) संहिता - प्रण इन्दो ।
पद - प्र । नः । इन्दो इति ।
क्रम - प्रणः । न इन्दो ।

Here in the first *Krama* unit, the *pada* नः stands in the *Saṁhitā* with प्रः hence is modified as णः ।. In the second *Krama* unit, न stands as it is, but, the *visarga* of नः is dropped as a result of its *Saṁhitā* with इन्दो.

(3) It is owing to the *Kramapāṭha* that we are able to understand the modifications of *Svara* during the *Sandhi* of the two *padas*. The *pada* has its own *Svara* (accent) and *Saṁhitā* determines the *svara* of the sentence e.g.

संहिता - प॒र्जन्या॑य॒ प्र गा॑यत दि॒वस्पुत्राय॑ मी॒ळ्हुषे॑ ।

पद - प॒र्जन्या॑य । प्र । गा॒ य॒ त॒ । दि॒वः । पु॒त्राय । मी॒ळ्हुषे॑ ।

क्रम - प॒र्जन्या॑य॒ प्र । प्र गा॑यत । गा॒ य॒ त॒ दि॒ व॒ः ।
दि॒वस्पु॒त्राय । पु॒त्राय॑ मी॒ळ्हुषे॑ । मी॒ळ्हु॒ष॒ । इति॑ मी॒ळ्हुषे॑ ।

The comparison of the accents in the above *Saṁhitā*, *pada* and *krama* in case of पर्जन्याय प्रगायत दिवः will at once reveal to us as to how the accents of the various *padas* have been modified in various readings.

(4) The *padas* undergo various types of modifications when they stand in *Saṁhitā*. Many times we cannot get a clear idea of the pure form of *pada* through the *Saṁhitāpāṭha* as well as their modification. It is only through the *Kramapāṭha* that we can get a clear idea about them. In all such cases in the *Kramapāṭha* the *krama* units are first recited in the *Saṁhitā* form and then the *padas* in that *krama* unit are distinctly shown by resorting to *'parigraha'* e.g.

(i) संहिता - ऋषिभिरीड्यः
पद - ऋषिऽभिः । ईड्यः ।
क्रम - ऋषिभिरीड्यः । ऋषिभिरिति ऋषिऽभिः ।

(ii) संहिता - मोषुणः
पद - मो इति । सु । नः ।
क्रम - मोषुणः। मो इति मो । सु इति सु

(iii) संहिता - तन्नः ।
पद - तत् । नः
क्रम - तन्नः । तदिति तत् ।

(iv) संहिता - तंनः ।
पद - तम् । नः ।
क्रम - तंनः । तमिति तम् ।

(v) संहिता - ईयते नरा च शंसं दैव्यम् ।
पद - ईयते । नराशंसम् । च । दैव्यम् ।
क्रम - ईयते नराच शंसं दैव्यम् ।
नराशंसमिति नराशंसम् । चेति च ।

In all the above examples of *Kramapāṭha*, the *krama* unit is first recited in *Saṁhitā* form and then the various *padas* in that unit are shown by *parigraha*, in which by *'Sthitopasthita'* method, the *pada* is again repeated after ' इति ' to show the *avagraha* or any other peculiarity in it. e.g. ऋषिभिरिति ऋषिऽभिः । is the case of *'parigraha'.* In this the form ऋषिभिः coming before इति appears as it is in *Saṁhitā.* This *pada* is again repeated after इति and shown as ऋषिऽभिः and thus its real *pada* form is exhibited.

It will thus be seen that in all cases of *Kramavarga* where the pure form of *pada* is not evident, that *pada* form is always shown by resorting to *parigraha.*

This much should give the student an idea of the method and purpose of the *Kramapāṭha.* Some more instances of *'parigraha'* will again be discussed in the Chapter on *'Prātiśākhya'* where the nature of *Krama-sandhi* will be made clear. In all cases of *'parigraha'* Śaunaka has given reasons, which may be studied from *Ṛk. Prātiśākhya, Paṭalas* X and XI.

The importance of the knowledge of *Padapāṭha* and *Kramapāṭha* for the correct and faultless recital of the *Saṁhitā* will be clearly appreciated from the following example. In the *Taittirīya Saṁhitā,* there is a *prapāṭhaka* commonly known as शतरुद्रिय. It contains a *Yajus* as -

नमः सूतायाहन्त्याय वनानां पतये नमः । (*तै.सं.* 4.5.9)

Its *padas* are : नमः । सूताय । अहन्त्याय । वनानाम् । पतये । नमः । and its *krama* reads as : नमः सूताय । सूतायाहन्त्याय । अहन्त्याय वनानाम्। वनानां पतये । पतये नमः । नम इति नमः ।

This gives us the clear understanding, that the *padas* are अहन्त्याय and वनानाम्. So the correct recital of the *Saṁhitā* will be नमः सूतायाहन्त्याय - then there will be a pause (विराम) which will be followed by the recital as वनानां पतये नमः ।

A Vedic reciter of the *Taittirīya Śākhā,* who generally is acquainted with the *padapāṭha* and the *kramapāṭha* of his *Śākhā,* will read as above.

Now, many *Ṛgvedins* have to recite this *Prapāṭhaka* as a part of their priestly profession, for, it is to be recited at the occasion of *Rudrābhiṣeka*. These *Ṛgvedin* priests generally study the *Saṁhitāpāṭha* of this *Prapāṭhaka* (which is generally separately printed as a matter of convenience). They do not study the *padapāṭha* and the *krama* of that *prapāṭhaka*. Naturally they do not get the correct idea of the *padas* of that portion. So many of them pause at a wrong place while reciting the *Saṁhitā* and recite as नमः सूतायाहृत्या - pause - यवनानां पतये नमः । I have myself heard such mistaken recital of the above *Yajus* many times and from many priests in *Mahārāṣṭra*. And it appears that such mistaken recital of this *Yajus* has been in vogue at least for the last two centuries as can be inferred from an anecdote quoted by Pt. Kashinath Shastri Lele of Wai in his introduction to the edition of Rudrādhyāya (cf. काशीनाथ शास्त्री लेले, रुद्राध्याय, मराठी भाषांतर, प्रस्तावना पान - २, ३).

Of course, the *Saṁhitāpāṭha* is the original *Veda* and for the *'Vedarakṣā'* it is absolutely necessary that it is recited correctly and has to be protected against formal decay. And for that, the knowledge of the *Padapāṭha* and the *Kramapāṭha* is also equally necessary.

■■

Chapter Three

THE PRĀTIŚĀKHYA

Śikṣā, Vyākaraṇa and Chandas - these three are the safeguards of the Vedic text, and as the *Ṛk-Prātiśākhya,* which is the most comprehensive and complete of all the *Prātiśākhya* works, contains all these three elements, we may hazard a generalisation that the *Prātiśākhya* is the safeguard of the *Saṁhitā* text, having been composed for the purpose of exhibiting all the operations necessary for changing the *padas* into *Saṁhitā.* We may, therefore, say that the oldest textbooks of the above three *Vedāṅgas* are the *Prātiśākhyas.*

On the origin of the *Prātiśākhyas,* Max Müller writes: "During the Brāhmanical period the songs of the *Veda* were preserved by oral tradition only; and as the spoken language of India had advanced and left the idiom of the *Veda* as a kind of antique and sacred utterance, it was difficult to preserve the proper pronunciation of the sacred hymns without laying down a certain number of rules on meter, accent and pronunciation in general. The necessity of such provision, however, could hardly have become felt until certain differences had actually arisen in different seats of Brāhmanical learning. Thus, when the attempt was made to prevent a further corruption, a certain number of local varieties in accent and pronunciation, and in recital of hymns, had actually crept in and become sanctioned by the tradition of different families or schools. These could not be given up, nor was there any means of determining which was the ancient and the most correct way of reciting the sacred songs of the *Veda.* Discussions having arisen on this subject, we find in the *Brāhmaṇa*s, occasional mention of the verses which, if improperly pronounced, become changed in their meaning. But even when the sense of the *Veda* is not affected, the respect paid by each teacher, by each family and by each Brāhmanical community to its own established oral tradition, was sufficient to give an imaginary value to the slightest peculiarities of the pronunciation, accent and meter.

"Twofold advantage was gained when the rules and the exceptions of the old sacred dialect were first reduced to a system. First, ancient dialectical differences, many of which were not so much attributable to the corruptions as to the freedom of old spoken language, were carefully preserved, and even apparent irregularities and exceptions were handed down as such, instead of being eliminated and forgotten. Secondly, a start was made towards a scientific study of Language by the collection of similar passages, general laws were elicited which afterwards served as a phonetic basis of a grammar like that of Pāṇini - a work which although ascribed to one author, must have required ages of observation and collection before its plan could be conceived and carried out by one individual.

"Even the *Prātiśākhyas* though they do not refer to grammar properly so called but principally to the phonetic laws of the language, presuppose a long continued study of grammatical subjects previous to the time of their composition. The best proof of this lies in the great number of authors quoted in the *Prātiśākhyas* themselves." (Max Müller: *History of Ancient Sanskrit Literature,* 1859, pp. 117-118).

The term *Prātiśākhya* has been explained as शाखायां शाखायां or शाखां शाखां प्रति, प्रतिशाखम्, प्रतिशाखं भवं प्रातिशाख्यम् । which indicated that there must have been a textbook of the nature of *Prātiśākhya* attached to each *Śākhā*. The extant *Prātiśākhyas*, however, reveal that they do not relate to any particular *Śākhā*. On the other hand, they contain general rules observed in all the *Śākhās* of a particular *Caraṇa*, noting of course the differences observed in particular *Śākhā*. Yāska also notes this fact when he says : पदप्रकृतीनि सर्वचरणानां पार्षदानि, (*Nir* - 1.17).

This shows that the *Prātiśākhyas* relate to the *Caraṇa* and not a particular *Śākhā*. The *Prātiśākhya* is termed as *Pārṣada* also, which implies that the treatise belongs to a special group (*Pariṣad*) in which, among other things, general principles of phonetics were adopted to the Vedic texts by oral tradition. *Caraṇa* is distinct from *Śākhā* in so far as it includes in it all the *Śākhās* in respect of a particular *Saṁhitā*. The *Saṁhitā* was first handed down by the main Ācārya, which later on was further handed down by different pupils to the progeny; and this handing down contained certain differences in readings at certain places in the *Sāṁhitā*. This led to different *Śākhās*. e.g. Vājasaneya Yājñavalkya handed down the original *Saṁhitā*. This was later on taught by such teachers as Mādhyandina, Kaṇva, Gālava, etc., leading to certain differences in readings and pronunciation. But, they all are the *Vājasaneyi Saṁhitās*. The term *Vājasaneyi* indicates the *Caraṇa* of which Mādhyandina, Kāṇva, etc. are the *Śākhās*.

That the *Prātiśākhya* relates to different *Śākhās* in one *Caraṇa* and that the arrangement of the readings is determined by the *Pariṣad* has been hinted at in the following statements of different writers:

(i) द्वित्रिशाखाविषयत्वेऽपि तदसाधारणतयोपपत्तेः । तथा बह्वृचानां शाकलबाष्कलात्मकशाखाद्वयविषयं प्रातिशाख्यं प्रसिद्धम् । - Gopāla Yajwā in the *Vaidikābharaṇa* on *T.Pr.* IV - 11.

(ii) धर्मशास्त्राणां गृह्यग्रंथानां च प्रातिशाख्यलक्षणं प्रतिचरणं पाठव्यवस्थोपलभ्यते । - Kumārila, *Tantravārtika*, I.17.

(iii) स्वचरणपरिषद्येव यैः प्रतिशाखानियतमेव पदावग्रहप्रगृह्यक्रमसंहितास्वरलक्षण-मुच्यते, तानीमानि पार्षदानि प्रातिशाख्यानि इत्यर्थः । - Durga on the *Nirukta*, I. 17.

That the *Prātiśākhya* at its earliest stage related to its own *Śākhā* and noted the *Saṁhitā* recitation therein, is indicated by such statements as: (1) एवमेहेति शाखायामिति शास्त्रप्रयोजनम् - (Uvaṭa on *Ṛk. Pr.* Introduction); (2) एवमिह इति च विभाषाप्राप्तं सामान्ये (*Caturadhyāyī*, I.1), and the like.

These statements allude to the specific purpose for which the *Prātiśākhya* literature came into existence. The teacher of the particular *Śākhā* was very strict in adhering to the peculiarities of that *Śākhā* in respect of both the ritual as well as recitation. If any one substituted anything from another *Śākhā* in place of any part of his recital or ritual, he was condemned, as is noted in the verse:

स्वशाखाश्रयमुत्सृज्य परशाखाश्रयं तु यः ।
कर्तुमिच्छति दुर्मेधा मोघं तत् तस्य जीवितम् ॥ (कर्मप्रदीप, I.3)

This was true not only in respect of recitation but in respect of *Gṛhya* rituals also. But gradually there arose a position in respect of rituals in which it was permitted to adopt the rituals in another *Śākhā* if that particular part of the ritual was not present in one's *Śākhā*, as is seen from the verse:

यन्नाम्नातं स्वशाखायां परोक्तमविरोधि यत् ।
विद्वद्भिस्तदनुष्ठेयमग्निहोत्रादिकर्मवत् ॥ (*Ibid* I.3)

This brought various *Śākhā*s nearer and gradually there started assimilation. The result was that the number of *Śākhā*s got gradually reduced and the more favoured ones continued to flourish. This naturally brought a stage of assimilation of their *Prātiśākhya* manuals also. Much of the matter in the *Prātiśākhya* manuals was common and they differed in very few respects. The *Prātiśākhya* relating to the most favoured *Śākhā* continued and the peculiarities of the other manuals were recognised in the same as the views of अन्ये, अपरे, एके. In this way, the *Prātiśākhya* which in its original position started as a manual of a particular *Śākhā*, was recognised as a *Pārṣada* of a *Caraṇa*. All the extant *Prātiśākhyas* represent this stage of assimilation.

The extant *Prātiśākhyas* take for granted the *Saṁhitāpāṭha* and the *Padapāṭha*. For the purpose of training (शास्त्रदृष्टि), they suppose that the *pada* is the *Prakṛti* and that the *Saṁhitā* is modification (*Vikṛti* विकृति). Taking these things as the basis, they attempt to evolve certain general rules which appear to govern the modified recital of the *padas* at the *Saṁhitā* stage. While noting those rules, they also note the cases which do not appear to follow the general rule, but, exhibit their peculiar tendency which forms the exception. They also note the individual cases where neither the rule nor the exception operates and enumerate each and every case of such type. Not a single instance is left unnoticed, the enumeration is so perfect. The general rules (न्याय), the exception (अपवाद) and the enumeration of the individual cases not covered by both (प्रतिकण्ठ), together form one topic in a *Prātiśākhya* work. This is the *Prātiśākhya* method of dealing with every topic. The *Ṛk-Prātiśākhya* states this in the following *kārikā*:

न्यायैर्मिश्रानपवादान् प्रतीयात्
सर्वशास्त्रार्थं प्रतिकण्ठमुक्तम् ॥ (*Ṛk. Pr.* II.4)

The purpose of the *Prātiśākhya* is to keep *Saṁhitāpāṭha* intact in respect of modifications both of *svara* and *varṇa,* and their utterance. Therefore, it has to deal with the topics which later on became the special subject matters of *Śikṣā, Vyākaraṇa* and *Chandas*. The *Prātiśākhya,* in a way, is the forerunner of these three *Vedāṅga*s. It is all these three combined in one. These three have a great bearing on the Vedic recitation. For our purpose, we shall keep the *Chandas* portion aside and say a few words about the other two. The phonetic discussions in the *Prātiśākhya* culminated into what is called the science of *Śikṣā,* while its *svara-saṁskāra* discussions formed the main basis on which the *sandhi*å rules of later grammar were developed. We will, therefore, say a few words in comparison of *Śikṣā* and the *Prātiśākhya* before we take up its grammatical aspect.

The main topics in *Śikṣā* are: the description of *Sthāna, Karaṇa,* and *Āsya-prayatna* of letters; the method of pronunciation and the methods to be adopted in the oral study of the Vedic text. These are no doubt included in the *Prātiśākhya,* but, that is not its only purpose. The other important and perhaps the main purpose of the *Prātiśākhya* is to explain the *svara-saṁskāra,* i.e., the modification of letters and accents as found in the *Saṁhitā.* These *saṁskāras* are of the nature of *āgama, ādeśa, lopa, vikāra,* and *prakṛtibhāva* of letters. We may, therefore, say that the *svara-saṁskāra* is the principal subject matter of the *Prātiśākhya,* while *Sthānānupradāna* etc. are the main topics of *Śikṣā.* The fact that all the details of *svara* and *saṁskāra* mentioned in the *Prātiśākhya* have been incorporated and fully utilised by later grammatical works indicates that the *Prātiśākhya* has greater proximity to Grammar than to *Śikṣā* and hence they can be treated as the earliest grammatical attempts available.

Some scholars like Winternitz opine that the *Prātiśākhyas* belong mainly to the *Śikṣā* branch of the *Vedāṅga.* In my opinion, it would be better to include them in the *Vyākaraṇa.* The modifications of *svara* and *varṇa* are among the principal topics of the *Vyākaraṇa* and as the earliest works dealing with these are the *Prātiśākhyas,* they have their proper place in the *Vyākaraṇa.* This is supported by some statements from the *Vājasaneyi Prātiśākhya.* The first *sūtra* of that work opens as स्वरसंस्कारयोः छन्दसि नियमः (Vaj. Pr.I.1), indicating that the main topic of the work is to explain *svara* and *saṁskāra.* Later on in the 29th *Sūtra* it introduces the topic pertaining to the *Śikṣā* saying अथ शिक्षाविहिताः I, i.e., the elements of *Sthāna, Karaṇa, Āsya-prayatna* etc. are now introduced. Here the work refers to *Śikṣā* as something which has purpose and subject matter different from its own and it is being now introduced. This clearly indicates that the main topic of discussion in the *Prātiśākhya* is *svara-saṁskāra,* while that of the *Śikṣā* is *Sthānānupradāna,* etc.

The following examples will show that the *svara-saṁskāra* dealt with by the *Prātiśākhya* has close affinity to grammatical operation. The rules रषाभ्यां नो णः समानपदे and अट्कुप्वाङ्नुम्व्यवायेऽपि (Pāṇini 8-4-1,2) are well known rules of Pāṇini bearing on the णत्व of न्. These have corresponding rules in the *Vāj. Prātiśākhya* as ऋषरेफेभ्यो नकारो णकारं समानपदे and स्वरयवहकपैश्च (3.84 and 95). The examples of the first *sūtra* are नृणाम्, पूष्णः, पूर्णः. These rules have no direct bearing on the *Prātiśākhya*, for it deals with the नकार of the *Pratyaya* standing before the *Prakṛti* as indicated by the word समानपदे in the *sūtra*. Consequently, the second rule should have no bearing as it also deals with the cases of समानपद. But compare the following *padas* and *Saṁhitās* in the *Yajurveda*:

Pada	*Saṁhitā*
पुरीष - वाहनः	अग्ने पुरीषवाहणः ।
नृ - मनाः	तृतीयमप्सु नृमणाः ।
प्र - वाहनः	विभूरसि प्रवाहणः ।

It will be seen that in the *pada* stage, न is not changed to ण, while, at the *Saṁhitā* stage, it is changed. At the *pada* stage, the compounds नृऽमनाः, पुरीषऽवाहनः, प्रऽवाहनः are read with *avagraha* and hence their समानपदत्व is disturbed. But when read in *Saṁhitā,* they are read without *avagraha* and hence their समानपदत्व is maintained. Hence Uvaṭa says:

स्वरैर्यकारवकारहकारैः कपवर्गाभ्यां च व्यवहिते नकारः णकारमापद्यते संहितायाम्।

This shows how the *svara-saṁskāra* rules of *Prātiśākhya* and the corresponding rules of Grammar have a close relationship.

Secondly, the Commentators look at *Prātiśākhya* as a special application of general Grammar in respect of particular *Śākhā*. Thus, Uvaṭa introduces his *Bhāṣya* on *Ṛk-Prātiśākhya* with the following verse:

पाणिन्यादिव्याकरणे सामान्येनोक्तलक्षणम् ।
तदेवमिह शाखायामिति शास्त्रप्रयोजनम् ॥

Explaining the purpose of *Ṛk-Prātiśākhya,* Uvaṭa says: The rules given by Pāṇini and others are of a general nature. The purpose of this *Prātiśākhya* is to show that those general rules are seen applied in this *Śākhā* in such and such manner. This means that while Pāṇini and others wrote general Grammar of Language, the *Prātiśākhyas* are Special Grammars of particular *Śākhās.*

Thirdly, Patañjali says in the *Mahābhāṣya* "सर्वपारिषदं हीदं शास्त्रम्" (*Mbh.,* Vol. III., P. 146) meaning that *Vyākaraṇa* is a science common to all the *Pārṣadas.*

All these points clearly indicate that the *Prātiśākhya* is more integrally related to the *Vyākaraṇa* than to the *Śikṣā.*

We are now in a position to state the main topics in the *Prātiśākhya.* It lays down rules for proper recitation of the *Saṁhitā, Pada* and *Krama.* It is attached to a *Caraṇa* of the *Veda* and covers all its *Śākhās.* It gives the general description of the *varṇas* employed in that *Veda,* both at the *pada* stage and the *Saṁhitā* stage. It deals with all the modifications of the *varṇa* and *svara.* All the individual cases in which peculiar phonetic and other changes take place, are especially pointed out. It is also understood from the *Prātiśākhya* as to how the *Saṁhitā* is reconstructed from the *padas;* where the *padas* are given in their original forms as unaffected by any *ādeśa, āgama, lopa,* shift position etc. and to explain all these as briefly as possible, it takes resort to certain *Saṁjñās* and *Paribhāṣās.* Other things may be treated as ancillary. All these topics may be broadly stated as (1) *Varṇasamāmnāya,* (2) *Saṁjñā-Paribhāṣā,* (3) *Svara-vidhāna* and (4) *Saṁskāra- vidhāna.* All the extant *Prātiśākhyas* will be seen to have these four broad divisions.

We may now turn to the extant *Prātiśākhyas* proper. The *Ṛgveda Prātiśākhya* is admittedly the oldest work. It is generally admitted by the scholars that the chronological order of the *Prātiśākhyas* is as follows:

1. The *Ṛgveda Prātiśākhya* ascribed to Śaunaka;
2. The *Taittirīya Prātiśākhya*;
3. The *Vājasaneyi Prātiśākhya* ascribed to Kātyāyana;
4. The *Śaunakīya Caturadhyāyī*;
5. The *Ṛk-Tantra*; and
6. The *Atharva Prātiśākhya*.

Secondly, all the extant *Prātiśākhyas* except the last one are pre-Pāṇinian; only the *Atharva Prātiśākhya* is post-Pāṇinian.

Of all the extant *Prātiśākhyas* the *Ṛk-Prātiśākhya* is complete and comprehensive in all respects. So, an analysis of this would give us a complete idea of *Prātiśākhya* works. This *Prātiśākhya* has eighteen chapters known as *Paṭalas*. The last three *Paṭalas* deal with the *Chandas*. The chapters 13 to 15 (both inclusive) deal with matters pertaining to *Śikṣā* and the method of *Pārāyaṇa*. We may leave these six chapters out of discussion as they do not pertain directly to grammar, and we may concentrate on the first twelve chapters. The broad division of the first twelve chapters will be:

Ch. I - Enumeration of *Varṇas*, *Saṁjñās* and *Paribhāṣās*,
Ch. II to IX - *Sandhis* or *Saṁhitās* of all types,
Ch. X and XI - *Kramapāṭha* and *Kramahetus*.
Ch. XII - *Padādis* and *Padāntas*.

The break up of the *Saṁhitā Kāṇda*, i.e., Chapters II to IX will be as under :-

Ch. II - *Svara Sandhi*; Ch. III - Accent in the *Saṁhitā*;
Ch. IV - *Vyañjana Sandhi*; Ch. V. - *Nata Sandhi*;
Ch. VI - *Varṇa krama Sandhi*; Ch. VII to IX - *Sāmavaśa Sandhi*.

It will be seen from the above that the first twelve chapters of the *Ṛk-Prātiśākhya* cover all the topics pertaining to *Svara-saṁskāra*, and the Study of *Pada, Saṁhitā*, and *Krama*, which is the subject-matter of the *Prātiśākhya* proper. This also covers the fourfold division of the subject-matter mentioned above. The other *Prātiśākhyas* also have all these topics arranged in their works according to their own plans. We may now take up each of these and try to understand their relevance in the grammatical studies.

The principal attempt of the *Prātiśākhya* is to combine the *padas* into *Saṁhitā* text. The *padas* are, therefore, taken as the basis or *Prakṛti*; and the *Saṁhitā* text, as modified text or the *Vikṛti*; the rules being termed as *'Vikāraśāstra'*. The *Ṛk-Prātiśākhya* states this as संहिता पदप्रकृतिः meaning that the *prakṛti* of the *saṁhitā* is the *padas* and *Uvaṭa* explains it as "संहितात्र विकारः ...प्रकृतिभूतत्वात् पदानां सिद्धत्वम् ।" How is the *Saṁhitā* formed from the *Padas*? The answer is given as पदान्तान् पदादिभिः संदधदेति यत् सा कालाव्यवायेन । meaning that the *Saṁhitā* comes into existence when the endings of the previous *padas* are recited by combining them with the beginnings of the subsequent *padas*, without interval of time. The first thing to be noted, therefore, is that the Sandhi rules of the *Prātiśākhyas* operate on the endings and the beginnings of the *padas*, and they have nothing to do with the modifications taking place in the formation of the *pada* as such, which is one of the principal topics in the later grammatical works. The *Ṛk-Prātiśākhya* says पदान्तादिष्वेव विकारशास्त्रम् meaning that the rules of *Sandhi* operate only on the endings and beginnings of the *padas* and nowhere else, i.e., in the formation of the *pada* itself.

Secondly, these rules are applicable only to those cases of the *padas* that are actually found in the *Padapāṭha* and not in any other form (पदेषु दृष्टेषु). For example, one of the *Sandhi* rules reads उकारोदय ओकारम् (ऋ. प्रा. 2.17) and lays down that when अ standing at the end of the *pada* is followed by उ standing at the beginning of the following *pada*, both together are pronounced as ओ in the *Saṁhitā*. e.g. अयाम + उप = अयामोप (I.33.1). Now we read in the *Saṁhitā* as वाय उक्थेभिर्जरन्ते (1.2.2). In this we have अ followed by उ at वाय उक्थेभिः. The above rule उकारोदय ओकारम् appears to have scope here. But that cannot be applied because the word form वाय is not found in the *Padapāṭha*, the form there being वायो.

The third thing to note is that in the *Ṛk-Prātiśākhya* we have only two stages; the *pada* stage where each *pada* is read in its original or pre-*sandhi* form, and the *Saṁhitā* stage, where we get it in the modified form. The intermediate stages which we find in later grammar are altogether absent in the *Ṛk-Prātiśākhya,* e.g. वायो + उक्थेभिः=वाय उक्थेभिः. Here we find the finished form in the *Saṁhitā* and the rule 2.28, states पूर्वौ चोपोत्तमात् स्वरौ स्वरपरौ अकारमापद्येते i.e. when ए and ओ standing at the end of the *pada* are followed by a vowel, they, i.e. ए and ओ are pronounced as अ in the *Saṁhitā* form. It is interesting to note here how *Pāṇini* would explain this *Saṁhitā* in his system. He would say:

वायो + उक्थेभिः ।

वायव् + उक्थेभिः । by एचोऽयवायावः । (P. 6. 1. 78)

वाय उक्थेभिः by लोपः शाकल्यस्य । पूर्वत्रासिद्धम् । (P. 8. 3. 19 & 8. 2. 1)

This middle step of वायव् उक्थेभिः is altogether absent in the *Ṛk-Prātiśākhya*. Let us take another example : यः + इन्द्रः = य इन्द्रः in य इन्द्र सोमपातमः (ऋ. 8.12.1). Here the *Ṛk-Prātiśākhya* says: ऽहस्वपूर्वस्तु सोऽकारम् (1.27) i. e. when the *arifita visarjanīya,* preceded by अ, is followed by any vowel at the *pada* stage, then at the *Saṁhitā* stage that *visarjanīya* along with the preceding अ will be changed as अ in the *Saṁhitā*. Now Pāṇini will put it as follows:

1. यः इन्द्रः

2. यस् इन्द्रः by विसर्जनीयस्य सः । (P. 8. 3. 34)

3. यरु इन्द्रः by ससजुषो रुः । (P. 8. 2. 66)

4. यय् इन्द्रः by भोभगोअघोऽपूर्वस्य योऽशि । (P. 8. 3. 17)

5. य इन्द्रः by लोपः शाकल्यस्य, पूर्वत्रासिद्धम् । (P. 8.3.19 & 8.2.1.)

All the intermediate steps 2,3, and 4 are absent in the *Ṛk-Pr.* Thus we find that the *Ṛk-Prātiśākhya* noted only the *pada* and the *Saṁhitā* stages in its *sandhi* rules and does not mention any intermediate stages in the analysis as we find them in Pāṇini.

If we take notice of the other *sandhis* as described in the respective *Prātiśākhyas*, we shall find that there has been a gradual progress in the building up step by step of the *sandhi* form. For example, in the *Vājasaneyi Prātiśākhya* we find: इडे एहि = इड एहि

This is derived as

1) इडे एहि
   इडय् एहि by मध्यक्षरमयवायावम् (4.48)
   इड एहि by यवयोः पदान्तयोः स्वरमध्ये लोपः (4.127)

2) इन्द्रः एकम्
   इन्द्रय् एकम् by कण्ठ्यपूर्वो यकारमरिफितः (4.38)
   इन्द्र एकम् by dropping य् acc. to 4.128 as above.

We have similar rules in other *Prātiśākhyas* to explain the above *sandhi*. Thus *Taittirīya Prātiśākhya* would say:

(1) अथ स्वरपरो यकारम् (विसर्जनीयः) 9:10,

(2) एकारोऽयम् । ओकारोऽवम् । ऐकार आयम् । औकार आवम् । 9.11,12,14,15.

(3) लुप्येते तु अवर्णपूर्वौ यकारवकारौ and optionally नोख्यस्य । 10.19,20.

The *Caturadhyāyī* has the following rules:

(1) स्वरे यकारः (2.40)

(2) सन्ध्यक्षराणामयवायावः (3.40)

(3) स्वराद्यवयोः पदान्तयोः (2.21)

(4) यवलोपे (प्रकृत्या) 3. 35.

In the *Ṛk-Tantra,* we have the following rules:

(1) सन्ध्यमयवायवम् (सू. 111)

(2) र मध्ये (सू. 159)

(3) अस्थात् यम् (सू. 117) when the विसर्जनीय changes to य्.

This would show how the intermediate steps were being noted in the later *Prātiśākhyas.*

We shall have occasion to study this progress in respect of every *sandhi* rule, when, in the second part, we shall study the *sandhi* rules of Pāṇini in the light of the corresponding *sandhi* rules in the *Prātiśākhyas.* The above two examples would be sufficient at this stage to show the line of progress towards which the *Prātiśākhyas* were heading in respect of the grammatical analysis of the *sandhis.* This would also show how the *Prātiśākhyas* have an intrinsic relation to grammar.

This is so far as the *sandhis* are concerned. But, in other few points also, the *Prātiśākhyas* show some sort of acquaintance with grammar. Thus, the rules of *avagraha* in the *Prātiśākhyas* show that the *Padakāras* had already divided the *samāsas* into their component parts. The same is seen in the case of *upasarga* and *ākhyāta,* some *taddhita* affixes and a few case affixes such as भ्याम्, भिः, भ्यः, under certain circumstances. This is the beginning of breaking up of the *pada* into its component parts. The *Padapāṭha* of the *Sāmaveda* ascribed to Gārgya shows some more peculiarities. Certain *padas* which are not separated into parts in the *Ṛgvedic Padapāṭha,* are shown separated in the *Padapāṭha* of the *Sāmaveda.* For example:

Pada in the *Ṛgveda*	*Pada* in the *Sāmaveda*
परीणसि	परि ऽ नसि
दूरात्	दुः ऽ आत्
उत्सः	उत् ऽ सः
समुद्रम्	सम् ऽ उद्रम्
प्राणः	प्र ऽ आनः

This is nothing but the splitting of the *pada* into further component units.

Certain *padas* in the *Sāmaveda Padapāṭha* reveal direct bearing on the *Uṇādi Sūtras*. For example:

स्वस्ति - सुऽअस्ति - सावसेः (उ. 638)
अद्भुतम् - अद्ऽभुतम् - अदि भुवो डुतच् (उ. 642)
चन्द्रमाः - चन्द्रऽमाः - चन्द्रे मो डित् (उ. 641)

These instances point out the importance of the *Padapāṭha* as the basis of the *Uṇādi Sūtras*. Now the *Uṇādi Sutras* are an intrinsic part of grammar. Dr. Sūryakānta has given many instances of similarity between the *Sāmaveda Padapāṭha* on the one hand and Yāska and Pāṇini on the other, and arrived at a sound conclusion when he said, "There is a remarkable affinity between the derivations implied by the *Sāmaveda Padapāṭha* and those given by Yāska and Pāṇini." (*Ṛk- Tantra*, Introduction, p.62).

We may now proceed to note certain general characteristics regarding the treatment of the fourfold topics in the *Prātiśākhyas*. They are: *Varṇasamāmnāya, Saṁjñā* and *Paribhāṣā, Svaravidhāna* and the *Saṁskāravidhāna*.

1. ***Varṇasamāmnāya***:- We are acquainted with the order of alphabets as given in Marāṭhī and Hindī. It is the same as that in Sanskrit and is known as लौकिक वर्णमाला. This has been followed by the *Vājasaneyi Prātiśākhya* and the *Prātiśākhyas* related to *Atharvaveda*. But the *Ṛk-Prātiśākhya*, the *Taittirīya Prātiśākhya* and the *Ṛk-Tantra* show a different tendency.

They do not include all the *varṇas* in the language, but, only those which they find necessary to note so far as the *sandhis* in their respective *Saṁhitās* are concerned. The *Ṛk-Prātiśākhya* notes the following vowels only, in the order given below:

अ, आ, ऋ, ॠ, इ, ई, उ, ऊ, ए, ओ, ऐ, औ = (12)

We find here two peculiarities: first, that ऋ, ॠ which should have come after ऊ have been placed after आ and before इ; and secondly, that no *pluta* vowels have been mentioned here as in other *Prātiśākhyas*. Likewise there is no mention of ऌ. Why so? That is because the author does not require the special mention of these vowels to explain the *sandhis* in the *Ṛgveda*. e.g. there are only three places in the *Ṛgveda* where *pluta* is found. They are अधस्विदासी ३ दुपरिस्विदासी ३ त् and भीरिव विन्दती ३.These have been noted in the *sūtra* I.31. The vowel ऌ does not occur in the *Ṛgveda* either at the end or at the beginning of any *pada*. The case of '*Kḷp*' has been noted in the *sūtra* XII.35. The vowel ḷ has been also mentioned at *sūtras* I-41; XII.1, and XIV.45. With these references as the special cases, the author of the *Ṛk-Prātiśākhya* has dispensed with the enumeration of ḷ in the series of vowels. The *sūtra* ऋकारादयो दश नामिनः स्वराः (1.65) indicates that Śaunaka places ṛ after ā. The order of the ऊष्मन् also is different from the ordinary order of letters. It is ह्, श्, ष्, स्, अः, क्, प् and अं = (8)

This order of the *Ūṣmans* has been indicated by the *sūtra* XIII. 10. This *sūtra* shows that the order of *Ūṣmans* according to Śaunaka is as shown above, and not as that of the लौकिक वर्णमाला.

This will give the idea as to how the authors of the *Prātiśākhya* works are interested in noting only those *varṇas* which they require for explaining the *sandhis* in their respective *Saṁhitās* and they are not interested in noting all the *varṇas* in the language. The same is true of the *Taittirīya* and the *Vāja- saneyi Prātiśākhyas*.

But, the most noteworthy enumeration is that of the *Ṛk-Tantra*. In the first *Prapāṭhaka;* it first gives the usual order of *varṇa*s and then states:

सन्निवेशोऽन्य: प्रत्याहारार्थ: । वर्णोऽनुबन्धो व्यंजनं यावतिथस्तावतां तदादीनां तत: पराणाम् ।

Then it gives an altogether unusual order of the *varṇas*. It is as follows: put - instead of, after each sound and retain the text as it is: ए, ओ, ऐ, औ, आ, ॠ, ॡ, ई, ऊ, ऋ, ऌ, इ, उ, आ: । र य व ला: । ङ ञ ण न मा: । घ झ द ध भा: । ग ज ड द बा: । ख छ ठ थ फा: । क च ट त पा: । ह श ष सा: । अ: ᳵ क ᳶ पा:। हुं कुं खुं गुं घुं अं आं. Then at the end it remarks इदमक्षरछन्दोवणेश: समनुक्रान्तम् meaning that this enumeration is as per *varṇas* in the *Chandas*. It was first noted by Brahmā and has come to us through the order of teachers noted as ब्रह्मा - बृहस्पति- इन्द्र - भरद्वाज - ऋषि - ब्राह्मणs.

This is known as अक्षरसमाम्नाय. Dr. Sūryakānta says that this was the order of letters adopted by Auḍavraji and Śākaṭāyana for their *Pratyāhāras*. This would indicate that the ideas of the *anubandha* and the *Pratyāhāra* and the peculiar order of letters goes as far back as Auḍavraji and Śākaṭāyana.

2. ***Saṁjñā* and *Paribhāṣā*:-** Every *Prātiśākhya* has formed its own *Saṁjñā*s and *Paribhāṣā*s. The *Saṁjñās* in the *Ṛk-Prātiśākhya* and the *Taittirīya Prātiśākhya* are in most places meaningful. But we find a tendency in the *Vājasaneyi Prātiśākhya* and the *Ṛk Tantra* to form artifical *Saṁjñās* such as *jit, mut, dhu, gha, san,* etc. This reminds us of the Pāṇinian *Saṁjñās* like *ṭi, ghu,* etc. The *Paribhāṣās* in each *Prātiśākhya* are the particular rules guiding us in interpreting the *sūtras*.

3. ***Svaravidhāna*:-** The importance of *svara* (accent) in *Vedic* study can never be minimised. A mistake committed in pronouncing an accent leads to different and disastrous meaning. The story of *Tvaṣṭṛ* in this respect is famous among the Vedic scholars. Venkaṭa Mādhava, a commentator of the

Ṛgveda, says that the accent throws light on the meaning in the same way as the lamp in darkness. (अन्धकारे दीपिकाभिः गच्छन्न स्खलति क्वचित् । एवं स्वरैः प्रणीतानां भवन्त्यर्थाः स्फुटा इति ॥ - स्वरानुक्रमणी, १८). It is for this reason that we appreciate the efforts of the Vedic teacher referred to in the *Mahābhāṣya,* who corrects his pupil by giving a slap because the latter uttered an *Anudātta* in place of *Udātta* (य उदात्ते कर्तव्येऽनुदात्तं करोति खण्डिकोपाध्यायस्तस्मै चपेटां ददात्यन्यत्वं करोति । म. भा. (Vol. 1.1). It is for this reason that every *Prātiśākhya* work gives detailed rules of accent.

The accents are of three types, viz., *Udātta, Anudātta,* and *Svarita. Udātta* and *Anudātta* are pure and independent accents. *Svarita* is a mixture of these two and hence it is a complex accent. Likewise, we hear of *Pracaya* in the *Prātiśākhya.* That also is not an independent accent, but a modification of *anudātta* when it follows *Svarita. Pracaya* is referred to by Pāṇini as *'Ekaśruti'.*

We need not go into the details of the nature of these accents. The Pāṇinian *sūtras* and the *Prātiśākhya* rules generally agree on this point. However, the treatment of *Svarita* in the *Prātiśākhyas* deserves special mention, for that is absent in the *Sūtras* of Pāṇini.

Svarita is a combination of *Udātta* and *Anudātta.* It is not an independent accent, nor does it come into existence independently, but only under certain circumstances, according to which, it has been divided by the *Prātiśākhyas* into the following types:

स्वरित
- उदात्तपूर्व
  - वैवृत्त
  - तैरोव्यंजन
  - तैरोऽवग्रह
- जात्य
  - नीचपूर्व
  - अपूर्वप्रश्लिष्ट
- सन्धिज
  - क्षैप्र
  - अभिनिहित

The उदात्तपूर्व *Svarita* is one where an *Anudātta* is changed into *Svarita* because it follows an *Udātta.* In this case, we always find an *Udātta* preceding the *Svarita* e.g. the *padas* अ्ग्निम् and ई ळे when read in the *Saṁhitā* form are uttered as अग्निमीळे. Here this *Svarita* has no independent existence but has come into being under the influence of the preceding *Udātta*. In modern terminology it is called 'dependent *Svarita*'.

In the *Saṁhitā* this is found in three circumstances. In many places we find in *Saṁhitā* a hiatus or *vivṛtti*. This hiatus at times is preceded by an *Udātta* and is followed by *Svarita* e.g. the *padas* य: । इ न्द्र are read in the *Saṁhitā* as य इन्द्र. Here there is a *vivṛtti* between य and इ न्द्र. Even then the *Udātta* in य has influenced the *Anudātta* इ in इ न्द्र and has changed it into *Svarita*. This is the case of *vaivṛtta svarita*. Another case is where there is a consonant intervening between the influencing *Udātta* and the resulting *Svarita*, e.g. when the *padas* अग्निम् । ई ळे । are read in the *Saṁhitā*, they are pronounced as अग्निमीळे. Here the consonant म् is intervening between the *Udātta* इ in अग्नि and the *Svarita* ई in ई ळे. In a way there is a sort of a curtain by which these two vowels are separated, and yet the result is *Svarita*. It is therefore called तैरोव्यंजन (तिरोऽन्तर्धानं व्यंजनं यस्य स: as Uvaṭa puts it).

The third case where the उदात्तपूर्वस्वरित is seen, is the case of *padas* with *avagraha*, e.g. the *pada* पुर:ऽहितम्. This is a compound in which पुर: is end *Udātta* and हितम् is *Anudātta*. In the *Saṁhitā* form, we read it as पुरोहितम् where the *Anudātta* is influenced by the preceding *Udātta* in रो giving rise to *Svarita* हि. The *Udātta* ओ and the *Svarita* इ are intervened by the consonant ह् and it is therefore तैरोव्यंजनस्वरित. But at the *pada* stage, it is read as पुर:ऽहितम् with an *avagraha* between the two *padas* पुर: and हितम् and yet the *Svarita* is heard. The influencing *Udātta* and the resulting *svarita* are here intervened by an *avagraha* and therefore it may be termed as तैरोऽवग्रह as suggested by Dr. Virendra Kumar Verma. It is necessary to treat this as a separate type of उदात्तपूर्व *Svarita*, because it is a special feature of the *Ṛgveda Padapāṭha*, followed by the *Padapāṭha*s of the

Vājasaneyins and the *Atharvaṇas*. The *Taittirīya Padapāṭha* does not have such a *Svarita*. It would read this *pada* as पुरःऽहि त म् ।

The second type of *Svarita* is termed as *'Jātya'* in *Prātiśākhya*. In the modern terminology, it is called 'Independent *Svarita*', because it does not depend on *Udātta* for its existence, like the उदात्तपूर्वस्वरित and its position does not alter whether it is in the *Saṁhitā Pāṭha* or the *Pada Pāṭha*. The term *Jātya* means 'by birth' or 'by nature'. It is a *Svarita* by its own nature and this does not depend on its position either in the *Saṁhitā* or the *Pada*. The examples are स्वं: । क्वं: । कन्यां. These *Svaritas* have either *Anudātta* before them, e.g. कन्यां, हृदय्यंया or they have nothing before them, e.g. स्वं:, क्वं. Accordingly, they are divided as नीचपूर्व or अनुदात्तपूर्व and अपूर्व.

It is invariably observed that the *Jātya Svarita* occurs on the vowel which comes after the conjunct consonant in which य् or व् is the second member, e.g., क्वं, क न्यां. Hence modern scholars hold that in its origin it is a case of *Kṣaipra sandhi,* even though it is not recognised as such, in these cases. They say that क्वं is originally कु + अ and क न्यां originally is कनी + आ. Thus, it is also a case of the combination where the *Udātta* vowel is changed into either य् or व् as the case may be. However, we may note here that the *Svarita* resulting in the body of the *pada* due to *Kṣaipra sandhi* is internal, while that resulting due to *Kṣaipra sandhi* between the two *padas* is external. Again, the purpose of the *Prātiśākhyas* being to explain the *sandhi* between the *padāntas* and the *padādis,* they are not interested in the splitting of the *pada* further into its elements, and as such though the *Svarita* in the *pada* might be due to the *Kṣaipra sandhi* in its final analysis, for the *Prātiśākhya* works, it is already there in the given *pada* as such, and hence for them it is *Jātya* only. And because, whether in the *Saṁhitā* or in *pada,* it does not change its nature, it is sometimes termed as *'Nitya-Svarita'.* It is important to note that both these are covered by *Pāṇini* in the *Sūtra*: उदात्तस्वरितयोर्यणः स्वरितोऽनुदात्तस्य (8.2.4).

The third type is that which may be called *Sandhija Svarita*. This is seen when the *Sandhis* called *Praśliṣṭa, Kṣaipra,* and *Abhinihita*, take place in the *Saṁhitā* modification. In all these cases the original *svara* of the vowel is also changed. The examples of all these three types are:

प्रश्लिष्ट - स्रु॒चिऽइंव । घृतम् । = स्रुचींव घृतम्

क्षैप्र - नु । इ॒ न्द्र॒ । = न्विंन्द्र

अभिनिहित - ते । अ॒ व॒ र्ध॒ न्त॒ । - तेंऽवर्धन्त

In all these cases, the *svarita* is the result of *sandhi* and therefore it is *Sandhija Svarita*. These distinctions in the *Svarita* were recognised by all the *Prātiśākhyas*. However, they are not so recognised in the Grammar. All these types are explained as *Svarita* only, though the rules to explain all these types are given in Grammar.

Another point to be noted in this connection is that of *'Kampa'*. When a *'Jātya'* or the *'Sandhija' Svarita* is immediately followed by an *Udātta*, there arises what is known in the *Prātiśākhya* as *Kampa*. When the *Svarita* vowel is short, the *kampa* is shown by the figure 1, and when the *Svarita* vowel is long the *kampa* is shown by the figure 3 in the written text of the *Saṁhitā*.

e.g. नि + अ॒न्यम् = न्य१॑न्यम् । अ॒ भि + इ॒दम् = अ॒ भी॒ ३॑ द॒ म्॒ ।

What do these figures indicate? We have seen that the *Svarita* is a combination of *Udātta* and *Anudātta*. In this combination, the first *mātrā* is *Udātta* and the rest is *Anudātta*. In the case of a short vowel the first half *mātrā* would be *Udātta* and the other half *mātrā* would be *Anudātta*. They will be of equal dimensions. Thus in the above example न्य१॑न्यम्, the अ in न्य is to be pronounced as *svarita*. The first half of it would be uttered as *Udātta* and the other half as *Anudātta*. Their proportion is 1:1, and that is shown by the figure 1. In case of long vowel e.g. अ॒ भी॒३॑दम्

the first half *mātrā* would be uttered as *udātta* and the remaining $1^1/_2$ *mātrā* would be uttered as *anudātta*, their proportion being 1:3. This is shown by the figure 3 in the written text. This is as it is traditionally followed in reciting the *Ṛk-Saṁhitā* according to the interpretation of *Pāṇinian* rule. The *Ṛk-Prātiśākhya* records another view also, according to which the first half of *Svarita* would be *Udātta* and the other half would be *Anudātta*.

The *Anudāttas*, one or more, immediately following this *svarita* are known as *Pracayas* in the *Prātiśākhyas*. In grammar they are known as *'Ekaśruti'*. There is no uniformity among the *Śākhās* in respect of the pronunciation of *Pracaya*. Some pronounce them as *udātta* while others, as *anudātta*.

4. ***Saṁskāra-Vidhāna*** : Now we come to the last but the most important aspect of the *Prātiśākhya* literature. It is the *Sandhi* rules mentioned in them. It has already been stated that the *Prātiśākhya*s take the *pada* as the given element and the *Saṁhitāpāṭha* is to be constructed from them. So the *Saṁhitā* for them is the modification resulting from the close proximity of the end-letter of the first *pada* and the beginning letter of the following *pada*. To appreciate their efforts in this respect, we shall divide our study into the following parts:

(a) which letters can stand at the end of a *pada* and which do not stand;

(b) which letters can stand at the beginning of a *pada* and which cannot stand;

(c) the classification of the types of *sandhis* in respect of the letters, which are seen either at the end or at the beginning of *padas*.

We shall study them in this order.

All the *Prātiśākhyas* have noted the letters which come at the end of the *padas* and also the letters which begin the *padas*. Of course by *pada* in this context, they mean the *padas* of the *Saṁhitā* to which the *Prātiśākhya* belongs. Most of the rules are common; there are very few rules which point out the individual peculiarities. Hence the following rule in the *Ṛk-Prātiśākhya* will cover most of the letters in which the *padas* end:

ऊष्मान्त:स्थर्सोष्मचकारवर्गा:

नान्तं यात्यन्यत्र विसर्जनीयात् (ऋ.प्रा. 12.1)

This rule lays down that the *Ūṣman* letters excepting the *visarga*, the *antasstha* letters, ṛ, and the letters of *cavarga* can never be seen at the end of a *pada*. This rule practically covers all the positions. The *Caturadhyāyī* (I.5) adds the letter ल् as coming at the end of the *pada*, but that is found only in the *Atharvaveda* and pertains to the *padas* like बाल्, फाल्, which are really not the words in the language, but, only onomatopoeic words. Thus the stem वाच् will never occur as वाच् at the *pada* stage but as वाक्, वाग्, वाचा, वाचि etc. will be found. Likewise, the stems अनडुह्, भास्, विभ्राज् will not be found in the *pada* stage as ending in ह्, स्, ज् respectively, but, the forms अनड्वान्, अनडुद्भि:, भा:, विभ्राट् will be there. It will now be seen that some of the *Prakriyāsūtras* of Pāṇini like चो: कु:, हो ढ: etc. have their relevance in this context. Likewise, the *Prātiśākhya* has noted the letters which never appear at the beginning of the *pada*. Thus:

ऋकारलृकारौ परमूर्धमूष्मणां

नादिं तकारादवरे च सप्त ॥ (ऋ.प्रा. 12.2)

This *sūtra* enumerates such letters. It says that there are no *padas* which begin with ऋ, लृ, जिह्वामूलीय, उपध्मानीय, विसर्जनीय and अनुस्वार and the letters from झ् to ण्. Dr. Verma says that there is no *pada* which begins with ङ्. This has not been noted either by the *Prātiśākhya* or Uvaṭa. These two rules determine the limits as to what letters the rules of *sandhi* would relate to.

They have also noted in a number of *sūtras* the letters which cannot form conjunct consonants within the body of the *padas*, e.g. the rule नान्योन्येन मध्यमाः स्पर्शवर्गाः संयुज्यन्ते (ऋ.प्रा 12.31) lays down that in the middle of a *pada* the letters of *cavarga, ṭavarga* and the letters of *tavarga*, can never be found combined with one another. Thus, we would never get a *pada* in the *Ṛgveda* in which we would get the conjunct consonant which is made of चवर्ग with either टवर्ग or तवर्ग or टवर्ग with either चवर्ग or तवर्ग and तवर्ग with either चवर्ग or टवर्ग in the middle of a *pada*. The rules of this section in the *Prātiśākhya* have a great bearing on the Pāṇinian rules in the *Tripādī* of the *Aṣṭādhyāyī*. Just to take an example:

In the word रामेण, we find न् changed to ण् on account of the influence of र्. We find the same position in कुर्वन्ति, where the *sūtra* रषाभ्यां नो णः समानपदे (P. VIII 4.1) will have scope. According to this rule, the न् in कुर्वन्ति should change to ण्. But it does not. Why so? The explanation according to Pāṇini would be as follows:-

In case of कुर्वन्ति, two *sūtras* have scope simultaneously. According to नश्चापदान्तस्य झलि, (P. 8.3-4) the न् should change to *anusvāra*, while according to रषाभ्यां नो णः समानपदे it should change to ण्. But रषाभ्यां (P. 8.4.1) is असिद्ध when नश्चापदान्तस्य is to be considered and hence न् will change to *anusvāra*. Then by अनुस्वारस्य ययि परसवर्ण (P. 8. 4. 58) that *anusvāra* will change to न् and this न् is present in the form कुर्वन्ति. Now this न् is *asiddha* for रषाभ्यां etc and hence it will not change to ण्. The *Ṛk-Prātiśākhya* on the other hand, would, say that if we change न् to ण्, in कुर्वन्ति, then there will arise an occasion for a conjunct consonant of the letter of टवर्ग with that of तवर्ग which is not possible according to the rule 12.31 (quoted above). These two explanations thus stand in intrinsic relation and will throw light on the order of the *Tripādī* rules in the *Aṣṭādhyāyī*.

The field of *sandhis* thus determined, we can now proceed to the topic of *Saṁhitā*. Here, we come across such rules as

संहितायामेकप्राणभावे (तै.प्रा. V.1); संहितायाम् (वा. प्रा. 3.1); and संहितायाम् (च.अ. 2.1) and संहितायाम् (Pāṇini-6.1.72).

All these are *Adhikāra sūtras* and govern their respective fields. In the *Ṛk-Prātiśākhya* we do not find such a rule. But, according to *Uvaṭa,* the *sūtra* संहिता पदप्रकृतिः (2.1) is an *Adhikāra* (संहिता पदप्रकृतिः इत्येतदाधिकृतं वेदितव्यम् आ सीमापटलात्). But, what is a *Saṁhitā*? It has been defined by the *Prātiśākhyas* and Pāṇini as follows:

1. ऋ. प्रा. - संहिता पदप्रकृतिः पदान्तान् पदादिभिः संदधदेति यत् सा कालाव्यवायेन (2.1,2);
2. तै.प्रा. - नानापदसंधानसंयोगः पदसंहितेत्यभिधीयते (24.2);
3. वा.प्रा. - वर्णानामेकप्राणयोगः संहिता (1.158);
4. ऋ. तंत्र - सन्निकर्षः संहिता (सू.62);
5. यास्क
6. पाणिनी } - परः सन्निकर्षः संहिता (नि.1.6,अ, P. 1.4.109).

It will be of interest to study these definitions together, and note their peculiarities.

According to the *Ṛk-Prātiśākhya*, the *Saṁhitāpāṭha* has *Padapāṭha* as its basis (प्रकृति) and the *Saṁhitā* is the modified text (विकार). The *Saṁhitā* is constructed when the finals of *padas* are combined with the initial letters of the *padas* that follow, and read as such without interval of time. So according to the *Ṛk-Prātiśākhya*, *Saṁhitā* is the recital of the *padas* in succession and without interval of time. The *padas* when read in this way undergo certain modifications. These modifications are noted by the *Ṛk-Prātiśākhya*. We may therefore say that the rules of *Saṁhitā* in the *Ṛk-Prātiśākhya* relate to *Pada-saṁhitā*. It is the *Saṁhitā* of the *padas* as such. Hence the *sandhi* rules of the *Ṛk-Prātiśākhya* are framed in a peculiar fashion, e.g., it says that a *pada* ending in आः, ऐ, औ would be pronounced as one ending in आ in the *Saṁhitā*, if it is followed by a *pada* beginning with a vowel (II.24. 25. 26). It does not give any *prakriyā* like that we find in other *Prātiśākhyas*. This *Saṁhitā* according to *Ṛk-Prātiśākhya* is of two types viz. *Ārṣī-saṁhitā* and *Krama-saṁhitā*. *Ārṣī-saṁhitā* is the *Saṁhitāpāṭha* of the *Ṛgveda* while the *Krama-saṁhitā* is found in the *Kramapāṭha*.

As we come to the *Taittirīya Prātiśākhya*, we find a different angle in the treatment of the *sandhis*. It does not recognise *Krama-sandhi* as a separate type. On the other hand it talks of पदसंहिता, अक्षरसंहिता, वर्णसंहिता and अङ्गसंहिता (अथ चतस्रः संहिताः । पदसंहिताक्षरसंहितावर्णसंहिताङ्गसंहिता चेति । - तै. प्रा. 24.1,2).

Here, we find a shift from the simple recital of the *Saṁhitā* to an analysis of *sandhi* in the manner of grammatical work. It defines the *Pada-saṁhitā* as नानापदसंधानसंयोगः पदसंहितेत्यभिधीयते (24.3), meaning that a *Pada-saṁhitā* is a conjunction of *padas* through the euphonic combination. It is the संयोग of *padas* through the method of सन्धान, i.e. संधिकार्य. In respect of other types it only says: यथास्वमक्षरसंहितादीनामप्येवम् (24.4) i.e. in respect of *Akṣara saṁhitā* and the rest, they should be understood likewise. The author does not indicate what particular section of the work relates to what particular type of *sandhi*. However, in the *Tribhāṣyaratna* we get the following remark:

अथ पञ्चमाध्यायमारभ्य आ नवमात्, एकादशद्वादशौ, त्रयोदशस्यादौ सूत्रचतुष्टयं च पदसंहिता । दशमोऽक्षरसंहिता । त्रयोदशचतुर्दशौ षोडशश्च वर्णसंहिता । 'व्यञ्जनान् स्वराङ्गान्' इत्येषा अङ्गसंहिता ।

From the above observation of the *sūtras* on the guidelines given by the above remarks in the commentary, we are able to say that the *Akṣara-saṁhitā* is the *svarasaṁhitā*, the *Varṇasaṁhitā* is the *Vyañjana-sandhi* and the *dvirvacana* of letters, and the *aṅga-saṁhitā* is the one in which the components of a conjunct consonant are stated as forming part of the vowels preceding or following the conjunct. Here we find that gradually the treatment in the *Prātiśākhya* is shifting from *Padasandhi* to *Varṇasandhi*.

The nature of this shift can be better appreciated if we compare the statements of the *Ṛk-Prātiśākhya* with the corresponding statements of the *Taittirīya Prātiśākhya*, with the help of examples. Let us take the following examples:

(1) याः । ओषधीः । सोमराज्ञीः । - पदपाठ.
याः ओषधीः सोमराज्ञीः । - संहितापाठ.
(2) अन्वेतवै । उ । - पदपाठ.
अन्वेतवा उ । - संहितापाठ.
(3) उभौ । उ - पदपाठ.
उभा उ । - संहितापाठ.

All these three *sandhis* are of one type according to *Ṛk-Prātiśākhya*. They are *Padavṛtti sandhis* as stated in the *Kārikā*:

विसर्जनीयोऽरिफितो दीर्घपूर्वः स्वरोदयः ।
आकारमुत्तमौ च द्वौ स्वरौ ताः पदवृत्तयः ॥ (II.24,25)

The import of the *kārikā* is that when a *pada* beginning with a vowel follows a *pada* ending in दीर्घपूर्व अरिफितविसर्जनीय or ऐ or औ, then in the *Saṁhitā* it is read as आ. What the *Ṛk-Prātiśākhya* says amounts only to the stating of two positions, viz, the position at the *pada* stage and that at the *Saṁhitā* stage. It does not bother as to how the *visarjanīya* is dropped, or how ऐ and औ are reduced to आ.

Now let us explain these very examples according to the rules in the *Taittirīya Prātiśākhya*. The explanation will be as follows:

(1) याः । ओषधीः ।
याय् ओषधीः - अथ स्वरपरोयकारम् (9.10)
(2) अन्वेतवै । उ
अन्वेतवाय् उ - ऐकार आयम् (9.14)
(3) उभौ/उ = उभाय् उ - औकार आवम् (9.15)

and then by अवर्णपूर्वौ यकारवकारौ (10.19) we shall drop the य् thus obtained, and get the required *saṁhitā* as या औषधीः; अन्वेतवा उ and उभा उ. Such modification is altogether absent in the *Ṛk-Prātiśākhya*.

In the *Ṛk-Prātiśākhya,* the *Saṁhitā* form is given all at once, while in the *Taittirīya Prātiśākhya,* it is obtained step by step by modification of the *varṇa.* It is on account of this shift that we get intermediate steps in the *Taittirīya Prātiśākhya,* while in the *Ṛk-Prātiśākhya* the *Saṁhitā* is stated directly and is named, not as *svara sandhi* or the *vyañjana sandhi,* but as पदवृत्तिसन्धि, वशङ्गमसन्धि etc. One peculiar thing we observe in the *Ṛk-Prātiśākhya* is that it has given different names to the *sandhis* as उद्ग्राह, आनूपदवृत्ति, अवशंगम etc. which are not seen anywhere else either in the *Prātiśākhya* or in Grammar. The scholars wonder as to why such peculiar names are used, and if once used, why were they later on dropped. To me the reason appears to be that in the *Ṛk-Prātiśākhya* the author gives the description of the resultant *sandhi,* while in the later *Prātiśākhyas* and in Grammar there is an attempt to explain the modifications that the *varṇas* undergo, step by step. The terms are not arbitrary; they are etymological as explained later on. This we shall explain when we shall deal with the classification of the *sandhis* in the *Ṛk-Prātiśākhya.* This shift in the way of explanation is first found in the *Taittirīya Prātiśākhya.*

Both, whether it be the *Ārṣī* or *Krama-saṁhitā* according to *Ṛk-Prātiśākhya* or the fourfold division of the *Saṁhitā* as made by *Taittirīya Prātiśākhya,* the modifications, in the last resort, take place on the *varṇas* only. The *Vājasaneyi Prātiśākhya,* therefore, relates its *sandhi* conception to the *varṇa* and defines *Saṁhitā* as वर्णानामेकप्राणयोगः संहिता (वा.प्रा. I-159). *Saṁhitā* is the pronunciation of the sounds in the same breath. This element of *'Ekaprāṇayoga'* is mentioned by the *Taittirīya Prātiśākhya* also when it says संहितायामेकप्राणभावे (5.1).

Both the *Taittirīya* and the *Vājasaneyi Prātiśākhyas* do not recognise *Krama-sandhi* as a separate type of *sandhi,* though they recognise the *Kramapāṭha,* while *Ṛk-Prātiśākhya* recognises it. Why so? It is because of the peculiar nature of these *Saṁhitās.*

The *Saṁhitāpāṭha* is the modified form of the *padas* in combination and recited without interval. The same is true of the *Krama*, for it also is the *Saṁhitā* of two *padas* at a time. The *Saṁhitā* is given by the *Saṁhitāpāṭha* and the *padas* are given by the *Padapāṭha*. Now *Krama* stands in the intermediate position of the two, उभयमन्तर as it is called. Hence while reciting the *Krama*, the given position of the *Saṁhitāpāṭha* and the *Padapāṭha* is not to be disturbed. In the *Kramapāṭha*, the *Krama vargas* (units of *krama*) are formed in the series of 1-2, 2-3, 3-4, etc. till we reach the end of the half *Ṛk*, and each *varga* is to be recited in *Saṁhitā*. Thus the *Krama-varga* is to agree with the *Padapāṭha*, while the Saṁhitā is to agree with the *Saṁhitāpāṭha* as is laid down in the *sūtra*.

अथार्ष्यलोपेन यदाह स क्रमः । समानकालं पदसंहितं द्वयोः ॥ (ऋ.प्रा. 11.1);

also पद्भ्यां द्वाभ्यामभिक्रम्य पत्त्यादायोत्तरं तयोः । उत्तरेणोपसंदध्यात्तथार्धर्चं समापयेत् । (10.7).

This is the general notion about the *Krama*. e.g.

संहिता - पर्जन्याय प्रगायत दिवस्पुत्राय मीळ्हुषे । (ऋ. 7-102.1)
पदपाठ - पर्जन्याय । प्र । गायत । दिवः । पुत्राय । मीळ्हुषे ।
क्रम - पर्जन्याय प्र । प्रं गायत । गायत दिवः । दिवस्पुत्राय ।
पुत्राय मीळ्हुषे । मीळ्हुष इति मीळ्हुषे ॥

It will be seen that this *Krama* has maintained all the conditions of the *Krama* laid down in the above *sūtra*. But at many places in the *Ṛgveda* there arises a difficulty. Let us study this with the help of examples:-

(1) संहिता - शुनश्चिच्छेपं निदितम् ।
पद - शुनःऽशेपम् । चित् । निऽदितम् ।
क्रम - शुनश्चिच्छेपं निदितम् ।
चिदिति चित् ।

(2) मो षुणः परापरा ।
पद - मो इति । सु । नः । पराऽपरा ।

क्रम - मोषुणः । स्विति सु ।
न इति नः ।

In these two examples, the first *kramavarga* is to be made of three *padas*. Otherwise the *Saṁhitā* will be disturbed. Here if we read the *krama* on the basis of the *Padapāṭha*, it will be शुनः शेपं चित् । चिन्निदितम् । This will violate the *Saṁhitāpāṭha*. In the second example it will have to be recited as मोषु । सुनः etc. Here also the *Saṁhitā* will be disturbed. Hence at such places the *krama-unit* is to be formed of three *padas*. It is for this reason that the *Ṛk-Prātiśākhya* has to note the *Krama* as a separate type of *sandhi*. This difficulty is not to be faced by the reciters of the *Yajurveda* and hence, even though they recognise *Kramapāṭha*, they are not required to treat the *Krama-saṁhitā* as a separate type of *sandhi*.

They have, however, to face another difficulty. The *Yajus* being in running prose, they are not able to determine the *avasāna*. A unit in the *Saṁhitā* is determined by the *avasāna*. In reciting the *Ṛk*. the *avasāna* is at the end of half of a *Ṛk*. There is no such sign of *avasāna* in *Yajus*, it being in prose. So they determine it by saying it in the '*Ekaprāṇabhāva*'. The term means 'so many *varṇas* as can be uttered in one breath.'

(एकप्राणेन भाव्यते जन्यते उच्चार्यते इति एकप्राणभावः ।
एकेन प्राणेन यावान् उच्चार्यते वेदभागः तावानेकप्राणभावः इत्यर्थः ।
त्रिभाष्यरत्न on 5.1)

We find it mentioned both in the *Taittirīya* and the *Vājasaneyi Prātiśākhyas*. The latter has, however, one improvement, viz, that it has included it in the definition of *Saṁhitā* instead of keeping it in the *Adhikāra-sūtra* as is done by the former work.

We do not find the definition of *Saṁhitā* in the *Caturadhyāyī*. The *Ṛk-Tantra* has given it as सन्निकर्षःसंहिता (सू. 62). *Sannikarṣa* is the same as '*sandhāna*' or '*yoga*' and means proximity of letters. The adjective '*ekaprāṇa*' is not a necessary adjective in the definition of *Saṁhitā*. It only determines the limit of the unit of the *Saṁhitā* and it may be different in different cases, e.g., it may be half a *Ṛk* in the *Ṛgveda, Ekaprāṇabhāva* in the *Yajurveda*, two *padas* in the *Krama* and in the *Sāmaveda* it may differ on the nature of the *Sāman*. The *Ṛk-Tantra* which is the *Prātiśākhya* of *Sāmaveda* has rightly done away with that term in the definition of *Saṁhitā* and has concentrated on the *'sannikarṣa'* of letters. It is interesting to note at this point that Pāṇini also has separated the concept of *'avasāna'* from that of *'sannikarṣa'*. He has made two different *sūtra*s for them, relating *Saṁhitā* to *'sannikarṣa'* and *avasāna* to *virāma* (Pāṇini, I.4.109, 110).

We see that the *Prātiśākhyas* define the term *Saṁhitā* in the context of their own *Caraṇa*. Now *Ṛk-Tantra* is a *Prātiśākhya* of *Sāmaveda*, and it also must have defined the term in its own context. But the definition has been of such a general nature that it can apply not only to the cases of the Vedic lore but also the cases in the *Bhāṣā*. It appears to be a definition constructed by a grammarian's pen rather than a mere reciter of the Veda.

And we need not wonder at this, for the author of the *Ṛk-Tantra* is traditionally said to be Śākaṭāyana and he was a grammarian of repute in the pre-Pāṇinian age. It is not unlikely that he might have included the definition into the *Prātiśākhya* from his grammar.

The definition of *Saṁhitā* in the terms of *'sannikarṣa'* must have favourably impressed the later world of scholars, for a scholar like Yāska has included it in his *Nirukta*, only by adding an adjective परः to it. He says, परः सन्निकर्षः संहिता । संहिता पदप्रकृतिः। पदप्रकृतीनि सर्वचरणानां पार्षदानि । (I.17)

As we read this definition of Yāska we are at once reminded of Pāṇini, for his definition of *Saṁhitā* agrees word to word with that of Yāska.

This study of the different definitions of *Saṁhitā*, thus, reveals that there has been a gradual evolution in the concept from *Ṛk-Prātiśākhya* to Pāṇini, ultimately merging in Pāṇini's concept of it.

The definition of *Saṁhitā* in terms of '*sannikarṣa*' reveals the fact that the essence of *Saṁhitā* lies in the juxtaposition of letters (sounds) and not in their modification. What is necessary in *Saṁhitā* is the juxtaposition of letters; the letters in juxtaposition may undergo modification or not. We generally suppose that there is *Saṁhitā* only where there is some modification. We say that in निर्गच्छति there is *sandhi* of निस् and गच्छति, but, we do not say so in case of अवगच्छति though we utter the words अव and गच्छति in close proximation. The fact, however, is that there is *Saṁhitā* here also, for, at the *pada* stage अव । गच्छति will not have proximity, while in अवगच्छति it is there. Hence the *padas* न । नि । मिषति । सुरण: । when read as ननिमिषतिसुरण: there is *Saṁhitā*, and the *Ṛk-Prātiśākhya* recognises it as such, in so far as they are read without interval (कालाव्यवायेन). The विकार or modification of letters is not the necessary element in *Saṁhitā*.

Now, we may pass on to the study of the types of *Saṁhitā* dealt with in the *Prātiśākhyas*. For this we shall take up *Ṛk-Prātiśākhya*, not only because it is the earliest one among the *Prātiśākhya* works, but more particularly because it has used different descriptive names of different types of *sandhis*. We find there such names as परिपन्नसन्धि, उद्ग्राह सन्धि etc. We wonder as to why these names are there, and we wonder still more when we find that they are dropped later on not only by the grammarians but even by the authors of the *Prātiśākhyas*.

THE TYPES OF SANDHI

The sounds are of two types: Vowels and Consonants. Accordingly, there can be four types of *sandhis*. They are named in the *Ṛk-Prātiśākhya* as under:

1. स्वर + स्वर———— स्वरसन्धि

2. स्वर + व्यंजन——— अनुलोम अन्वक्षर सन्धि

3. व्यंजन + स्वर ——— प्रतिलोम अन्वक्षर सन्धि

4. व्यंजन + व्यंजन ———— आस्थापित सन्धि

In the *Varṇa-samāmnāya* the vowels come first and then come the consonants. So when in a *sandhi* a vowel is followed by a consonant, the position of the letters is '*anuloma*'; but when this position is reverted, i.e. when the consonant is followed by a vowel in the *sandhi*, the position of the letters is '*pratiloma*'. Both these types are *Anvakṣara* (अक्षरमनुगत:), i.e. according to the *akṣara*. In the *Prātiśākhya* the word अक्षर is used for vowel. In this *sandhi* the concept is based on whether the consonant follows or precedes the vowel; hence the name *Anvakṣara*. When a consonant is followed by a consonant, the *sandhi* is called *'Āsthāpita'*, because here the consonants are placed near each other. The term *Svara-sandhi* does not require any explanation.

Out of these four types, the *Ṛk-Prātiśākhya* has disposed of both the types of *Anvakṣara-sandhi* in the beginning of the second chapter, as there is very little to be said about them. In the *Anuloma Aṇvakṣara sandhi*, a *pada* ending in a vowel is followed by a *pada* beginning with a consonant e.g. the *padas* न । नि । मिषति । सुरण: । are read in *saṁhitā* as न निमिषति सुरण: । The special cases of this *sandhi* are एष देवो अमर्त्य: (ऋ. ९.३-१); उत स्य वाजी क्षिपणिम् (4-40-4) and स सुत:पीतये वृषा. Here the *padas* एष:, स्य:, स:, appear in the *padapāṭha* with *visarga*, but, in the *saṁhitā* form they are read without it, resulting in the position in which a vowel is followed by a consonant. In the *Pratiloma anvakṣara sandhi,* a *pada* ending in a consonant is followed by a *pada* beginning with a vowel. In this type, the only rule is that the first *Sparśa* letters are changed into the third letter of their class. e.g. अर्वाक् । आ = अर्वागावर्तया हरी (४.३२.१) हव्यवाट् । अजरम्। = हव्यवाळजरं पिता न: । (५.४.२)

SVARA-SANDHI

Coming to *Svara-sandhi,* the *Ṛk-Prātiśākhya* mentions the following types:- (1) प्रश्लिष्ट; (2) क्षैप्र; (3) भुग्न; (4) अभिनिहित; (5) पदवृत्ति; (6) उद्ग्राह; (7) उद्ग्राहवत्; (8) उद्ग्राहपदवृत्ति; (9) प्राच्य-पाञ्चाल पदवृत्ति and (10) प्रकृति भाव.

1. ***PRAŚLIṢṬA SANDHI***: The *Praśliṣṭa Sandhis* include the cases of *Savarṇa-dīrgha-ekādeśa, Guṇa-ekādesa* and the *Vṛddhi-ekādeśa sandhis* of Pāṇini. e.g. मधु + उद्कम् = मधूदकम्; आ + इन्द्र = एन्द्र; आ + एनम् = ऐनम्.

These are called *Praśliṣṭa* because there is *praśleṣa* or complete fusion, or union of the two vowels. It should however be noted that in the *Ṛgveda* there is no case of ṛ being combined with अ or आ.

2. ***KṢAIPRA SANDHI***: This is the *yaṇ-sandhi* of Pāṇini. e.g. अभ्यार्षेयम्, अधीन्वय । It is called *kṣaipra* because here the *sandhi* form is pronounced quickly, i or u being changed to y or v respectively, which requires only half a *mātrā*. So that the i + a which make two *mātrās* together are ultimately changed to one *mātrā* in the *sandhi* form, hence *Kṣaipra*. Here also we do not get the case of ṛ changing to r, for in the *Ṛgveda* there is no *pada* ending in ṛ.

3. ***BHUGNA SANDHI***: When a *pada* ending in o or au is followed by a *pada* beginning with a vowel other than u or ū, the *sandhi* by the *padavṛtti* or *udgrāha* rule would be that ओ or औ are pronounced as अ or आ. But in case where such *pada* is followed by one which begins with a vowel other than u or ū, व् is inserted as an *āgama*, i.e. ओ or औ are pronounced as अव् or आव् e.g. वायवायाहि (वायो + आयाहि); ऋतावृधावृतस्पृशा (ऋतावृधौ + ऋतस्पृशा). This is called *Bhugna* because the vowels ओ and औ are bent to अव् and आव्. √ भुज् means 'to bend.' It should be noted here that while other *Prātiśākhyas* and *Pāṇini* directly give अव्, आव् as *ādeśas* of ओ and औ, the *Ṛk-Prātiśākhya* changes them

first to अ or आ; then in case the *pada* that follows begins with a vowel other than उ or ऊ then only व् is inserted as *āgama*.

4. *ABHINIHITA SANDHI*:- In this *sandhi* the ए or ओ at the end of a *pada* absorbs the अ standing at the beginning of the next *pada*. e.g. दाशुषेऽग्ने, सोऽयम्. *Abhinihita* means 'absorbed fully'. It should be noted here that the ए or ओ in the *saṁhitā* form is not the same as one appearing at the *pada* stage. It has in its womb the अ which it has absorbed. So it is a '*sandhija*' ए or ओ. The *abhinihita-sandhi* is the same as the *Pūrvarūpa-ekādeśa-sandhi* of *Pāṇini* according to the *sūtra* एङः पदान्तादति. (P. 6. 1. 109) There also the *Pūrvarūpa-ekādeśa* coming in the place of ए + आ or ओ + अ as the case may be, is also *sandhija*. The *Abhinihita sandhi* in the *Ṛgveda* requires special attention, because, while in the Pāṇinian system, it takes place in all the cases where *padānta* ए or ओ is followed by अ, in the *Ṛgveda* it does not take place nearly in a quarter of the cases where the occasion arises. The *Ṛk-Prātiśākhya,* therefore, has taken note of every case where such *sandhi* has not taken place.

The four types of *sandhi* as mentioned above, are such that in them there is some type of modification either of the nature of *ekādeśa* or a change in the previous vowel. The remaining six are such that there results in the *Saṁhitā* form a *vivṛtti,* i.e., hiatus. Dr. Verma therefore calls them as विवृत्ति-फलकसंधि. They are as follows:

5. (Based on hiatus) *PADAVṚTTI-SANDHI*: This *sandhi* results in the following three cases (i) When an अरिफित *visarga* standing at the end of a *pada* is preceded by a long vowel and is followed by a *pada* beginning with a vowel. In such a case the *visarga* along with the previous long vowel is changed to आ, e.g., या ओषधीः (याः + ओ). (ii) When the *padānta* ऐ is followed by a vowel, the ऐ is changed to आ e.g. अन्वेतवाउ (अन्वेतवै + उ). (iii) When *padānta* औ is followed by a vowel, the औ is changed to आ e.g. उभा उ (उभौ + उ). This *sandhi* is called पदवृत्ति because there is *vṛtti*, i.e. *vivṛtti* between the two *padas* as they stand in the *saṁhitā*. This *vivṛtti* being the result of the *saṁhitā*, it is called *Padavṛtti sandhi*, i.e. based on hiatus.

6. *UDGRĀHA-SANDHI*: When an *'ariphita visarga'* stands at the end of a *pada*, and it is preceded by अ and is followed by a vowel except अ, it is changed to अ along with the preceding अ e.g. य इन्द्र (यः + इन्द्र). Likewise, when the *padānta* ए or ओ is followed by a vowel except अ, these ए or ओ are also changed to अ e.g. अग्न इन्द्र (अग्ने + इन्द्र), वाय उक्थेभिः (वायो + उक्थेभिः). These are termed as *Udgrāha-sandhi* because here the *visarga* as well as the elements इ and उ appearing in ए and ओ are as though cut off and separated in the *saṁhitā*. उद्ग्रह means to cut off and separate.

7. *UDGRĀHA-PADAVṚTTI-SANDHI*: This is the name given to the *Udgrāha-sandhi* when the vowel that follows happens to be a long one. e.g. क ईषते (कः + ईषते), तिरन्त आयुः (तिरन्ते + आयुः). The reason to treat this as a separate *sandhi* is that the *vivṛtti* in this case is *dīrgha vivṛtti* (cf. दीर्घपरा उद्ग्राहपदवृत्तयः)

8. *UDGRĀHAVAT SANDHI*: This is a special case where अ or आ are followed by ऋ. In this case, the preceding अ or आ is changed to a short अ, e.g. प्र ऋभुभ्यः (प्र + ऋभुभ्यः), मधुन ऋतस्य (मधुना + ऋतस्य). This is called *Udgrāhavat* because just as in the *Udgrāha-sandhi* the previous *pada* is changed to अकारान्त, here also it is changed to अकारान्त. One thing should be noted in this case that in the later grammatical works and also later *Prātiśākhyas*, in such cases, there is *Guṇa-sandhi* in the form of अर्. But, in the *Ṛgveda*, that is altogether absent and hence there is no *Guṇa sandhi* as an option here.

9. *PRĀCYA-PĀÑCĀLA-PADAVṚTTI-SANDHI*: This *sandhi* is a special case arising out of the *Udgrāha sandhi* and resulting in an exception to the *Abhinihita sandhi*. The *Pūrvarūpa* of *Udgrāha-sandhi* is a *visarga* preceded by अ or ए or ओ. When they are followed by अ standing at the beginning of the next *pada*, the *visarga* along with the अ preceding, is changed to ओ and then it remains unchanged e.g. यो अस्मै (यः + अस्मै). Likewise the ए and ओ standing at the end of the *pada* remain un-changed under similar circumstances. Even though there is an occasion for *Abhinihita sandhi*, it does not take place here. As a result, there is *vivṛtti*. This *vivṛtti* is of two types. The *vivṛtti* between ए and अ as in ते अग्रेपा, is termed as *Prācya Padavṛtti* and the *vivṛtti* between ओ and अ as in प्रो अयासीत् and यो अस्मै is called *Pāñcāla-Padavṛtti*. These have been separately mentioned in the *Ṛk-Prātiśākhya* because there is a difference of opinion respecting the pronunciation of this *sandhi*. According to Elder Śākalya, the *saṁhitā* in these cases will be pronounced as ते एँग्रेपाः, प्रो ओयासीत्, यो ओस्मै under the influence of the preceding ए and ओ; while according to Śākalya it will be pronounced as usual.

10. *PRAKṚTIBHĀVA-SANDHI*: There is *Prakṛtibhāva sandhi* in cases where the *Pūrvarūpa* has a *Pragṛhya* vowel. It should not be supposed that there is no *sandhi* here, for they are pronounced in *saṁhitā*. The *saṁhitā* in this case is termed as प्रगृहीत पदसंहिता . There are many special cases of *Prakṛtibhāva sandhi* and also many cases of exception to it. They all have been noted by the *Ṛk-Prātiśākhya*. Here we need not go into their details.

VYAÑJANA SANDHI

The *Vyañjana-sandhi* is known as *Āsthāpita-sandhi* in *Ṛk-Prātiśākhya*. It is of the following types:

(1) अवशंगम सन्धि;

(2) वशंगम सन्धि;

(3) परिपन्न सन्धि;

(4) विसर्जनीय सन्धि;

(5) आनूपदवृत्ति;

(6) आगम added in संहिता;

(7) लोप occurring in *Samhitā*.

We shall take them one by one:

1. ***AVAŚAṄGAMA SANDHI***: In the *Vyañjana-sandhi* a consonant standing at the end of a *pada* is followed by another consonant standing at the beginning of the next *pada*. In such a position either of them is influenced by the other or it is not. When it is influenced i.e. modified by the other, the *sandhi* is called *Vaśaṅgama*. But when neither of them influences the other, it is called *Avaśaṅgama sandhi*. The examples of *Avaśaṅgama sandhi* are: वषट्ते (वषट् + ते); आरैक्पन्थाम् (आरैक् + पन्थाम्); इमम्मे (इमम् + मे). Here we do not find any change in either of the two consonants coming in contact.

2. ***VAŚAṄGAMA SANDHI***: In this *sandhi* either or both of the consonants undergo modification. These are found in the following cases:

(a) A *sparśa-vyañjana* followed by a *saghoṣa-vyañjana* is changed to the third letter of its own class. e.g. अर्वाग्देवा: (अर्वाक् + देवा:); यद्वा (यत् + वा); षड्भि: (षट्ऽभि:). This is *jaśtva sandhi* according to Pāṇini.

(b) The first *sparśa* letter followed by the fifth letter of any class, is changed to the fifth letter of its own class. e.g. अर्वाङ्नरा: (अर्वाक् + नरा:); बण्महान् (बट्+महान्); तन्न: (तत्+न:). But the word ककुद्मान् is an exception to this.

(c) According to father Śākalya, when the sparśa letter is followed by श्, that श् is changed to छ् e.g. विपाच्छुतुद्री (विपाट् + शुतुद्री), अर्वाक्छफाविव (अर्वाक् + शफौऽइव).

(d) When the third letter of any class stands at the end of a *pada*, it being itself a modification of the first letter of that class, and is followed by the letter ह्, that ह् is changed to the fourth letter of the class. e.g. मद्यग्घुवान: (मद्यक् + हुवान:); अवाड्ढव्यानि (अवाट् + हव्यानि).

(e) When म् is followed by a *sparśa* letter of a different class, that म् is changed to the *anunāsika* of that class, e.g. यङ्कुमारम् (यम् + कुमारम्), अहञ्च (अहम् +च), तन्ते (तम् + ते).

(f) When the letter म् standing at the end of a *pada*, is followed by an *antastha* letter except र्, that म् is changed to the *anunāsika antassthā*. e.g. यय्ँयय्ँयुजम् (यम् + यम् + युजम्); एषाल्ँक्ष्मी: (एषाम् + लक्ष्मी:).

(g) If न् is followed by ल्, it is changed to *anunāsika* लँ e.g. जिगीवाल्ँलक्षम् (जिगीवान् + लक्षम्).

(h) Such न् is changed to ञ् if it is followed by a letter of च class or श् e.g. वज्रिञ्छ्नथिहि (वज्रिन् + श्नथिहि), मघवञ्छग्धि (मघवन् + शग्धि).

(i) The letter त् is changed to ज् or ल् if followed by ज् or ल् e.g. यज्जिगासि (यत् + जिगासि), अङ्गाल्लोम्न: (अङ्गात् + लोम्न:)

(j) The letter त् is changed to च् when followed by *aghoṣa tālavya* letter e.g. तच्चक्षु: (तत् + चक्षु:); यच्छर्धि: (यत् + शर्धि:); तच्छंयो: (तत् + शंयो:).

(k) When त् or न् are changed to च् or ञ् respectively, the श् that follows it is changed to छ् e.g. तच्छंयो:, वज्रिञ्छ्नथिहि.

The cases in which श् is changed to छ् according to father Śākalya, are not approved by Śākalya so that according to Śākalya the *Saṁhitā* will be तच्शंयो: and वज्रिञ्श्नथिहि. All these eleven types are the cases of *Vaśaṅgama-sandhi* for here some form of modification is seen in the *Saṁhitā*.

3. *PARIPANNA SANDHI*: When म् is followed by म् or *Ūṣman* letter, that म् is changed to *anusvāra*. e.g. होतारं रत्नधातमम्। *Paripanna* means 'completely lost'. In this *sandhi* म् is completely lost and an *anusvāra* comes in its place; hence the *sandhi* is *Paripanna* e.g. वसुं सूनुं सहस: ।

4. *VISARJANĪYA SANDHI*: *Visarjanīya-sandhi* has special importance among the *Vyañjana-sandhis*. It is the only *Ūṣman* that stands as the end of a *Pada*, and it stands at the end of the *Pada* only. In different circumstances it is changed to different letters viz. र्, श्, ष्, स्, क्, प्

At times, it is elided. In the *Prātiśākhya*, the *visarjanīya* is said to be of two types: viz., the *Riphita-visarjanīya* and the *Ariphita-visarjanīya*. The topic of the *Riphita-visarjanīya* is dealt with in twenty-eight *sūtras* (I.76-103) in the *Ṛk-Prātiśākhya*. Without going into its details we may say that a *visarga* which comes after *Nāmi* Svara, i.e. after any vowel except अ or आ, is *Riphita-visarjanīya*. The *visarga* which comes after अ or आ is not *Riphita*. But there are many cases where even the *visarga* coming after अ or आ is also treated as *Riphita*, e.g. प्रात:, अक: etc. All such cases are enumerated by the *Prātiśākhya*.

An observation of the cases of *Riphita visarga* shows that the nucleus of the *Riphita visarga* is र् while that of *Ariphita visarga* is स्. Both these letters (i.e. र् or स्) do not stand at the end of a *pada*, but, get themselves modified into *visarga*. Secondly, *Riphita-visarjanīya*, when followed by a *saghoṣa- vyañjana*, is always changed to र्. Thirdly, in the *Padapāṭha* a *Riphita visarjanīya* is followed by इति. However, this इति is added only in such cases where in the *Saṁhitā*, it is not changed to र्. If it is changed to र् in the *Saṁhitā*, then it is not shown with इति in the *Padapāṭha*. This means that इति is added to it in the *Padapāṭha* only when its *Riphita* character is not evident in the *Saṁhitā*. With these general observations on the character of *visarga* we may now proceed to different modifications of *Visarga*.

(A) When a *Riphita visarga* is followed by a vowel or a voiced consonant, it is changed to र्. This is called *Repha- Sandhi*. When it is follwed by आ it is dropped. This is called *Akāma-sandhi.* If the *Riphita-visarga* is preceded by a short vowel and it (*visarga*) is dropped as followed by र्, the preceding short vowel is lengthened. This is *Niyata-sandhi.* In the Pāṇinian system these two cases are covered by ढ्रलोपे पूर्वस्य दीर्घोऽण: (P. 6. 3. 111)

The examples of these are: अग्नीरस्मि (अग्नि: + अस्मि); प्रातर्मित्रावरुणा (प्रात: + मित्रा); अग्नी रक्षांसि (अग्नि: + रक्षांसि) respectively.

(B) In respect of *Ariphita visarjanīya* the following changes are to be noted:

(i) *NIYATA-SANDHI:* When a *saghoṣa* consonant follows, the *Ariphita-visarjanīya* along with the preceding vowel is changed to आ, e.g. पुनानायन्ति. This is *Niyata-sandhi. Niyata* means passed or lost.

(ii) *PRAŚṚTA-SANDHI:* When a *saghoṣa* consonant follows, the *Ariphita-visarjanīya* preceded by a short vowel is changed to ओ along with that vowel, e.g. देवो देवेभि: This is *Praśṛta sandhi. Praśṛta* means bent down. Here, the *visarjanīya* is bent down or rests in ओ.

(iii) *VYĀPANNA-SANDHI:* In this *sandhi,* the *visarga* is changed to *Ūṣma-varṇa. Vyāpanna* means changed to some other sounds. Here the *visarga* is changed to some other *Ūṣman* sound. This takes place in case of both the types of *visarga.* This *sandhi* is of two types:

(a) When a *visarjanīya* is followed by an *aghoṣa-sparśa,* which is itself not followed by an *Ūṣman,* the *visarga* is changed to *Ūṣman* of that class, e.g. ऋषि क: । य ककुभ: । अग्निश्च । देवास्तम् । वायु पूषा ।

(b) When a *visarga* is followed by *Aghoṣa Ūṣman,* then it is changed to that *Ūṣman* which follows, e.g. वश्शिवतम: । देवीष्षळुर्वी:। नरस्सपत्ना: ।

(iv) *VIKRĀNTA-SANDHI:* This occurs where a *visarga* remains as it is. *Vikrānta* means left as it is. It is of two types:

(a) When an *aghoṣa-sparśa* of *Ka-varga* or *Pa-varga* follows, they themselves not being followed by *Ūṣman*, the *visarga* optionally remains as it is. When it remains as it is, it is *Vikrānta Sandhi.* Otherwise it will be *Vyāpanna Sandhi.*

(b) When a *visarga* is followed by an *aghoṣa Uṣman* (which itself has not come in place of dental letter, i.e., which is not a result of *Nati*), then the *visarga* remains as it is. In that case it is *Vikrānta Sandhi*, e.g. यः ककुभः । यः पञ्च । वः शिवतमः । देवीः षट्। नरः सपत्नाः ।

(v) *ANVAKṢARAVAKTRA SANDHI:* When an *Ūṣman* which is itself followed by an *aghoṣa* consonant, follows the *visarga*, the *visarga* is dropped. e.g. समुद्र स्थः (समुद्रः + स्थः); वस्पट् (वः + स्पट्); कस्वित् (कः + स्वित्). 'This is called *Anvakṣaravaktra* because it is similar to *Anvakṣara-sandhi*, as in the case of एषः, स्यः, सः. In both these the *visarga* is dropped, the only difference being that in the *Anvakṣara Sandhi* the *visarga* is dropped before any consonant, while here it is dropped before an *Ūṣman* followed by an *aghoṣa* consonant.

(c) *UPĀCARITA SANDHI:* The change of the *visarga* into स् or ष् in case it is preceded by a *Nāmin* vowel, is termed as *Upācarita-sandhi. Upācarita* means changed to nearmost. Of all the *Ūṣmans*, स् and ष् are the nearmost to the *visarga*. This *sandhi* is of two types:

(i) When the *visarga* is preceded by a vowel other than अ or आ and is followed by क् or प्, it is changed to ष्, e.g., निष्कृतिः (निःऽकृतिः), छर्दिष्पौ (छर्दिःऽपौ)

(ii) When अ or आ precedes the *visarga* and is followed by क् or प्, the *visarga* is changed to स्, e.g. शश्वतस्कः यस्पतिः This *Upācarita-sandhi* takes place in the middle of a *Pada* as well as between the two *padas*. Both these types have been enumerated by *Ṛk-Prātiśākhya* in nearly thirty-three *sūtra*-s (4.42 to 64) along with their exceptions. We need not go into those details.

5. *Changes of NAKĀRA*: Of all the consonants the नकार (consonant न्) is the most susceptible to change. It assumes different forms under different circumstances. All these changes have been noted by *Ṛk-Prātiśākhya*. They are named as (a) *Ānpada-vṛtti-sandhi*, (b) *Vivṛttyabhiprāya-sandhi*, (c) *Sparśa-repha-sandhi* and (d) *Sparśoṣma-sandhi*. In all these changes, the vowel preceding the *padānta* न् necessarily changes to nasalised vowel (सानुनासिकस्वर). We shall now observe these different changes of नकार:

(a) *Ānpadavṛtti-sandhi*: This *sandhi* pertains to the *padas* which end in आ. *Ānpada* means pertaining to the *pada* ending in आन्. *Padavṛtti* means the *vivṛtti* between the two *padas*. So, when the *sandhi* pertains to *Ānpada* and ultimately results in *Padavṛtti*, it is termed as *Ānpadavṛtti sandhi*. This is of two types:

(i) When it is followed by a vowel, then न् is dropped and the previous vowel is nasalised as stated earlier, e.g. सर्गाँ इव (सर्गान् + इव), महाँ इन्द्रः (महान् + इ). This *sandhi* takes place in case of न् standing at the end of a *pada* or *padya*.

(ii) This *sandhi* is found to have taken place in the case of certain *padas* when न् stands at the end of a *pada* and is followed by a vowel of the next *pada*. Such words have been noted by the *Ṛk-Prātiśākhya* 4.66 e.g. अज्ञान्, अग्रसानान् etc.

(b) *Vivṛttyabhiprāya Sandhi*: The *Saṁhitā* forms पीवो अन्नाँ रयि वृधः । दधन्वाँ यः, जजुर्वा यः, स्ववाँ यातु, दद्वाँ वा etc. are termed *Vivṛttyabhiprāya sandhis*. In these cases, the न् is dropped, not because a vowel follows it, but because an *Antasstha* follows it. Here न् is dropped and the previous vowel is nasalised and there is a *vivṛtti* between the two *padas*. This *vivṛtti*, however, is not in keeping with the *Vivṛtti lakṣaṇa* which applies to the *vivṛtti* between the two vowels, for there on one side there is a vowel while on the other there is *Ardhasvara*. So it is termed *Vivṛtti-abhiprāya*, meaning *Vivṛtti-sadṛśa*.

(c) *Sparśarepha sandhi*: When the न् is preceded by long ई or ऊ and is followed by a vowel, it is seen changed to *Repha*, e.g. रश्मीँरिव (रश्मीन् + इव); अभीशूँरिव (अभिशून् + इव). In these *cases* the *sparśa* letter is changed to *Repha*; hence, *Sparśarepha*. Some special cases in which न् is changed to *Repha* (and which do not fall under the general rule) are also noted under this type.

(d) *Sparśoṣma sandhi*: In the *Saṁhitā* forms like महाँश्चरति, तांश्चक्रे the *padānta* न् gets the modification like that of a *visarga*. Hence, it is regarded as a special type. The *Sūtras* 4.73-75 note all the exceptions to the modifications of the *Nakāra*.

6. *ĀGAMA*: The topic of *Āgama* is treated under two heads viz., *Śauddhākṣara sandhi* and *Antaḥpāta sandhi*. The *Śauddhākṣara sandhi* relates to the *Āgama* of *Ūṣman* letter (*ś, ṣ, s*) and *R*, and the *Antaḥpāta sandhi* to other *Āgamas* viz. k.c.t.

Though both these are *Āgamas*, still, they differ in the following two points. The *Antaḥpāta Āgama* comes between the two *padas*, while *Śauddhākṣara Āgama* may come between the two *padas*, two *padyas*, or even where अवग्रह does not take place. Secondly, *Antaḥpāta* comes only between the two consonants, while *Śauddhākṣara* comes between the vowels.

7. *LOPA*: According to the *Prātiśākhya*, *Lopa* also is a type of *Sandhi*. Hence, it is described in the *Sandhi paṭala*. e.g. यमी गर्भम् (यम् + ईम् + गर्भम्), समी वत्सं न मातृभिः ।

8. *NATI-SANDHI*: *Nati* is a name given to cerebralisation of a letter of *ta-varga* to *Mūrdhanya* letter, when a letter of *ta-varga* follows a *Nāmi svara*. This pertains to the letters न् and स् changing to ण् and ष् respectively. All the general and special cases of *nati* have been noted in the *Prātiśākhya*. In cases where the *visarga* is followed by स्, we have first to change that स् to ष् by *nati*, and then the *visarga* to ष् by *Vyāpanna sandhi*. (cf. नतिरत्रपूर्वा ततो व्यापत्तिर्भवतीति विद्यात्). *Ṛk-Prātiśākhya* has noted all the cases of *Nati* in the *Ṛgveda* including exceptions.

9. *SĀMAVAŚA-SANDHI*: Where we see a short vowel in the *Padapāṭha*, but the same is seen lengthened in the *Saṁhitā*, such *Saṁhitā* is called *Sāmavaśa sandhi*. The purpose of this *sandhi* is to meet the metrical requirements. These have been treated in chapters vii, viii and ix of the *Ṛk-Prātiśākhya*. This is called *Pluti* also. These *sandhis* are exceptions of the *Anuloma-anvakṣara-sandhi*. The chapter vii deals with *Padānta Pluti* and the remaining two chapters deal with *Padamadhya* and other *plutis*.

10. *VARṆAKRAMA*: The *Varṇakrama* is the doubling of a consonant. This takes place both in the *Saṁhitā* as well as in the middle of a *pada*, e.g. आत्त्वा रथम् (आ + त्वा + रथम्). *Padamadhya* वर्णक्रम is गच्छति. Śākalya, however, discourages all such cases of doubling as far as possible. Even though all the rules of the *Prātiśākhyas* pertain to the *padasandhis*, yet, this *Varṇakrama* is a *Varṇasandhi* and is an exception to the general rule of the *Prātiśākhya* and hence operates on the middle of the *pada* also.

The above analysis of the treatment of *sandhis* in the *Ṛk-Prātiśākhya* would at once reveal that the author of this work gives only description of the letters as they stand at the end of the previous *pada* and at the beginning of the *pada* following, as they are found at the *pada* stage; and then states as they are seen in the form of the *Saṁhitā*. He does not speak of one or more stages in the process (*prakriyā*) by which the finished form is arrived at in the *Saṁhitā* as is seen in case of later *Prātiśākhyas* and grammarians. His treatment of *sandhi* therefore is only descriptive and as it relates to the *padāntas* and *padādis* only, it becomes the description of पदसन्धि. He has actually called them by that name (ततोऽन्याः

पदसंधिषु 2.14). Not that he is not aware of the *sandhis* in the middle of the *pada*, or the *varṇa-sandhis* for he talks of them when occasion arises for them both in respect of the *padamadhya* and the *varṇas*, but he is not concerned with them in general and as a principal topic under consideration. His main purpose is to place before his students the *padas* as they appear in the *Padapāṭha* and the modifications in them when they are read in the *Saṁhitā* form.

But, as we come to other *Prātiśākhyas*, we find that they are dealing with the *sandhis* in the fashion in which they would be dealt with by a grammarian, e.g. by reducing the *padas* to the *sandhi* form by processing them, i.e. by entering into the *prakriyā* step by step. In the earlier part of this chapter, we have seen this by taking an example of the *Padavṛtti-sandhi* in the case of a *visarga* preceded by a long vowel (दीर्घपूर्वविसर्ग), ऐ and औ. The following example of *Ānpadavṛtti* is still more telling. Let us take the following example of the *Ānpadavṛtti sandhi* and see how various *Prātiśākhyas* have explained it.

महान् । इन्द्रः । नृऽवत् (प.पा.) = महाँ इन्द्रोनृवत् (संहिता)

Here the *Saṁhitā* of महान् + इन्द्रः has been महाँ इन्द्रः ।

(i) The *Ṛk-Prātiśākhya* explains it as follows: नकार आकारोपधः पद्यान्तोऽपि स्वरोदयः लुप्यते (4.26) and नकारस्य लोपरेफोष्मभावे पूर्व-स्तत्स्थानादनुनासिकः स्वरः (4.35), meaning that the न् standing at the end of a *pada* (or even at the end of a *padya*) is dropped if it is followed by a vowel; when such न् is dropped or is changed to *Repha* or *Ūṣman*, the vowel preceding its position is nasalised. This is simply the description of the finished *sandhi* form and there is no attempt to arrive at the finished form through any kind of process.

(ii) Now, the *Taittirīya Prātiśākhya* explains it as follows: मर्त्यानुदयानमृतान्दुर्यानसोमपूर्व.... पोषान्महाँश्च (9.21). The words in this *sūtra* change their न् to य् when followed by a vowel. So महान् +

इन्द्रः will be changed to महाय् + इन्द्रः. Now, this य् will be dropped by the rule लुप्येते तु अवर्णपूर्वौ यकारवकारौ (10.19) and while doing that the preceding vowel will be nasalised by the rule नकारस्य रेफोष्मयकारभावात् लुप्ते च मलोपाच्च पूर्वस्वरोऽनुनासिकः (15.1). So the whole process by which we get the finished form in the *Saṁhitā* will be, महान् + इन्द्रः = महाय् + इन्द्रः = महाँ इन्द्रः ।

(iii) The *Vājasaneyi Prātiśākhya* also has the similar process. The relevant *sūtras* are: आकारोपधो यकारम् (3.142); यवयोः पदान्तयोः स्वरमध्ये लोपः (4.127); अनुनासिकमुपधा प्रागनास्थायाः and स्वर औपद्यवि (3-130, 131).

This brings us to the position महाँ इन्द्रः which is found in the process adopted by the *Taittirīya Prātiśākhya*. But the *Vājasaneyi Prātiśākhya* goes a step further and sees the possibility of further *sandhi* at this stage, which it prohibits by the *sūtra* न परकालः पूर्वकाले पुनः (3.4).

(iv) The *Atharva Prātiśākhya* would apply the *sūtras* as: आकारोपधस्य उपबद्धादीनां स्वरे विसर्जनीयः (2.27); स्वरे यकारः (2.41); स्वराद्यवयोः पदान्तयोः (2.21); नकारमकारयोर्लोपे पूर्वस्यानुनासिकः (1.67). Here न् is changed to the *Visarjanīya*, the *Visarjanīya* to य् and then य् is dropped.

(v) Pāṇini would explain it as दीर्घादटि समानपादे (रुः) (P. 8-3.9); then that रु will be changed to य् by भोभगोअघो (P. 8.3.17) etc. and finally the य् will be dropped. The nasalisation of the preceding vowel will be affected by अत्रानुनासिकः पूर्वस्य तु वा । (P. 8.3.2)

This shows how the later *Prātiśākhyas* get into the domain of the grammatical process. The word *Ānpadavṛtti* is only a descriptive name, describing the *Padavṛtti* (*padavivṛtti*) in case of *pada* ending in आन् stating that in the position महाँ इन्द्रः, there is *vivṛtti*. This is just to say that there is no further *sandhi*. But the *Vājasaneyi Prātiśākhya* has stated it in the form of a rule न परकालः पूर्वकाले पुनः (3.4) the import of which is just the same as that in the Pāṇinian *sūtra* पूर्वत्रासिद्धम्. (P. 8.2.1.) The effect of the *vivṛtti* which is the prohibition of further *sandhi* in case of आनुपदवृत्ति being thus achieved by a *sūtra* of general nature, the later *Prātiśākhyas* have no necessity of sticking to the descriptive names of the *sandhis* used in the *Ṛk-Prātiśākhya*. The names of *sandhis* in *Ṛk-Prātiśākhya* are descriptive of the *sandhi* but the rules of later *Prātiśākhyas* are of prescriptive nature being the rules of general application.

The *sandhi* rules given by the later *Prātiśākhyas* are of the nature of later grammatical rules and in the last stage, they practically merged into the Pāṇinian rules of *sandhi*. We need not, therefore, go into their details here as they will have to be considered when we shall study the Pāṇinian rules in the second part of our study. We may, however, make a general observation here that the later *Prātiśākhyas* gradually tended more and more to adopt the line of the grammatical mode of the *Prakriyā* and many a time they are found entering the field of purely grammatical nature such as the change of न् into ण् in the body of a *pada* itself.

Even though the *Prātiśākhyas* were not the works of purely grammatical nature like Pāṇini's work, still, they appear to be fully conscious of the science of grammar. The *Ṛk-Prātiśākhya* calls the grammarians *Śābdāḥ* and mentions the division of words into *Nāma, Ākhyāta, Upasarga* and *Nipāta*, giving their definitions. The *Caturadhyāyī* makes a special reference to the relation between grammar (which it terms as *Sāmānya śāstra*) and the *Prātiśākhya*, when it says एवमिह च विभाषाप्राप्तं सामान्ये. It is, therefore no wonder that the *Prātiśākhyas* quote many authorities some of whom are found mentioned in the later stage in the study of grammar also. It would be good for us here to mention them in this chapter and refer to their special views.

DIFFERENT *ĀCĀRYAS* AND THEIR VIEWS MENTIONED IN THE *PRĀTIŚĀKHYAS*

1. *ṚK-PRĀTIŚĀKHYA*:

1. Āgastya: This name occurs in the introductory verse 2 commented upon by *Viṣṇumitra*. He has reconciled the apparently contradictory views of Māṇḍukeya and Mākṣavya in respect of *Saṁhitopāsanā*. The opinion of this *Ācārya* is found mentioned in *Aitareya Āraṇyaka*, 3.1.1 also

2. Ācārya, Ācāryāḥ: The opinion of *Acāryāḥ* is recorded in 1.63, 64 in respect of the nasalisation of the *padānta* vowel coming at the *Avasāna*, e.g. ईड्यो नूतनैरुतँ (ऋ. 1.1.2). The *Śākalas* observe this rule only in three cases of *pluta* in the *Ṛgveda* (and not anywhere else) out of regard for these teachers. This has reference in Pāṇini at 8-4-58.

3. Anyatareya: His opinion regarding the *Anudātta* pronunciation of *Pracaya* when it is followed by an *Udātta* or *Svarita* is recorded in 3.22. According to him, when a *Pracaya* is followed by an *Udātta* or *Svarita,* it is to be pronounced as *Anudātta*. The same is the view of Śākalya also. This also agrees with the Pāṇinian *Sūtra* नोदात्तस्वरितोदयम् (P. 8.4.67) etc. Can we say that this *Anyatareya* is the same as *Aitareya?*

4. Gārgya: The following views of Gārgya have been recorded in the *Ṛk-Prātiśākhya*. (i) Any *sparśa* except *anunāsika* standing at the end of a *pada* is to be changed to the third letter of that class, e.g. संपद् (while according to Śākaṭāyana it is to be the first letter संपत्) (1.15). Compare Pāṇinī झलां जशोऽन्ते (8.2.39); (ii) After a *yama,* there is a nasalised *svarabhakti* (6.36); (iii) If there is a *Kramavarga* (unit) of three *padas* in which every *pada* influences the following *pada* in the *Saṁhitā*, then according to Gārgya the first *kramavarga* is to be of three *padas* and the succeeding *kramavarga* has also to be of three *padas* e.g. उदूषुणः (सं.पा.); उत्। ऊँ इति । सु । नः । (प.पा.). - उदूषु । ऊषुणः (क्रम. पा.). The reason for

this is stated at 11.26 that it is only after showing the *kramavarga* twice that the original form of the *pada* would be shown in the *kramapāṭha*. Thus उद्‌षु । ऊषुण: । ऊँ इत्यूँ । सु इति सु। (iv) The changes into *ṣatva, ṇatva*, the *Sāmavaśa-sandhi* and the *Upācarita-sandhi,* are termed by Gārgya as *Samāpadya* (13.31).

5. Pāñcāla: His name occurs in reference to Pāñcāla-*Padavṛtti* which has been noted in the previous pages.

6. Pūrva-nimitta-māninaḥ: Those reciters of the *Ṛgveda* who regarded the *pūrvapada* as the *nimitta* for forming the *Kramavarga* in the case of the *padas* वीरास एतन मर्यास: चित्कंभनेन स्कभीयान् and योनिमारैगप. Who they were is not known.

7. Pūrve: These were the old teachers. They held that in case of *Parigraha* when the word is repeated after *iti*, there should be *sandhi* between the word *iti* and the word following iti except in case of the word स्व:. Thus, we have स्व१रितिस्व: (X.17).

8. Prācya: They have been mentioned in connection of *Prācya-padavṛtti.*

9. Mākṣavya: His opinion regarding the *Saṁhitopāsanā* has been mentioned in the introductory verse 2.

10. Maṇḍūkeya: His opinion regarding *Saṁhitopāsanā* is recorded in the introductory verse 2. (ii) According to Maṇḍūkeya, in a *Praśliṣṭa sandhi* of the vowels, and where *Udātta* is followed by an *Anudātta*, the accent in *sandhi* form is a *Svarita*. Compare Pāṇini: स्वरितो वा अनुदात्ते पदादौ । (P. 8.2.6)

11. Yāska: There is no *Eka-padā Ṛk* in *Ṛk-saṁhitā* except one by Vimada - ṛṣi, i.e, 10.20.1, according to *Yāska*.

12. Vedamitra: According to him, the *sthāna* of *ḍa-kāra* is *Jihvāmūla-tālu,* and it is this *ḍa-kāra* that is changed to *ḷa-kāra* when found in between two vowels, e.g. अग्निमीळे (R.V.1.1.1) The same is the case with *ḍhakāra* which is changed to *ḷha-kāra*.

13. Vyāḷi: (i) The *Ṛk-Prātiśākhya* 3.23 records a particular view of Vyāḷi. The general rule is that one or more *Anudātta*s which follow *Svarita* are changed to *Pracaya*. But, Vyāḷi notes a special practice to the effect that when in the *Parigraha* a *pada* is repeated after *anārṣa iti* and that word has one or more *anudātta*s following *iti*, then instead of their being changed to *Pracaya*, they would be kept as *anudātta* only, if they are themselves followed by *Udātta* or *Svarita*, e.g. स॒ त्या॒ नृ॒ ते इति स॒ त्या॒ नृ॒ ते॒ । अ॒ ल॒ लाँ भर्वन्ती॒रित्यल॒ ला॒ भर्वन्तीः । But श॒ त॒ क्र॒ तो॒ इति शतक्रतो ।

(ii) In the case of the *Pluta-svara*, according to some teachers the last *mātrā* is *Anudāttatara*, but, according to Vyāḷi, both the *mātrās* in *pluta* have the same accent (3.28). (iii) According to Vyāḷi, *Abhinidhāna* does not take place anywhere (6.43). (iv) In the case of *Samāpadya*, Vyāḷi agrees with Gārgya and Śākalya. He also holds with them that *ṣatva*, *ṇatva*, *Sāmavaśa* and *Upācarita* are the cases of *Samāpadya*. (v) Vyāḷi treats *Anunāsika* as *Nāsikya* and optionally *Mukhanāsikya* (13.37).

14. Śākaṭāyana: (i) According to Śākaṭāyana, the *sparśa* letter except *anunāsika* is changed to the first letter of its class when it stands as a *padānta* (this is against the opinion of Gārgya who holds that it is the third of the class). Hence Pāṇini has option in this case. (ii) In the *Sandhya* letters, i.e. ए, ओ, ऐ, औ, their first half is अ and the second half is इ (इ, ई) in the case of ए, ऐ and उ (उ, ऊ) in the case of ओ, औ (13.39).

15. Śākalāḥ (the followers of Śākalya): The following views of Śākalas are noted in the *Ṛk-Prātiśākhya*: (i) According to Śākalas, the final vowel at the end of a hemistich is to be nasalised provided it has 3 *mātrās* (1.64). (ii) The particle उ is made *dīrgha* and *sānunāsika* in the *Padapāṭha* and is followed by *iti* (1.75). (iii) There is no *varṇakrama* in the case of conjunct consonants which follow a long vowel (6.14). (iv) लकार undergoes *Abhinidhāna* even when *Ūṣman* follows (6.20).

(v) *Abhinidhāna* is *asaṁyukta* according to Śākalas, i.e. the consonants in *abhinidhāna* are not pronounced like conjunct consonants (6.24). (vi) The opinion about *Abhinidhāna* held by the Śākalas was optionally accepted by others in cases of such conjuct consonants which differed in *Prayatna* or *Sthāna - Prayatna* (6.27). (vii) Śākalas have *catuḥkrama* in such cases as उद्घुष्णः (11.19). (viii) Many *Ācāryas* follow the Śākala method of having *Kramavargas* of different types (11.21). (ix) In the *Padapāṭha*, the *padas* are shown in two ways. They are shown as they are originally, and in some cases they are shown with *iti*. The *padas* without *iti* are termed *Sthita* and those with *iti* are called *Upasthita*. In the *Kramapāṭha* the Śākalas follow the practice of *Sthitopasthita*, i.e. first they show it with *iti* and immediately in the *sthita* form, e.g. आरैगित्यारैक् । स्वितिसु । प्रातरिति प्रातः । It is only in this way that the original form of the *pada* is maintained and exhibited in the *Krama* (11.61).

16. Śākalya: The following views of Śākalya are noted in *Ṛk-Prātiśākhya*: (i) *Svarita* should be used in *Ikārapraśleṣa*, *Kṣaipra* and *Abhinihita*, when the *Pūrvarūpa* is *Udātta* (3.13). (ii) When *Pracaya* is followed by *Udātta* or *Svarita*, it should be uttered as *Anudātta*. This is the view of Śākalya as well as Anyatareya (3.22). (iii) *Ch* coming after c is not changed to ś (4.13). (iv) *Ṣatva, Ṇatva, Sāmavaśa* and *Upācarita* are included in *Samāpadya* according to Śākalya, Gārgya and Vyāḷi (13.31).

17. Śākalya-pitā: *Ch* preceded by any first *Sparśa varṇa* is changed to Ś (4.4.)

18. Śākalya-Sthavira: The *Akāra* in the *Prācya padavṛtti* and *Pañcāla padavṛtti* is to be pronounced as एँ and ओ respectively (2.81).

19. Śābdāḥ: These are the *Vaiyākaraṇa*s. They divided the words into four divisions, viz. *Nāma, Ākhyāta, Upasarga* and *Nipāta* (12.17).

20. Śūravīra and his son: Mentioned in the context of *Saṁhitopāsanā* in the introductory verse 3.

21. Śaunaka: The author of the *Ṛk-Prātiśākhya*, mentioned in the introductory verse 1.

22. *Others*: Certain teachers are mentioned by such words as *Anye, Eke, Apare, Kecit*. They cannot be identified. Their opinions are recorded in the following *sūtras*.

i. *Anye* - 17.43

ii. *Apare* - 6.45, 51; 11.6.14, 20, 58, 59; 13.18.

iii. *Eke* - 1.46; 3.22, 27; 4.16; 6.27, 50, 52, 54, 55; 13.12, 14, 15, 19, 32, 38; 15.33; 16.25; 18.57.

iv. *Kecit* - 1.40; 3.20; 17.43, 50.

2. *TAITTIRĪYA PRĀTIŚĀKHYA*:

1. Āgniveśya: In 9.4 he rejects the change of *Visarga* to *Jihvāmūlīya* and *Upadhmānīya*, e.g. यः कामयेत or अग्निः पशुः ।

2. Āgniveśyāyana: The *Anudātta* followed by the *Udātta* or the *Svarita* remains as *Anudātta* only and does not become *Svarita*, even if it is preceded by *Udātta*. This is the general rule. However, Āgniveśyāyana does not agree with it. In 14.32 he says that even here स्वरितात् परोऽनुदात्तः स्वरितः holds good. His rule is the *pratiprasava* against नोदात्तस्वरितपरः. His opinion corresponds to that of Gārgya, Kāśyapa and Gālava mentioned by Pāṇini in नोदात्तस्वरितोदयमगार्ग्यकाश्यपगालवानाम् (P. 8. 4. 67).

3. Ātreya: According to him, when an *Anunāsika* is followed by ल्, it is changed to ल् and the *anunāsikatva*, i.e., nasalisation is shifted to the previous letter, e.g. तान् + लोकान् = ताँल्लोकान् (5.31). The *sūtra* 17.8 states Ātreya's view on pronunciation of letters.

4. Ukhya: His views are recorded in 8.22, 10.20, 16.24.

(i) 8.22 states the case of एष्टः रायः = एष्टारायः This *sandhi* is said to have various alternatives. According to Sāṅkṛtya, it becomes एष्टो रायः, while, according to Ukhya, it is एष्टुरायः (एष्टः = एष्टर्, *Riphita-visarjanīya* according to 8.8.)

(ii) When य् and व् stand at the end of a *pada* as modification of *visarga*, or ए and ओ, or ऐ and औ, that is not dropped according to Ukhya, e.g. आपः + उन्दन्तु = आपयुन्दन्तु.

(iii) 16.24 states Ukhya's view on the pronunciation of र ह्यै in which ऐकार is uttered with excessive effort (नितान्त).

5. Uttamottarīya: This teacher also refers to the *sandhi* of एष्टः + रायः which according to this teacher is एष्टर् रायः ।

6. Kāndamāyana: Referred to in 9.1, 15.7,8. (i) The *visarga* followed by *Ūṣman* or *Aghoṣa* is dropped according to him (9.1) e.g. चतुः + स्तनाम् = चतुस्तनाम् ।

(ii) 15.7, 8, state that according to this teacher, the *Pluta* vowel is to be nasalised in the *Padapāṭha*, e.g. अस्तु ही इत्यब्रूतम् = अस्तु । हिँ३ । इति । अब्रूतम् ।

7. Kauṇḍinya: Referred to in 5.38, 18.34, 19.2. (i) The *sūtra* 5.38 states that according to Kauṇḍinya, the ह् preceded by the first *sparśa* becomes the fourth letter of that class, e.g. अर्वाक् । हि । एनम् = अर्वाग्घ्येनम् । (ii) 18. 3, 4. states that ओंकार has to be uttered as sustained *Pracaya* and in the middle tone. (iii) 19.2 states that an *Anudātta* preceded by a *Pracaya* and followed by an *Udātta* or a *Svarita* is called *Vikrama*.

8. Kaundanya (Sthavira): When the न् is converted to र् or *visarga* or य् (dropped) or when म् is lost, the nasal quality of the previous letter is *Tīvratara*. (xvii.4).

9. Kauhaliputra: 17.2 states that the nasal quality in all the cases is the same, according to this teacher.

10. Gautama: the ह् preceded by the first *sparśa* is changed

to the fourth of the class (5.38).

11. Pauṣkarasādi: He is referred to in 5.37, 38; 13.16; 14.2; 17.6

(i) The *sūtra* 5.37 refers to the change of श् to छ्. According to Pauṣkarasādi, if that श् is followed by a consonant and is preceded by a न् which is not changed to ञ्, then that श् is not changed to छ् e.g. आदित्यान्श्मश्रुभिः ।

(ii) Rule 5.38 relates to the change of ह् to the fourth letter of class.

(iii) 13.16 states that ड् is not changed to ळ् if preceded by a mixed vowel ऋ, e.g. मृडाति. But मृळाति in *Ṛg*.

(iv) 14.2 states that a conjunct consonant becomes doubled even if it is preceded by ल् or व्.

(v) 17.6 states that *Svarita* and *Vikrama* are to be pronounced with greater effort.

12. Plākṣāyaṇa: Referred to in 9.6; 14.11, 17; 18.5.

(i) 9.6 states that the *visarga* is changed to *'sasthāna'* if followed by a surd.

(ii) 14.11 relates to *Abhinidhāna* in case the following mute is nasal.

(iii) 14.17 states that an *Ūṣman* is not doubled when followed by the first mute.

(iv) 18.5 states that ओंकार is to be uttered as *Svarita*.

13. Plākṣi: (i) Referred to in 5.38; 9.6; 14.10, 17; 18.5. For 9.6; 14.17 and 18.5 see Plākṣāyana. Plākṣi holds the same views.

(ii) 5.38 states about the change of ह् to the fourth of the class.

(iii) 14.10 states Plākṣi's view about *Abhinidhāna* in case an *Aghoṣa* follows.

14. Badabhīkara: Referred to in 14.13. stating about the change of the second letter in place of the first when the following spirant is not of the same *sthāna*.

15. Bhāradvāja: According to Bhāradvāja the Anunāsika element is very faint in Anusvāra (17.3).

16. Mācākīya: *Padānta* य् and व् are dropped when followed by उ or ओ (10.22) e.g. आप: + उन्दन्तु = आपय् उन्दन्तु = आप उन्दतु; ता:ओषधी: = ता ओषधी:; But ते एनम् = तयेनम्, वायविष्टये.

17. Vātsapra: 10.23. According to Vātsapra, the य् and व् referred to in the previous note are indistinctly uttered.

18. Vālmīki: Referred to in 5.36, 9.4, 18.6. (i) According to Vālmīki, श् is not changed to छ् when preceded by प्, e.g. अनुष्टुप्-शारदी:. (ii) 9.4 states that *visarga* is not changed if followed by क् or प्. (iii) 18.6 states that the letter ओं is to be uttered *Pluta* and *Udātta*.

19. Śāṅkhyāyana: Only *Pluta pada* is to be nasalised (15.7).

20. Śaityāyana: Referred to in 5.40; 17.1, 7; 18.2

(i) 5.40 states that the fourth letter is interposed, e.g. अवीघ्ह्यसि.

(ii) 17.1 states that the *Anunāsika* element is *tīvratara* in case of *Anusvāra* and the fifth letter of class.

(iii) 17.7 states that each letter has its own peculiar effort.

(iv) 18.2 states that a letter may be uttered *Udātta, Anudātta* or *Svarita*.

21. Sāṅkṛtya: Referred to in 8.21; 10.21; 16.16.

(i) 8.21 states that एष्टा + राय: should be uttered as एष्टो राय:।

(ii) 10.21 states that व् is dropped while य् is not dropped.

(iii) 16.16 states the cases that long ई or ऊ would become short when followed by an *anusvāra*. But, this does not apply to आ. Thus according to him हविंषि, आयुंषि, but वयांसि.

22. Harita: surd spirant is not doubled (14.18)

23. In addition to the above teachers we have (i) *Ācāryāḥ* in 1.46, (ii) *Eke Ācāryaḥ* in 1.47; 2.19; 27.47; 5.39; 8.19; 9.19; 14.33; 15.2,6; 18.1; 19.3; 21.23. (iii) *Pūrve* in 15.9, (iv) *Sarve* in 8.7 and (v) *Mīmāṁsakāḥ* in 5.41. The *Taittirīya Prātiśākhya* refers to the maximum number of opinions in different cases.

3. *VĀJASANEYI PRĀTIŚĀKHYA*:

1. Aupaśivi: According to him the penultimate vowel is nasalised when a vowel follows (3.132).

2. Kāṇvāḥ: 1.123, 149, 150. This is a *Śākhā* of the *Śukla Yajurveda* and not the name of particular persons. The *Prātiśākhya* has noted the peculiarities of this *Śākhā* which are:

(i) The posture of hand is oblique when the *Svarita* is preceded by *Anudātta* (1.123).

(ii) The word following *iti* is pronounced as obliquely grave, when followed by a word accented finally or in the middle. In other cases the grave becomes like an *Udātta*, i.e., *Prācaya* (1.149, 150).

3. Kātyāyana: In 8.68 he is mentioned as the author of the *Prātiśākhya* and is honoured as स्वरसंस्कारप्रतिष्ठापयिता.

4. Kāśyapa: According to him म् and न् are dropped (and the penultimate vowel is nasalised in cases where *Anusvāra* is prescribed by 4.1,2) (4.4)

5. Gārgya: 4.165 states that according to Gārgya, ख् and य् in the root ख्या become क् and श् respectively except in the words

सख्य, उख्य and मुख्य.

6. Jātukarṇya:

(i) Referred to in 4.123, 158; 5.22. 4.123 states that according to Jātukarṇya the ह् followed by a र् is not changed to the fourth of the preceding *sparśa*, nor does the preceding *sparśa* to the third.

(ii) 4.158 states that according to Jātukarṇya, the word कश्यप has no य् in it when the word does not refer to *Ṛṣi*.

(iii) 5.22 states that according to Jātukarṇya the words पारावतान् and आग्निमारुता: are separated by *avagraha*.

7. Dālbhya: According to Dālbhya, ण् and न् when followed by स् are not intervened by क् and त् respectively (4.15).

8. *Brāhmaṇa (Śatapatha)*: 1.129 states that while the *Yajur mantras* recognise the three usual accents, the *Brāhmaṇa*, i.e. *Śatapatha Brāhmaṇa* recognises only two, i.e. *Udātta* and *Anudātta*, both known as *Bhāṣika*.

9. *Mādhyandināḥ*: 8.45 and 46 refer to the mode of the *Mādhyandina Śākhā* that the ळ्, ळ्ह, जिह्वामूलीय, उपध्मानीय, नासिक्य, long ॡ and *pluta* vowels are not recognised by the *Mādhyandināḥ* i.e. the followers of the *Mādhyandina Śākhā*.

10. Śākaṭāyana: Referred to in 3.9, 12, 88; 4.4, 127, 189.

(i) The *sūtra* 3.9 states that according to Śākaṭāyana, the *visarga* is changed to the homogeneous letter when श्, ष्, स्, (मुत्) follow.

(ii) 3.12 states that according to Śākaṭāyana, the visarga is changed to the *Jihvāmūlīya* and the *Upadhmānīya* respectively when क्, ख and प्, फ् follow.

(iii) 3.88 states that according to Śākaṭāyana the *Saṁhitā* of the *padas* परि and न: becomes परिण:.

(iv) 4.4 states that according to Śākaṭāyana, the *Padānta* न् and म् are dropped and the penultimate vowel is nasalised in the cases mentioned in the rules 4.1 and 2.

(v) 4.127 states that according to Śākaṭāyana the final व् of असौ is not dropped when the *asasthāna* vowel follows.

(vi) 4.189 states that according to Śākaṭāyana, the word सु joined to the next word in a *Krama* group should also be repeated with *iti* interposed.

11. Śākalya: According to Śākalya, the *visarjanīya* does not undergo any change when followed by श् ष् स् (3.10) or by क्, ख्, प्, फ् (3.10, 11).

12. Śaunaka: A *sparśa* letter except the fifth is changed to second when a mute letter (श्, ष्, स्) not of the same *sthāna* follows (4.120).

13. Other authority referred to is एके in the *sūtras* 3.92, 229; 4.55, 126, 144, 186; 5.23, 44, and 7.8.

4. *CATURADHYĀYĪ OR ATHARVAVEDA-PRĀTIŚĀKHYA*:

1. Śākaṭāyana: In all cases where य् and व् are to be dropped according to others, according to Śākaṭāyana they are to be uttered with 'leśavṛtti' in respect of the contact (2.24).

2. Śaunaka: The words which are declared to end in the first mute are, according to Śaunaka, to end in the third. But that is not the authorised usage. (1.8).

3. Kavayaḥ: विकंपितं तत्कवयो वदन्ति । (3.65).

4. *Eke*: According to some, the *Prayatna* of vowels is *Spṛṣṭa* (1.33).

5. *ṚK-TANTRAM*:

1. Auḍavraji: The *sandhi* of *Ucca*, i.e. *Udātta* is always *Udātta* (*Sūtra* 60)

2. Naigi: According to Naigi, it may be *Udātta* or *Svarita* in case of the *Sandhi* of *Udātta* and *Anudātta* (*Sutra* 59).

3. *Eke*: Referred to in *Sūtras* 102, 108, 160, 175, 188

Chapter Four

THE NIRUKTA

The basic question the *Nirukta* asks is: "Why it is that when a man conveys his ideas, he does so by using particular words only?" When he is trying to find out and state the import of words, he is attempting what may be called *Nirvacana,* and the general rules which underlie this process of *Nirvacana* ultimately develop into the science called *Nirukta*. It may be argued why a bud is called *kuḍmala,* while the same when opened is called *puṣpa*. An attempt to answer such enquiries is the starting point of *Nirvacana*.

On close observation, it will be found that this enquiry has its beginning in the Veda itself. For example, compare:

अग्निर्देवासो, अग्नियमिन्धते वृत्रहन्तमम् (ऋ. - 616-48)

with the *Śatapatha Brāhmaṇa* 2.2.4.2, which says: तदा एनम् एतदग्रे देवानामजयन्त तस्मादग्निः । अग्निर्ह वै नाम एतद् यदग्निः । (Also see, *Śatapatha Br.* 6.1.1.1).

On the basis of minute observation of the Vedic expression, the ancient Vedic scholars found that a word or sound-group expressing anything in the final stage bears some relation with the sounds expressing action (क्रिया). They arrived at the conclusion that the names of substances and qualities have their ultimate basis in the क्रिया denoted by roots (धातु). This they found in the Veda itself. e.g. अर्कमर्चन्ति अर्किणः (ऋ1.7.1); स्तोतृभ्यो मंहते मद्यम् (1.11.3); यज्ञेन यज्ञमयजन्त (1.164.5); ये सहांसि सहसा सहन्ते (6.66.9); पूर्वीरश्नन्तावश्विना (8.5.31); ऋत्विज् - 'यजिष्ठो देवाँ ऋतुशो यजाति (10.2.5), नचिकेता 'एतमर्थं न चिकेताहमग्निः (10.51.4), धान्यमसि धिनुहि देवान् (वा.सं. 1.20); नवनीतम् - नवं नीतम् (तै.सं.2.3.10.1) नदी - यददः संप्रयतीरहावनदता हते । तस्मादा नद्यो नाम स्थ ता वो नामानि सिन्धवः (अ.वे.3.13.1).

Such examples may be multiplied. The *Brāhmaṇas* have followed this line and they gave *Nirvacana* in their own way. The words explained in this way in the Vedic text number more than eight hundred. This attitude is found in the *Āraṇyakas* and the *Upaniṣads* also. Of course, the words they selected for *Nirvacana* were such as were of importance to them. This ultimately developed into the *Nirukta-śāstra*.

The only work on this science available to us today is the *Nirukta* of Yāska. But, the references to the earlier writers on this science in that work indicate that there must have been a long line of the *Ācāryas* who lived before Yāska. The names of the *Nairuktas* that have come down to us are: Āgrāyaṇa, Audumbarāyaṇa Aupamanyava, Aurṇavābha, Kātthakya, Kautsa, Krauṣṭuki, Gārgya, Gālava, Carmaśiras, Taiṭīki, Vārṣyāyaṇi, Śatabalākṣa, Śākaṭāyana, and Śākapūṇi (the son of Śākaṭāyana). The last name in the list is, of course, that of Yāska.

Another branch of the study of language was known as *Vyākaraṇa*. Starting from Bṛhaspati, it came through Indra - Bharadvāja - Padakāra Śākalya and others, reaching Pāṇini.

Both the *Nirukta* and the *Vyākaraṇa* deal with the word but from different angles. Both take the word as it is found in the language, they neither add to nor detract anything from it. They are not makers of the word. The *Nirukta* takes the word and tries to find out the *Kriyā* from which it has sprung, with a view to finding out how the meaning evolved. The *Vyākaraṇa* takes the word as it is and tries to find out its formation. Hence the *Vyākaraṇa* has to deal with the steps of the evolution of the form of the word, which is known as the *Prakriyā*. It has, therefore, to postulate some imaginary or conceptual steps, as stated in the *Vākyapadīya*. उपाया: शिक्ष्यमाणानां बालानामुपलालना: । असत्ये वर्त्मनि स्थित्वा तत: सत्यं समीहते ॥ (वा.प. 2.238).

The *Nirukta* has not to deal with such steps. A *Nairukta* will say that the word दम्पती is the present form in vogue for दमपती.

But a *Vaiyākaraṇa* will say that it is from जाया + पति, the word जाया being changed to either जम् or दम् (जायाशब्दस्य जम्भावो दम्भावो वा निपात्यते 11. *Bālamanoramā* on P. 2. 2. 31). Likewise, in the case of *ārdhadhātuka* affixes, the *Vyākaraṇa* has to postulate भू as the substitute of अस्, वच् as that of ब्रू, ख्या as that of चक्ष् and so on. We also find that the different teachers of Grammar have imagined differently in this respect. For example, Āpiśali takes स् as the root and says that अ comes as an आगम in *laṭ* and *loṭ*, and आ comes as an *āgama* in *liṭ* and *laṅ* while Pāṇini, Gārgya, Śākaṭāyana and Yāska take अस् as the root and say that in the *Nivṛttisthāna* अ is dropped. In the *Vyākaraṇa svara* and *saṁskāra* are of great importance; while, in the *Nirvacana* Yāska says: न संस्कारमाद्रियेत, (Nir. 2.1.4.) if it comes to that.

The words *nirukta* and *nirvacana* have been derived from the root निर् + वच्. Durga takes the word in the sense of bringing out the meaning from the words which are *Parokṣa-vṛtti* or *Atiparokṣa-vṛtti*. Thus, he says: अपिहितस्यार्थस्य परोक्षवृत्तावतिपरोक्ष-वृत्तौ वा शब्दे निष्कृष्य विगृह्य वचनम् निर्वचनम् (Durga on Nir. 2.1)

This is of course the *Yaugika* meaning. But the word is also used in *Yogarūḍha* sense which means 'Science which does that work.' We have now to find out how that meaning has come to be.

i) We find the roots निर् + वच् and निर् + मन्त्र used in the *Atharvaveda* and it has been rendered by Sāyaṇa in the sense of 'bringing out'. Thus, the expression यक्ष्मणां सर्वेषां विषं निरवोचमहं त्वत् in *Atharva, Śaunaka Śākhā* (9.13.12), is found in the *Pippalāda-śākhā* as यक्ष्मोधामन्तरात्मनो बहिर्निमन्त्रयामहे (16.75.2). Here, the word निरवोचम् corresponds to निर्मन्त्रयामहे. Sāyaṇa renders it as मन्त्रेण निर्वीर्यं करोमि यद्वा तदीयं विषं निर्गतं ब्रवीमि ।

ii) In the *Kāṭhaka* and *Maitrāyaṇī Saṁhitās*, the words निरुक्त and अनिरुक्त have been used as adjectives and they have the *yaugika* sense. In the *Śatapatha* also, the word is used in the same sense as will be seen from the following passages:-

(1) तं गर्भिण्या वाचा मिथुनया प्रजनयति यन्निरुक्तं चानिरुक्तं च तन्मिथुनम् । (का.सं.6.5).

(2) एतद्वै देवानां स्तोत्रमनिरुक्तं यत् सर्पराज्ञा ऋचः, तस्यै तदुक्थमनिरुक्तं यच्चतुर्होतारो मनसा प्रस्तौति । (का. 9.15).

(3) अनिरुक्तः प्रातःसवः, प्रजापतिमेव तेनाप्नोति, वियोनिर्वै वाजपेयः प्राजापत्यः, स निरुक्तसामा, यदनिरुक्तः प्रातःसवः, तेन सयोनि रथंतरं साम भवति (मै 1.11.9).

(4) यजुषा हविर्धानं मिनोति, निरुक्ताहिद्यौः, यजुषा सदो, निरुक्ताहीयम्, अयजुषा आग्नीध्रम्, अनिरुक्तमिव अन्तरिक्षम् (ap. 3.8.9).

(5) उच्चैर्निरुक्तमभिष्टूयात्, प्राणो वै स्तुभो निरुक्तो ह्येषः । (श.ब्रा. 8.3).

(6) उच्चैर्निरुक्तमनुब्रूयात् । एतद्वै वाचो नन्वसितम् पाप्मनो यन्निरुक्तम्... (श.ब्रा. (1.1).

(iii) It is in the *Devatādhyāya Brāhmaṇa* that we find the word निर्वचन used in the technical sense, as अथातो निर्वचनम्. The relevant passage is as under:

अथातो निर्वचनम् ॥३ ॥ ॥ गायत्री गायतेः स्तुतिकर्मणः ॥२ ॥ ॥ गायतो मुखादुदपतत् इति ह ब्राह्मणम् ॥३ ॥ ॥ उष्णिग् उत्स्नानात्, स्निह्यतेर्वा कान्तिकर्मणः, अपि वा उष्णीषिणी वा इति औपमिकम् ॥४ ॥ ककुप् च कुब्जश्च कूजतेर्वा उब्जतेर्वा ॥५॥ अनुष्टुभनुष्टोभनात् ॥७ ॥ अन्वस्तौदिति ह ब्राह्मणम् ॥८॥ etc. This passage has a corresponding section in Yāska's work at 7.13. Many scholars, however, hold that this *Devatādhyāya Brāhmaṇa* is not a work of the *Brāhmaṇa* stage, but it is of the post-*Nirukta* period.

(iv) It is in the *Muṇḍakopaniṣad* that we get the mention of *Nirukta* as a definite science. This is the direct mention of निरुक्त as a *Vedāṅga*. The passage is: तत्रापरा ऋग्वेदो यजुर्वेदः सामवेदोऽथर्व- वेदः शिक्षा कल्पो व्याकरणं निरुक्तं छन्दो ज्योतिषमिति । अथ परा यया तदक्षरमधिगम्यते । (मु 1.5)

(v) In the *Chāndogyopaniṣad* 7.1.2, *Devavidyā* has been mentioned as one of the sciences (विद्या). The word देवविद्या has been rendered as *Nirukta* in the *Śāṅkara-bhāṣya* (देवविद्यां निरुक्तम्). This is a very important reference. We find in the *Brāhmaṇa* works that the words *nirukta* and *anirukta* are used in relation to the nature of deities. The word *nirukta* has been used there in the sense of देवतास्वरूप निर्वचन, and not in the sense of शब्दनिर्वचन. A discussion which pertains to the nature of a deity or to the things related to it has been termed as *nirukta* in the *Brāhmaṇa* works. We can, therefore, say the word *nirukta* has been used in the *Brāhmaṇa* works in the sense of *Devavidyā*.

Yāska's *Nirukta* also supports this surmise. This work serves two functions, viz., the *Nirvacana* of the Vedic words, and the *Nirvacana* of the nature of the Vedic deity. The first six chapters deal with the *Nirvacana* of *Śabda*, the remaining eight chapters relate to देवतास्वरूपनिर्वचन. It is also evident that Yāska's work gives greater importance to देवतास्वरूपनिर्वचन.

Brāhmaṇa works also contain the instances of शब्दनिर्वचन. However, the word *Nirukta* does not appear to have been used there in that sense. This does not mean that they did not know the art or science of *Śabda-nirvacana*. We may not be far from truth if we say that the original purpose of this science was to explain the nature of the deity (देवतास्वरूप-निर्वचन) through the medium of the शब्दनिर्वचन and hence it was termed as *Devavidyā*. As time went on it developed into the science of शब्दनिर्वचन as we understand it today.

The modern scholar of the *Nirukta*, who is under the impression that it is a science of etymology of words only, is at a loss to know why the chapters on the *Daivata-kāṇḍa* are added by Yāska to his work. Many of us feel that these chapters might be a later addition. The above discussion will now show that this science has its beginning in the effort towards देवता-परिज्ञान which developed into *Devavidyā*. It was through the मन्त्रार्थचिन्ता that they wanted to know the nature of the deity. This *mantrārtha* required the knowledge of the import of the words and hence they required the *Śabdanirvacana*. The etymology of words was a means rather than the purpose of the science of *Nirukta*. Yāska states this in clear terms when he says : "इत्ययं मन्त्रार्थचिन्ताभ्यूहो अभ्यूढ:, अपि श्रुतित:, अपि तर्कत: । न तु पृथक्त्वेन मन्त्रा निर्वक्तव्या:, प्रकरणश एव तु निर्वक्तव्या: । (नि. १३-१२)

Yāska's *Nirukta* is a commentary on the work called the *Nighaṇṭu,* which by itself is a collection of Vedic words. The *Nighaṇṭu* may be termed as the first dictionary of the world. It is a collection of 1771 words and appears to have some plan in the arrangement of words. Out of the five chapters in which the work is divided, the first three *adhyāyas* consist of the synonyms of various words. The synonyms are first noted and at the end of each group of synonyms, the total number is noted. Yāska has called the first three *adhyāya*s by the name *Naighaṇṭuka-kāṇḍa*. In the fourth *adhyāya*, words having more than one meaning as well as words having uncertain meaning have been collected in three sections. Yāska calls this the *Aikapadika-kāṇḍa*. The fifth and the last *adhyāya* is a collection of the names of deities and is termed by Yāska as *Daivata-kāṇḍa*.

The arrangement of the words in the first three *adhyāyas* appears to have some plan. In the first *adhyāya,* words which are names of physical things such as पृथ्वी, अन्तरिक्ष, दिशा, मेघ, नदी etc. have been given in seventeen sections. They together make 415 words. In the second *adhyāya* the words denoting man and the things and actions relating to him, have been noted in twenty-two sections. They together make 516 words. The third *adhyāya* has thirty sections and consists of 420 words. They contain some adjectives, the names denoting *Bhāva* such as *Prajñā* etc., and names of actions. Thus the *Naighaṇṭuka-kāṇḍa* consists of 1341 words.

The fourth *adhyāya* has 279 words of the nature of

अनवगत-संस्कार, i.e., the words the derivation of which is uncertain. They do not reveal any internal plan.

The fifth *adhyāya* has 151 names divided in six sections. The first three sections enumerate 52 names of the deities connected with the Earth (पृथ्वीस्थानीय देवता). The fourth section deals with the names of the deities belonging to the Mid region (अन्तरिक्षस्थानीय देवता). These names are 32. The fifth *adhyāya* deals with the minor deities of the Mid region (अन्तरिक्ष) and the names of the female deities. They together number 36. The sixth and the final section enumerates 31 names of the deities belonging to *Dyauḥ* (द्युस्थानीय देवता).

A peculiarity in this enumeration is to be noted. Many nouns and verbs have been noted in the list in the form in which they appear in the *mantras*. Thus we get them in different case forms. The verbs also are noted in the forms of different *lakāras*. In the case of a few verbs different forms of the same verb are given.

Many scholars have criticised the author of the *Nighaṇṭu* for this confusion. It, however appears to me that he had a mind to explain them in the context in which they occurred in the *mantras*.

Yāska has not explained every word from the *Nighaṇṭu*. Out of 1771 words in the *Nighaṇṭu*, he has written on 660 words only. In the *Naighaṇṭuka-kāṇḍa* which has 1341 words Yāska explains only 230 words. His comments also are very short. He has followed the *samāsa* style rather than the *vyāsa* style of writing in respect of the words in the *Nighaṇṭu*. The explanation of the actual words in the *Nighaṇṭu* begins in the fifth section of the second *adhyāya*. The whole of the first *adhyāya* and the first four sections of the second *adhyāya* are given to the introduction and to the theoretical topics. The whole of the *Naighaṇṭuka-kāṇḍa* forming three chapters of the निघण्टु have been covered by Yāska in less than two chapters, for it ends with the third *adhyāya* of the *Nirukta*.

From among the synonyms, Yāska has commented only on the first word of the series and left out the rest of the words. The result is that we are not now in the know of various shades of meanings of these synonyms. For example there are 122 words in the sense of गति. In the *Nighaṇṭu* 2.10 there are 28 words in the sense of धन. Each of these words has in it its peculiar notion apart from its general meaning. These senses would have been clear to us had Yāska commented on them in the same way as he has done in the case of the word गो.

Yāska has, however, been very liberal in respect of the words in the ऐकपदिककाण्ड. He has explained every word in that section. In respect of the दैवतकाण्ड also, he has made many points clear. Thus, even though the words जातवेदस्, वैश्वानर, द्रविणोदस्, all mean Agni, still he has brought out various shades of meaning in the case of those words.

All scholars agree that the present *Nirukta* has two parts, viz., the *Nighaṇṭu,* which is a collection of Vedic words and a commentary on it, and the commentary beginning with the words 'समाम्नाय: समाम्नात:, स व्याख्यातव्य:' is written by Yāska. But, who is the author of the *Nighaṇṭu*?

In this respect scholars - both ancient and modern hold two opinions. Durga opines that the *Nighaṇṭu* is older than the *Nirukta* and its author is different from Yāska. He says:

"तस्यैषा गवाद्या देवपत्न्यन्ता पञ्चाधायी सूत्रसंग्रह: । सा पुनरियं साक्षात्कृतधर्मभ्यो महर्षिभ्य: उपदेशेन मंत्रार्थमुपश्रुत्य श्रुतर्षिभि: अवरशक्तिदौर्बल्यमवेक्ष्य तदनुजिघृक्षया वाक्यार्थ - सामर्थ्यादभिधेयानुन्नीय उन्नीय मंत्रार्थावबोधनाय छन्दोभ्य: समाहृत्य समाहृत्य समाम्नाता ।" - दुर्ग, भूमिका. At 1.20, he further says: ते (ऋषय:) इमं ग्रंथं गवादिदेवपत्न्यन्तं समाम्नातवन्त: I; again at 4.12 while writing about अकूपारस्य दावने he says: *तेन ज्ञायते अन्यैरेवायमृषिभि: समाम्नाय: समाम्नात: । अन्य एव चायं भाष्यकार: ।*

स्कन्दस्वामिन् also holds the same view. He says on समाम्नाय: समाम्नातः as follows: समाम्नायशब्देनात्र गवादिर्देवपत्न्यन्त: शब्दसमूह: उच्यते, न वेद: । समाम्नात: संभूय आभिमुख्येन आम्नात: अभ्यस्त: । ग्रन्थीकृत्य पूर्वाचार्यै: पठित इत्यर्थ: । Prof. Rath, Sāmāshrami, Prof. Karmarkar, Dr. Belwalkar and Prof. V. R. Rajwade hold the same opinion.

मधुसूदनसरस्वती, on the other hand, holds that both the *Nighaṇṭu* and its commentary are the work of Yāska. He says in his commentary on महिम्नस्तोत्र, verse 7: एवं निघण्ट्वादयोऽपि वैदिकद्रव्य-देवतात्मकपदार्थपर्यायशब्दात्मकानिरुक्तान्तर्भूता एव । तत्रापि निघण्टुशब्दात्मक: पंचाध्यायात्मको ग्रंथो भगवता यास्केनैव कृत: । The word एव in this expression indicates that मधुसूदनसरस्वती was conscious of the opposite view.

Earlier than मधुसूदनसरस्वती, Veṅkaṭa Mādhava appears to have held that the निघण्टु was prepared by Yāska. He says in his भाष्य on ऋग्वेद 7.87.4 "तत्रैकविंशतिर्नामानि काचिद् गौर्बिभर्ति इति पृथिवीमाह । तस्या हि यास्कपठितानि एकविंशतिर्नामानि ।

This view is held by Dayānanda Saraswati, Pt. Bhagavaddatta, Pt. Seetarama Sastry, and Pt. Shiva Narayana Shastry.

We need not go into the details of this controversy. It has been fully stated and examined by Pt. Bhagavaddatta (vide, his वैदिक वाङ्मय का इतिहास, भाग २, पृ. १८३). It may however be stated here that the internal evidence from the *Nirukta* goes in favour of the view that the author of the *Nighaṇṭu* is *Yāska* himself. That evidence may be stated here for the benefit of students. In *Nirukta* 7.13 Yāska says:

अथोताभिधानैर्हविश्चोदयति । इन्द्राय वृत्रघ्ने । इन्द्राय वृत्रतुरे । इन्द्रायांहोमुचे इति । तानप्येके समामनन्ति । भूयांसि तु समाम्नानात् । यत्तु संविज्ञानभूतं स्यात् प्राधान्यस्तुति तत् समामने । अथ कर्मभि: ऋषिर्देवता: स्तौति वृत्रहा पुरंदर: इति । तानप्येके समामनन्ति । भूयांसि तु समाम्नानात् ॥

The import of this passage is as follows: Some *Nairuktas* include the names of the deities along with their adjectives in their respective *Samāmnāyas*. But even then all the adjectives are not exhausted. I, therefore, include in my *Samāmnāya* only such words as are usually used as principal names (सविज्ञान- भूतं प्राधान्यस्तुति). Others include the names of the deities which are indicators of their actions such as वृत्रहा, पुरन्दर: etc., but, they also cannot include all such words.

This shows that the *Nairuktas* used to prepare their own *Nighaṇṭus* and used to explain them. Yāska also prepared his own and commented on it. On the word समामने Durgâ writes अहं तु न समामने. This directly points to the समाम्नाय prepared by Yāska, which clearly indicates that the list was prepared by the author of the *Nirukta* himself.

There are many references to the fact that the *Nairuktas*, who came earlier than Yāska, also had their own *Nighaṇṭus*. All such references have been collected by Pt. Bhagavaddatta in his above mentioned work in the chapter on the *Nirukta*. A few of them are noted below for information of the readers:-

(i) While commenting on तमिमं समाम्नायम् Nir 1.1.2. Durga writes तं च यो असमाम्नात: छन्दस्येवावस्थित: गवादि: अन्यैर्वा निरुक्तै: समाम्नात: तमिमं च निघण्टव: इत्याचक्षते । अन्ये अग्याचार्या: इति वाक्यशेष: ।

This shows that Durga also holds that the *Nighaṇṭu* was prepared by older *Nairuktas*.

(ii) On तानप्येके समामनन्ति (*Nir.* 7.13. 9) Durga writes एके नैरुक्ता: तान्यपि गुणपदानि वृत्रांहोमुक्प्रभृतीनि अग्न्यादौ देवपदसमाम्नाये पृथक् पृथक् समामनन्ति ।

This also shows that the *Nairuktas* were preparing their own *Nighaṇṭus*.

The *Nirukta* begins with the words समाम्नाय: समाम्नात: स व्याख्यातव्य: । Rajwade holds that the words समाम्नाय: समाम्नात: refer to the *Nighaṇṭu* which according to him Yāska got readymade and the next sentence refers to the *Nirukta* which is the work of Yāska. According to those who hold that both the works are from Yāska's pen the import will be: 'The words have been enumerated (समाम्नाय: समाम्नात:) and now it is to be explained. Again while explaining the statement 'इमं ग्रंथं समाम्नासिषु: Nir. 1.1.2', Durga says that the words इमं ग्रन्थं refer to the *Nighaṇṭu* which Yāska is commenting upon, while according to the thinkers of the other school, they would mean 'this science of *Nirukta*', and not any particular work.

The science of *Nirukta* has its roots in the *Devavidyā*. We find in the *Brāhmaṇas* an attempt to derive the names of deities, such as Indra from the root *indh,* Agni from *agri* and so on. The principal work among the *Nairuktas* before Yāska in this respect appears to have been done by Śākapūṇi. Yāska regards Śākapūṇi as a great authority in this respect. He has quoted the opinions of Śākapūṇi at 23 places out of which 14 appear in the *Daivata-kāṇḍa*, and 9 in the *Pūrvaṣaṭka*. Even there at one place (2.8) it refers to *Devatā*. Thus out of 23 places 14 appear in respect of *Devatā* and only 8 in other respects. The importance of *Devavidyā* in the earlier stages of *Nirukta* can be seen from one more fact, viz. that in the earlier *Nighaṇṭus* even the *paryāyas* and the adjectives were also enumerated. Gradually the importance of this science (निर्वचन) was recognised in understanding the meaning of the Veda, and the science got a wider field. Instead of being limited to the *Devavidyā* alone, it was extended to *arthanirvacana* also as it was also required for proper understanding of the Veda. Yet the *Devavidyā* had its proper place in this new set up also, for it was equally important for understanding the Veda. It is this stage of the science to which Yāska's work belongs, for the latter half of it includes the *Devavidyā* while the first half includes other things. Thus, the science of *Nirukta* which was confined to the *Devavidyā* alone in its earlier stages, came to be regarded as the science of Etymology required for understanding the Veda.

This determines the scope of *Nirukta*. The main purpose of *Nirukta* is to understand Veda (मंत्रार्थचर्चा). This requires *Nirvacana* and *Devatāparijñāna*. See: अयं मन्त्रार्थचिन्ताभ्यूहो अभ्यूढः । अपि श्रुतितः, अपि तर्कतः - (13.2) also see (1.15).

So, *Nirukta* has three purposes: 1. मन्त्रार्थचिन्ता 2. देवता-परिज्ञान and 3. निर्वचन. We shall now see what Yāska has done in these respects:-

1. *Mantrārthacintā*: Yāska first settles the meaning of the word from *Nighaṇṭu* and then points out the *mantra* in which it appears to have been used in that sense, i.e. the sense which he has determined. At times he quotes a part of the *Vedic* verse and at times the whole verse. Nearly 800 verses either in whole or in part have been quoted by Yāska in his discussion and explained briefly. While giving the meaning of the verses he either gives its synonyms in the *Laukika-bhāṣā* in respect of Vedic words, or determines their import by etymology. At times he gives the legend connected with the verse, or the tradition connected with it. If there are different opinions about the import of the verse, he quotes them and, if necessary, examines them and gives his own view.

If the *mantra* can be interpreted from a different angle he refers to it. There were various points of view from which verses were interpreted. Yāska refers to them as *Aitihāsika, Ādhidaivata, Adhyātma,* and *Adhiyajña*. Yāska gives importance to *Adhidaivata* view, but he does not simply ignore others.

Nearly 440 verses have been explained by Yāska in this way. At times, he quotes the verse and leaves it as निगदव्याख्यात or he simply refers to it saying इत्यपि निगमो भवति ।

2. *Devatāparijñāna*: The treatment of this topic covers chapters 7 to 12 of *Nirukta*. In this topic Yāska's discussion is of two types. In the opening part of the seventh chapter, Yāska acquaints us with the general notions of *Devavidyā*.

The topics under this heading are:

(i) How to recognise the deity of the *mantra*,

(ii) The division of the *mantras* on the basis of style,

(iii) The division of the *mantras* on the subject they deal with,

(iv) The number of deities and the basis of settling the number,

(v) Whether the deities have form and

(vi) The *gauṇa-pradhāna-bhāva* of the deities in the *mantra*.

From the 12th section of the 7th *adhyāya*, Yāska acquaints us with the nature of the deities mentioned in the *Nighaṇṭu*, and this goes on upto the end of the work. In this he follows the following method. (i) First, he gives the *nirvacana* of the name of the deity, (ii) He then enters into a discussion on the *Ādhidaivika* nature of the deity. (iii) He then quotes the *mantra* and shows how it supports his view. In the *nirvacana* of *Agni* he, for example gives five alternatives viz. अग्रणीर्भवति and अग्रे यज्ञेषु नीयते (these two are of the *ādhidaivika* type), अङ्गं नयति सन्नयमान: and अक्नोपनो भवति (these two are of the *ādhibhautika* type), and the *nirvacana* given by Śākapūṇi (which is of the *ādhyātmika* type). The same he has done with the word '*Deva*'.

According to Yāska, deities are not something supernatural. They are things of the world such as Agni, Vāyu, Sūrya, etc. These all are the manifestations of the *Ātman*. Agni, Indra, Varuṇa etc. are the names given to these manifestations on account of their functions.

The *sthāna, karma,* and the associating deity (सहचरी देवता) of deities are generally settled. But, in many *mantras* the same are found used in respect of different deities. This raises controversy. *Yāska* discusses this point from various angles and gives his opinion that, that deity is to be treated as principal (*pradhāna*) which has been the subject of praise in the *sūkta*, or in whose name the oblation is ordained. That deity is *pradhāna* in respect of his *sthāna* and *karma*. But, if it is shown to reside in *sthāna* and *karma* which is different from his own, it is to be treated as subsidiary (*gauṇa*); (यस्तु सूक्तं भजते, यस्मै हविर्निरूप्यते सोऽयमग्निर्निपातमेवैते उत्तरे ज्योतिषी एतेन नामधेयेन भजते - 7.18, 20, 31).

The *Adhyāyas* 13 and 14 are treated as *Pariśiṣṭas*. They contain the topic of *Atistuti*. *Stuti* is the description proper of the deity in respect of its *sthāna* and *karma*. The description of the deity which goes beyond the sphere of *sthāna* and *karma* of the deity is *Atistuti*. In the 13th chapter, Yāska discusses some *mantras* containing *Atistuti*. The 14th chapter is a beautiful description of *Ātmavidyā*. Here, Yāska describes the nature of *Mahān Ātmā* and the *Jīvātmā* according to the *Sāṁkhya* viewpoint. He also describes the *garbha-gati* of the *Jīvātmā* on the basis of *Āyurveda*. The *Jīva* by performing the meritorious deeds, becomes *Brahman* and ultimately is freed from the cycle of rebirth. In the end Yāska shows how the *Mahān Ātmā* is described in the Veda by various names. The *mantras* in this *adhyāya* have been explained by Yāska from the *ādhidaivata* and the *ādhyātmika* angles. The *Nirukta* ends with the salutation as follows: नमः पारस्कराय नमो यास्काय । ब्रह्मशुक्लमसीय ब्रह्मशुक्लमसीय ॥ 14. 37.

3. *Nirvacana*: Yāska has devoted the first *adhyāya* and the first four sections of the second *adhyāya* to prepare the ground for *nirvacana*. He has given the classification of the words to be derived. There, he deals with such questions as whether the names (संज्ञा) are *ākhyātaja* or not, whether the *mantras* have meaning, and tells us about the three sections of the *Nighaṇṭu*. In the beginning of the second chapter, he deals with the principles of *Nirvacana*. This mostly pertains to the form rather than to the sense of the word. Then from the 5th section of the second chapter, he gives the *nirvacana* of the important words from the *Nighaṇṭu* (*Naighaṇṭuka-kāṇḍa*), which he finishes by the end of the third *adhyāya*.

In the fourth *adhyāya,* he begins the *nirvacana* of words in the *Naigama-kāṇḍa,* which is also known as *Aikapadika-kāṇḍa* (ऐकपदिकमित्यनेन नाम्ना अन्येऽप्याचार्याः आचक्षते । निरूढा हि इयमस्मिन् प्रकरणे संज्ञा इत्यभिप्रायः । - Durga on IV. 1).

This section contains the discussion of such words which are known as *anekārthaka* or *anavagata-saṁskāra.*

Yāska does not limit his discussion to the derivation of the words in *Nighaṇṭu* only. While explaining the word *Nighaṇṭu* he quotes the *mantras* and while explaining the *mantra* he explains other words also. He first gives the meaning of the word as found in the Veda and then in the *Bhāṣā* if that word is found there also. Yāska gives various shades of meanings of the word and refers to the traditions and social opinions which are found related to it. Such examples are *Kaccha, Kīkaṭa, Prepsā, Apatya.* Describing Yāska's style in the *Naigama-kāṇḍa,* Durga says:

तत्त्वं पर्यायशब्देन व्युत्पत्तिश्च द्वयोरपि ।

निगमो निर्णयश्चेति, व्याख्येयं नैगमे पदे ॥ (Nir, 4.1.2)

Yāska first gives the *paryāya* of the word to be explained, then the derivation of both the words, then he gives the *mantra,* and on the basis of that he gives his final view. As a matter of fact this style is not restricted to *Naigama-kāṇḍa* only; it is found in the whole work.

Yāska gives derivation in two ways which may be termed as *Śabda-nirvacana* and the *Artha-nirvacana* respectively. In the *Śabda-nirvacana* some root is conceived as *prakṛti* and the *vikāra* or the *prādeśika guṇa* is taken into consideration, e.g. *Putra = put + tra; Aśva = aś + va.* In such cases, the importance is given to the form of the word. This has close affinity to the Grammar. *Artha-nirvacana* is that in which the meaning is taken into consideration rather than the form of the word. In this, *Prakṛti* and

Vikāra are ignored, if required, for example कीकट = किं क्रियाभिः; निघण्टु = आहनन; व्याघ्र = व्यादाय हन्ति; समुद्र = समुद्द्रवन्ति एनमापः - etc.

Words have their primary meaning. But they also have other shades which are connected with the primary meaning. Yāska explains both these meanings. As Durga puts it: अत्र अर्थस्य अप्रतीयमानस्य पर्यायाभिधानेन विभज्य प्रतिपादनं व्याख्या । शब्दस्यापि व्युत्पादनं व्याख्या । एवमेते द्वे व्याख्ये । तयोः अर्थपरिज्ञानमेकस्याः कार्यम् । शब्दपरिज्ञानमेकस्याः । एतदुभयमपि एकस्मिन्नैगमे पदे यथासंभवं व्याख्यास्यते । - Durga on 4.1.2.

THE PURPOSE OF THE STUDY OF THE *NIRUKTA*

(i) The earlier seers who had realised *Dharma* by themselves, handed down the *mantras* to the younger generation of the seers by oral tradition (*Upadeśa*). Still, younger generations were not so much inclined to learn by the old method of *Upadeśa*. Hence, the *Vedas* and the *Vedāngas* were written down. Among them were the *Nighaṇṭu* and the *Nirukta*. Yāska wrote his *Nighaṇṭu* and *Nirukta* in the tradition of earlier writers avoiding their faults. The purpose of the *Nighaṇṭu* and *Nirukta* is expressed as '*Bilma-grahaṇa*' i.e. to explain the knotty portions only and not every word of it. cf- साक्षात्कृतधर्माणः ऋषयो बभूवुः । ते अवरेभ्योऽसाक्षात्कृतधर्मभ्यः उपदेशेन मंत्रान् संप्रादुः । उपदेशाय ग्लायन्तोऽवरे बिल्मग्रहणाय इमं ग्रन्थं समाम्नासिषुः वेदं च वेदाङ्गानि च । (I. 6.5).

(ii) It is not possible to understand the import of the *mantra* unless the meaning of the *padas* is understood. The *padārtha* has to be understood in the context of the *mantra*. Hence, the *Nirukta* which explains the *pada* in its proper context, is useful for *mantrārtha-pratyaya*. (अथापीदमन्तरेण मन्त्रेषु अर्थप्रत्ययो न विद्यते । नि. 1.5).

(iii) The *Vyākaraṇa* and the *Nirukta* are the two sciences which deal with the explanation of words. Out of them, the *Vyākaraṇa* deals with the word in respect of its form and explains its formation by conceiving प्रकृति, प्रत्यय, and स्वर. But, so far as the meaning is concerned, it has to derive much from the *Nirukta*. As a matter of fact, the *artha-nirvacana* is the sole field of the *Nirukta*. Take, for example, the word *Nistriṁśaḥ*. The *prakṛti* is conceived as *'nis + triṁśat'* and the *pratyaya* is taken to be अ as *Samāsānta* affix. The modifications are then explained. This is according to .e *Vyākaraṇa*. But 'निर्गत: त्रिंशत: अङ्गुलिभ्य:' is its *nirvacana* and falls into the field of the *Nirukta*. '*Kaupīna*' is just a piece of cloth. But, as long as we do not get in touch with its *artha-nirvacana,* we shall not be in a position to grasp its full import. See, for example: शालीन य-कौपीने अधृष्टाकार्ययो: (P.5.2.20) शालीनकौपीनशब्दौ निपात्येते यथासंख्यम् अधृष्टे अकार्ये चाभिधेये । ...शालीनकौपीने अधृष्टाकार्ययो: पर्यायौ यथाकथंचिद् व्युत्पादयितव्यौ । (Kāśikā). Likewise, the *Vyākaraṇa* would say that in the words तिलतैल, सर्षपतैल, गोगोष्ठ etc. the portions तैल and गोष्ठ are affixes. But, we know, they are not the affixes in the real sense. They are independent words treated as affixes by the *Vyākaraṇa*. This can be learnt from the *Nirukta* alone. The same is the case with the affixes शालच् and शंकटच् (P.5.1.28). They are really the words treated as affixes. See *Kāśikā* : वे: शालच्शंकटचौ (P.5.2.28) विशब्दात् शालच्शंकटचौ प्रत्ययौ भवत: । .... परमार्थतस्तु गुणशब्दा एते यथाकथंचित् व्युत्पाद्यन्ते । नात्र प्रकृतिप्रत्ययार्थयोरभिनिवेश: । The nature of their being full words can be known from *Nirukta* alone. The full purpose of *Vyākaraṇa* cannot be realised without the help of the *Nirukta* (अर्थमप्रतीयत: नात्यन्तं स्वरसंस्कारोद्देश: (नि. 1.13) Thus, the *Vyākaraṇa* is incomplete without the aid of the *Nirukta*. तदिदं विद्यास्थानं व्याकरणस्य कार्त्स्न्यम्, स्वार्थसाधकं च (नि. 1.13). But, the same cannot be said of the *Nirukta*. For, so far as the words in *Pratyakṣa-vṛtti* are concerned, the *Nirukta* will follow the *Vyākaraṇa*; but, in the case of the *Parokṣa-vṛtti* words, it will chalk its own way. Yāska has stated this in very clear terms. "तद्येषु पदेषु स्वरसंस्कारौ समर्थौ प्रादेशिकेन गुणेनान्वितौ स्याताम् तानि तथा निर्ब्रूयात् । अथ अनन्वितेऽर्थे अप्रादेशिके विकारे अर्थनित्य: परीक्षेत् केनचिद्वृत्तिसामान्येन । अविद्यमाने सामान्येऽपि अक्षरवर्णसामान्यात् निर्ब्रूयात् । नत्वेव न निर्ब्रूयात् । (नि. 2.1) the *Vyākaraṇa* deals with the *Vyutpanna* words only. In the case of other words it takes resort to *nipātana, vyatyāsa* and *ādeśa*. But the *Nirukta* takes into consideration both the *vyutpanna* and the *avyutpanna* words. It suggests various derivations and looks at the word from various angles and attempts to find out the root = meaning of the word.

(iv) The *Vyākaraṇa* divides the *Pada* as *subanta* and *tiṅanta*. This is only a technical division. Even the *Avyayas* have been imagined to have *vibhakti* and then dropped, for being included in the *pada* as defined by the grammar. However, the fact is that the *pada* can be determined only on the basis of *artha* (cf अर्थः पदमैन्द्राणाम् and प्रधानमर्थः शब्दो हि तद्गुणायत्त इष्यते and अर्थात् पदं स्वाभिधेयम् - बृ. दे. - 2.99, 2.177). The *arthajñāna* and the *padavibhāga* are intrinsically related according to *Nirukta*. For example in the sentences अवसाय पद्वते रुद्र मृळ (ऋ. 1.169.1) and विमुच्यावयो अवसायाश्वान् (ऋ. 1.104.1), the *pada avasāya* is differently shown, for, in one case, it is dative and in the other case, it is *tiṅanta* and that has been determined on the basis of meaning. In the same way, in the lines दूतो निर्ऋत्या इदमाजगाम (ऋ. 10.165.1) and निर्ऋत्या आचक्ष्व (8-221) whether the word निर्ऋत्या is to be taken as *dative, ablative* or *genitive* is to be determined by reference to the meaning. Hence, the *padavibhāga* in the Veda rests on the meaning; this is the position of *Nirukta* (अथापीदमन्तरेण पदविभागो न विद्यते - नि. 1.6).

(v) The *Mantras* are to be employed in the sacrifice, only after their meaning is known. The meaning of the *mantra* cannot be known unless one has *Devatā-jñāna* and that can be had only from the *Nirukta*. (अथापि याज्ञे दैवतेन बहवः प्रदेशा भवन्ति । तदेतेन उपेक्षितव्यम् (नि. 1.6).

(vi) The *Nirukta* says that there is no use of mere recitation of the *mantras*. The reciter of the *mantras* without knowing their meaning is just like a pillar which bears weight only (स्थाणुरयं भारहारः किलाभूत्, अधीत्य वेदं न विजानाति अर्थम् - नि. 1.6.2).

(vii) In addition to the above, the study of the *Nirukta* throws light on the concepts of वर्णागम (Prothesis), वर्णविपर्यय (Metathesis), वर्णविकार (Assimilation, Dissimilation), वर्णान्तर (Elision), आदिस्वरलोप

(Aphesis), मध्यस्वरलोप (Syncope), सवर्णलोप (Haplology), in Phonetics, as well as रूपविज्ञान (Morphology), अर्थविज्ञान (Semantics), वाक्यविज्ञान (Syntax) and निर्वचनविज्ञान (Etymology).

NĀMĀNI ĀKHYĀTAJĀNI

The statement नामानि आख्यातजानि is the fundamental notion of the *Nirvacana* in the *Nirukta*. It is necessary for us to understand the underlying idea in this statement. We shall first try to understand the import of the term *ākhyāta* and then see how it is the basis of the name (संज्ञा or नाम), according to the *Nirukta*. Grammatically, the word *'ākhyāta'* is आ + ख्या + क्त. Now, we get the first reference to this in *Śatapatha Brāhmaṇa* 10.1.2.5. as तस्मात् यत्रैतानि सह क्रियन्ते, महदेवोक्थम् आतमां ख्यायते, आत्मा हि महदुक्थम् । Here we get the expression आतमां ख्यायते. So we may say आतमां ख्यायते (अनेन) तदाख्यातम् । All other words in the sentence are connected in sense with it, but, the *artha* of the sentence becomes complete (सुसमाप्त) only by the use of the word which is of the nature of *ākhyāta*. In Grammar this आख्यात is termed as तिङन्त. Hence, *ākhyāta* is to be equated with *tiṅanta* and not with the Dhātu. The word *ākhyāta* has been significantly used by Yāska in the following places.

1. चत्वारि पदजातानि, नामाख्याते च उपसर्गनिपाताश्च (1.1)

2. तत्र परोक्षकृता: सर्वाभिर्नामविभक्तिभि: युज्यन्ते प्रथमपुरुषैश्च आख्यातस्य (7.1.1)

3. कतमानि तानि चत्वारि पदानि । .... नामाख्याते च उपसर्गनिपाताश्च इति वैयाकरणा: । (13.9

This term *ākhyāta* had become a technical term before Yāska as can be seen from the above statements and also from the words आख्यातज (i.12) and आख्यातेभ्यो गम्यते (7.14).

This means that according to the *Nirukta*, a *Samjñā* i.e., the name of a thing, has its origin in the action (व्यापार) of that thing. The *Vyākaraṇa* uses the word* *Dhātuja* for *Ākhyātaja* in the same sense (cf. नाम च धातुजमाह निरुक्ते व्याकरणे शकटस्य च तोकम् । - महाभाष्य), (*Mbh.* on, P. 3.3.1. Vol. II. P. 138). i.e. generated by the व्यापार, for, according to them, a *Dhātu* is that which denotes *Vyāpāra*. Whenever a derivation is given in the *Nirukta,* it is always by reference to *Karman* or *Bhāva* i.e., a *Kriyāpada* or *Bhāvavācaka-samjñā,* and never to a *Dhātu.* For example, the name पृथिवी is related to प्रथनव्यापार and not to the root प्रथ; the word सत्य is related to the action of being or knowing. This leads us to the conclusion that the *nirvacana* would be different in the case of the same *saṁjñā* because of its relation to different *kriyās* (not *Dhātus*). This explains how the word निर्ऋति has two *nirvacanas* (2.7) and the word अग्नि has three *nirvacanas* (cf. त्रयाणामाख्यातानामभिधेयाक्रियात्र लक्ष्यते । ता उपादाय हेतुत्वेन अग्नि शब्दः अत्र आत्मानं लभते ।... एतद्धातुवाच्याः क्रियाः एष करोति इति दुर्ग Nir. 7. 14. 6. Therefore, the *Pravṛtti-nimitta* of a *samjñā* or *Nāman* is *Kriyā* or *Vyāpāra* denoted by the *ākhyāta.*

Skanda-Svāmī says: आख्यातं तिङ्पदम्। तेनात्र एकदेशो धातुः लक्ष्यते। धातुजानि इत्यर्थः । अथवा आख्यातेन स्वार्थो लक्ष्यते । तेन एकदेशभूता क्रिया। तज्जानि तन्निमित्तप्रवृत्तानि इत्यर्थः । Skand on *Nir.* 1.12.

In this statement, the second alternative (and not the first one) states the correct position of the *Nirukta*. The basis of naming a thing (नामकरण) is *Kriyā*. When it has to be shown in the *prakriyā,* it is shown in Grammar by taking a root (धातु) or its part, or its *ādeśa,* and by adding a *Nāmakaraṇa* affix to it. The *ākhyātaja* concept refers to the psychological and hence the internal cause of naming, while the *Dhātuja* concept is an attempt to exhibit that psychological fact in a word-form. So, the word *ākhyāta,* according to Yāska is *Kriyāpada* and not *Dhātu*. Hence, he defines *Ākhyāta* as 'पूर्वापरीभूतं भावमाख्यात-शब्देनाचष्टे - व्रजति, पचति इति' (नि. 1.1), meaning that those word-forms which denote पूर्वापरीभूतभाव, i.e. साध्यभाव are termed as *Ākhyāta*. For example, व्रजति, पचति etc. The same must have been the view of his predecessors like Śākaṭāyana, Gārgya and others, or else, as in other matters, he would have mentioned their views and rejected them.

Pāṇini also uses the word *ākhyāta* in the sense of *tiṅanta* in P. 4.3.72 (द्वयजृद्ब्राह्मणर्क्प्रथमाध्वरपुरश्चरणनामाख्याताट्ठक्) and also in the *gaṇasūtra* on P. 2.1.72 (आख्यातमाख्यातेन क्रियासातत्ये - e.g. अश्नीतपिबता, खादतमोदता etc.) and the *Vārtikakāra* also in the *Vārtikas,* आकार आख्याते परादिश्च (on P.1.2.37) and आख्यातं साव्ययकारकं विशेषणं वाक्यम् (P. 2.1.1).

Now, we may come to the definition भावप्रधानमाख्यातम्, meaning that 'the word is an *Ākhyāta* which has *Bhāva* as its principal sense.' Here comes a question. Agreed that an *Ākhyāta* is *Bhāvapradhāna,* for example व्रजति, पचति. But there are nouns also which also are *Bhāvapradhāna.* For example, व्रज्या, पक्तिः etc. If both these are *Bhāvapradhāna,* how to determine that व्रजति is an *Akhyāta* (and not *Nāman*) while व्रज्या is a *Nāman* and not *Ākhyāta*? The reply given by Yāska is as follows:

पूर्वापरीभूतं भावमाख्यातेनाचष्टे - व्रजति पचतीति उपक्रमप्रभृति - अपवर्गपर्यन्तम्। मूर्तं सत्त्वभूतं सत्त्वनामभिराचष्टे - व्रज्यापक्तिरिति (*Nir.* 1.1). This shows that the *Ākhyāta* denotes a *Bhāva* which is पूर्वापरीभूत i.e. which is an action in process, while when the process is complete and nothing remains there as of the nature of process, it becomes *Mūrta,* i.e. *Siddha.* Such a *siddha-bhāva* is as good as *Sattva* and hence it is denoted by *Nāman.* We may therefore say that *Ākhyāta* denotes *Bhāva* in साध्यावस्था while *Nāman* denotes *Bhāva* as सिद्धावस्थापन्न. *Bṛhaddevatā* also states the same thing when it says:

क्रियासु बह्वीष्वभिसंश्रितो यः पूर्वापरीभूत इवैक एव ।
क्रियाभिनिर्वृत्तिवशेन सिद्धः आख्यातशब्देन तमर्थमाहुः ॥
क्रियाभिनिर्वृत्तिवशेन जातः कृदन्तशब्दाभिहितो यदा स्यात् ।
संख्याविभक्तिव्ययलिङ्गयुक्तो भावस्तदा द्रव्यमिवोप लक्ष्यः ॥

Bṛhaddevatā 1.44. 45.

Bhartṛhari also says in the *Vākyapadīya*:

गुणभूतैरवयवैः समूहः क्रमजन्मनाम् ।
बुद्ध्या प्रकल्पिताभेदः क्रियेति व्यपदिश्यते ॥ वा. प. 3.8.4.
सत्त्वस्वभावमापन्ना व्यक्तिर्नामभिरुच्यते ।
असत्त्वभूतो भावश्च तिङ्पदैरभिधीयते ॥

Hence, Bhaṭṭoji says: "फलव्यापारयोर्धातुः" where फल refers to सिद्धावस्था and व्यापार refers to साध्यावस्था. (*Vaiyakaraṇa-bhūṣaṇasāra, Dhātvarthanirṇaya Kārika*. I.)

Nāma, Ākhyāta, Upasarga and *Nipāta* - these are the four types of words recognised by the *Nairukta*s and the *Vaiyākaraṇa*s. Out of these the *Upasarga* and the *Nipāta* can be enumerated. The *Ākhyāta*s are many, still, the grammarians have tried to enumerate them in the *Dhātupāṭha*, which may generally be accepted even though there may be a few additions or subtractions in the list. But, the *Nāmans* can never be a matter of enumeration (*Pratipadapāṭha*), they are so innumerable. The word *Nāman* has been used in the *Śatapatha Brāhmaṇa* 1.4.4.1 to denote a *Dravya*. It is *arthābhidhāyaka* (*Arthābhidhāyakam nāma - Ṛk-Pr*). In the passage, त्रयं वा इदं नाम, रूपं, कर्म । तेषां नाम्नां वागित्येतत् एषामुक्थम्, अतो हि सर्वाणि नामानि उत्तिष्ठन्ति । एतदेषां साम, एतद्धि सर्वैर्नामभिः समम् । तदेषां ब्रह्म, एतद्धि सर्वाणि नामानि बिभर्ति ॥ the word *nāma* is used in the sense of a *saṁjñā* or a *śabda* or a *pada* to denote some *artha*. But, gradually it came to mean a word denoting *dravya*, i.e. *saṁjñā*. Now, the question is why it is that a particular *dravya* is denoted by a particular name? What is the basis of Name?

The *Nirukta* (1.12-14) indicates that the ancient *ācāryas* like Śākaṭāyana, Gārgya and others had given a thought to this problem. The *Bṛhaddevatā* (1.23-25) throws some light on this problem saying that according to some *Nairuktas*, old teachers, Madhūka, Gālava, Śvetaketu, there are nine causes behind naming the things. They are: *Nivāsa, Karman, Rūpa, Maṅgala, Vāṇī, Āśis, Yadṛcchā, Upavasana* (habit), and *Āmuṣyāyaṇa*.

It says:

तत्खल्वाहुः कतिभ्यस्तु कर्मणो नाम जायते ।
सत्त्वानां वैदिकानां वा यद्वान्यदिह किंचन ॥

नवभ्य इति नैरुक्ताः पुराणाः कवयश्च ये ।
मधूकः श्वेतकेतुश्च गालवश्चैव मन्वते ॥
निवासात् कर्मणो रूपात् मङ्गलाद्वा च आशिषः ।
यदृच्छयोपवसनात् तथाऽऽमुष्यायणाच्च यत् ॥ (बृ. दे. १.२३-२५)

Śaunaka further says that the teachers Yāska, Gārgya, and Rathītara enumerate only four out of these nine, viz, *Āśis, Arthavairūpya, Vāṇi* and *Karman,* as the basis of name:

चतुर्भ्य इति तत्राहुर्यास्कगार्ग्यरथीतराः ।

आशिषोऽथार्थवैरूप्यात् वाचः कर्मण एव च ॥ (1.26)

These four are seen in the present *Nirukta*. Thus:

1. आशीः (i) कितवः, किं तवास्ति शब्दानुकृतिः,
कृतवान् वा आशीर्नामकः । (नि. 5. 2)

2. वाक् (ii) काक इति शब्दानुकृतिः । तदिदं शकुनिषु बहुलम् (3.18)
(iii) कृकवाकोः पूर्वं शब्दानुकरणम्, वचेरुत्तरम् (12.13)

3. कर्मन् - Yāska holds नामान्याख्यातजानि as a *Siddhānta*. He always refers to कार्मनामिक words.

4. अर्थवैरूप्य The word कच्छ has two meanings:tortoise and bank of a river. Yāska explains them thus:

(i) कच्छं पाति, कच्छेन पाति इति वा, कच्छेन पिबति इति वा । कच्छः = खच्छः = खच्छद : ।

(ii) अयमपि अपरो नदीकच्छः एतस्मादेव । कम् उदकम्, तेन छाद्यते (4.18).

However, Śaunaka gives his view that all the *Saṁjñās* are derived from action (*Karman or Kriyā*) only. All other causes can be shown to be varieties of *Kriyā* only. He says:-

सर्वाण्येतानि नामानि कर्मतस्त्वाह शौनकः ।
आशीरूपं च वाच्यं च सर्वं भवति कर्मतः ॥
यदृच्छयोपवसनात् तथामुष्यायणाच्च यत् ।
तथा तदपि कर्मैव तच्छृणुध्वं च हेतवः ॥

प्रजाः कर्मसमुत्था हि कर्मतः सत्त्वसंगतिः ।
क्वचित्संजायते सच्च निवासात्तत्प्रजायते ॥
यादृच्छिकं च नामाभिधीयते यत्र कुत्रचित् ।
औपम्यादपि तद्विद्यात् भावस्यैवेह कस्यचित् ॥
नाकर्मकोऽस्ति भावो हि न नामास्ति निरर्थकम् ।
नान्यत्र भावान्नामानि तस्मात् सर्वाणि कर्मतः ॥
मंगलात् क्रियते यच्च नामोपवसनाच्च यत् ।
भवत्येव तु सा ह्याशीः स्वस्त्यादेर्मंगलादिह ॥
अपि कुत्सितनामायमिह जीवेत्कथं चिरम् ।
इति क्रियन्ते भूतानां नामानि विदितान्यपि ॥ (बृ.दे. 9.27.33)

These verses point to the fact that the earliest thinkers thought of nine causes for giving names to objects. Later on they were reduced to four, and ultimately to one, viz. *Kriyā*. It is not necessary that the *Kriyā* must reside in the same thing as bears the name related to that *Kriyā*. It is sufficient that the name can be related to *Kriyā* whether by near or by distant relation. It will be seen that all the causes given here are psychological in nature and have no direct relation to the *Dhātu*.

In the Pāṇinian system the *Nāman* is termed as the *Prātipadika*. The *Prātipadika* is of two types: it is *Vyutpanna* or it is *Avyutpanna*. *Vyutpanna prātipadika* is one which can be shown as an outcome of some *vṛtti* such as *kṛt*, *taddhita* or *samāsa*. According to the *Nairuktas*, names are of three types, viz., the *Pratyakṣa-vṛtti*, the *Parokṣa-vṛtti*, and the *Atiparokṣa-vṛtti*. *Pratyakṣa-vṛtti* names include the *Vyutpanna-prātipadika*s of the grammarians. Yāska calls them the *'Avagata-saṁskāra'* names. *Parokṣavṛtti* names are those where there is *vṛtti-prakriyā*, but it is not evident, it is hidden, e.g., *aśva, gauḥ, puruṣa,* etc. Yāska calls them the *'anavagatasaṁskāra'* names. In the *atiparokṣa-vṛtti* names the *prakṛti* and the *pratyaya* cannot be ascertained at all. *Durga* calls them by the names: *Pratyakṣa-kriyā, Parokṣa-kriyā* and *Avidyamāna-kriyā* respectively.

The *Avyutpanna prātipadika* is that which denotes the sense by *rūḍhi*, such as *kāka, kokila, ḍittha, ḍavittha* and so on. The words Rāma, Kṛṣṇa etc. are of double nature. When used by *yadṛcchā* they are *avyutpanna*, but, when they are used with the sense agreeing with derivation (व्युत्पत्तिलभ्य) they are treated as *Vyutpanna*.

This shows that Pāṇini does not recognise *Kriyā* as the sole basis of names. However, he gives his recognition to the *Kriyā-vyutpanna* names in the *sūtra*: उणादयो बहुलम्. (P. 3.3.1). On the examination of the *Taddhita Sūtras* and the *Samāsa Sūtras* of Pāṇini, we find that he recognises all the various bases of names referred to above. This will be clear when we examine those *sūtras* in the second part.

On the point of नामान्याख्यातजानि the *Nairuktas* are at one, but the grammarians are of divided opinion. Śākaṭāyana is the principal grammarian who holds the principle नामान्याख्यातजानि and he agrees with the *Nairuktas*, but Gārgya does not hold this view. Even though some names are *ākhyātaja*, all are not so, as he holds (न सर्वाणीति गार्ग्यः).

Yāska's discussion with Gārgya in this respect, is of importance. It throws light on the position of the *Nairuktas* in this respect. The following is the gist of the argument:

Gārgya is a grammarian. To the grammarian, *Vyutpatti* is the most important element. The structure of the word (संरचना), the sense (अर्थाभिधान), and the *Rūḍhi*, etc. must be in keeping with the *Vyutpatti*. Hence, Gārgya lays stress on it. The *Nairukta* is not so much attracted by the *Vyutpatti* or by the structure of the name, as by the meaning conveyed by it. As a matter of fact the meaning of a word is not determined by grammar, it is known by its use in the language (लोकविदित). Hence the *Lokavidita-artha* is all important to the *Nairukta*. To justify it he would even ignore the *vyutpatti*. Why is a particular word used in a particular sense? Gārgya cannot satisfy us on this point. But, Yāska straightaway says: "It is the *Loka-pravṛtti*, and that ends the matter." Yāska has used this weapon of the *Loka-pravṛtti* to answer every objection raised by Gārgya, and has ultimately proved his point.

Secondly, there was a tendency among the grammarians to relate everything to *Dhātu*, for, they always understood *Dhātu* by the terms *Kriyā*, *Karman*, *Bhāva* and *Ākhyāta*. Hence, Gārgya's objection. But, to a *Nairukta*, *Ākhyātaja* means *Karmaja* or *Kriyājanya* and not *Dhātuja*. Yāska has nowhere traced the word to a *Dhātu*, but always to *Kriyā*.

Even in the Vedic literature, names have been traced to *Kriyā*. Even the name *Naciketas*, which is a *Rūḍha* word, is traced to नाहं चिकेत (ऋ. 1.79.4, 10.51.4). Dr. Fateh Singh has traced 833 Vedic words to *Kriyā*. *Aitareya Brāhmaṇa* records 42 such *Vyutpattis*.

The *Ākhyātaja* theory of the *Nairuktas* appears to have Vedic basis. We are giving below some *Vedic* quotations which will show that the concepts नामान्याख्यातजानि as well as the *Pratyakṣa-vṛtti* and *Parokṣa-vṛtti* were derived by *Nairuktas* through the study of the Vedic lore which consisted of the *Saṁhitā* and the *Brāhmaṇas*. The following quotations from the Veda will reveal this point:

Quotations from the *Ṛgveda* which imply *Nirvacana*.

1. वाय उक्थेभिर्जरन्ते त्वामच्छा जरितार: (1.2.2)

2. इन्द्रमर्केभिरर्किण: (1.7.1)

3. गीर्भिर्गृणन्तमृग्मियम् (1.9.9), also गिरा गृणीहि कामिन: (5.3.16), गीर्भिर्गृणन्त (5.8.4) also 8.46.3)

4. गायन्ति त्वा गायत्रिण: (1.10.1)

5. स शक्र उत न: शकत् (1.10.6)

6. यज्ञेन यज्ञमयजन्त देवा: (1.164-50)

7. जेषि जिष्णोहितं धनम् (6.45.15)

8. ये संहासि सहसा सहन्ते (6.66.9)

9. सोताहि सोममद्रिभि: (8.1.17)

10. यातमश्वेभिरश्विना (8.5.7) elsewhere पूर्वीरश्नन्तावश्विना (8.5.31)

11. ध्रुवे सदसि सीदति (9.40.2)

12. सिन्धोरिव प्रवणे गातुमाशवो वृषच्युता मदासो गातुमाशत (9.69.7)

The ऋग्वेद is a work of Poetry and not that of *Śāstra*. Yet in his poetic fervour, the seer uses the names and directly relates them to the *Kriyās*. Here, the name and the *Kriyā* stand before each other, e.g. जरितार:-जरन्ते, गीर्भि:-गृणन्ते, गायत्रिण:-गायन्ति, सदसि - सीदति and so on. These are all प्रत्यक्षवृत्ति words, hence, अवगतसंस्कार also. The निर्वचन and the poetic fervour appear to go hand in hand.

The following are the instances of परोक्षवृत्तिनिर्वचन from the *Ṛgveda*.

1. अर्चन्ति अर्कमर्किण: (1.10.2)

2. स्तोतृभ्यो मंहते मघम् (1.11.3)

3. पिपर्ति पपुरिर्नरा (1.46.3)

4. स न: पप्रिपरियाति (8.16.11)

5. सं वाजमञ्जन्तु अक्तुभि: (6.69.13)

6. जरितुर्वर्धया गिर: (9.40.5)

7. यजिष्ठो देवानृतुशो यजाति (10.2.5), सृचायजाना ऋतुभिर्ध्रुवेभि: (1.84.10), विद्वान् ऋतून् ऋतुपते यजेह (10.2.1), स यज्ञियो यजतु यज्ञिया ऋतून् (10.11.1)

8. आदर्दिरासो अद्रयो न विश्वहा (10.78.6).

9. एतमर्थं न चिकेताहमग्निः (10.51.4) नाहं देवस्य मर्त्यश्चिकेत (1.79.4).

This is the निर्वचन of नचिकेतस्.

10. The निर्वचन of गिर्वणस् -

यदि स्तोतारः शतं यत् सहस्रं गृणन्ति गिर्वणसं शंतदस्मे (6.34.3), शृणुतं जरितुर्हवम्, इन्द्राग्नी वनतं गिरः । ईशाना पिप्यतंधियः (7.94.2), इमां मे मरुतो गिरम्, इमं स्तोममृभुक्षणः। इमं मे वनताहवम् ।(8.7.9).

Here गिर्वणस्, वनतं गिरः and वनता गिरम् carry the same sense.

From the above examples, the following conclusions can be drawn :-

i. The nouns are traced to the verbs (क्रियापद or आख्यात). This suggests the principle: '*Nāmāni Ākhyātajāni*'.

ii. The name and the verb to which it is related agree in sense. Hence the word *papuri* in the case of *Āditya* is related to the action denoted by *piparti*, while *papri* in the case of Indra is related to the action denoted by *pārayāti*. This suggests the principle: *Arthanityaḥ parīkṣeta*.

iii. The *pratyakṣa-vṛtti* names and the *parokṣa-vṛtti* words were derived in the same fashion. They did not stick to the limitation of the later *Nairuktas* that only the *anavagata-saṁskāra* word should be derived.

iv. They were conversant with certain phonetic changes such as *arc-arka, añj-akta, ṛtutyaj-ṛtvij, maṁh-magha*. They appear to have the knowledge of the palatal law and the *saṁprasāraṇa*.

v. The word *Aśvin* is related to *aś* and *aśva*. It shows that the word could be explained from different angles. For the learned, it was *aś+vin,* while, for others, it was *'aśva+in'* based on some mythology.

vi. The word *girvaṇas* shows that they also derived the compounds.

vii. The word *Naciketas* shows that they used to derive the '*Yādṛcchika*' words also.

viii. The later *Nairuktas* were fully conversant with these derivations. The derivations of the word *arka, gāyatra, giraḥ, megha, soma,* given in the *Nirukta*, fully agree with this *vedic nirvacana*. The derivations of *Āśvin* and *papuri* agree in sense though they differ in *vikaraṇa*. The name of *ṛtvij* has been derived in the *Nirukta* in two ways, out of which one agrees with the Vedic derivation. ऋत्विक् कस्मात् । ईरण: । ऋग्यष्टा भवतीति शाकपूणि: । ऋतुयाजी भवतीति वा । (नि. 3.19).

Yajña has been derived in the same way but under the name of different *Nairuktas*. The words *arkebhiḥ, arkam,* and *arkiṇaḥ* show that the word *arka* meant prayer, one who prayed, and the god who was prayed to. This has been stated by Yāska as 'अर्को देवो भवति यदेनमर्चति । अर्को मन्त्रो भवति यदनेन अर्चति.

Other *Saṁhitās* also have similar derivations. They, however, do not have such freshness as we find in the *Ṛgveda*. Some examples from other *saṁhitās* also may be noted here:

वाजसनेयि संहिता

1. देवस्त्वा सविता पुनातु वसो: पवित्रेण (1.3)

2. धूरसि धुर्व धुर्वन्तं धुर्व तं योऽस्मान् धुर्वति (1.8)

3. भृगूणामङ्गिरसां तपसा तप्यध्वम् (1.18)

4. धान्यमसि धिनुहि देवान् (1.20)

5. विष्णो वेष्योऽसि (1.30)

6. अग्निरिड ईडित: (2.3)

7. मयीदमिन्द्र इन्द्रियं दधातु (2.10)

8. यं परिधिं परिधत्थाः (2.10)

9. वेदोऽसि येन त्वं देव वेद (2.21)

10. केतपूः केतं नः पुनातु (11.17)

सामवेद संहिता

11. विप्राय गाथं गायत (4.16)

12. संवर्तयति वर्तनिं सुजाता (4.51)

13. उरोर्वरीयो वरुणस्ते कृणोतु (1870)

अथर्ववेद संहिता

14. यत्रैषामग्ने जनिमानि वेद

गुहा सतामत्रिणां जातवेदाः (1.8.4)

15. अयं देवानामसुरो विराजति

वशा हि सत्या वरुणस्य राज्ञः (1.10.1)

16. इदं रजनि रजय (1.23.1)

17. वृश्चामि ते कुलिशेनेव वृक्षम् (2.12.3)

18. तान् वो अस्मै सत्रसदः कृणोमि (1.30.4)

19. रणाया रिष्यन्तो दक्षमाणा सदैव (2.4.1)

20. यस्य ते वासः प्रथमवास्य हरामः (2.13.5)

21. विश्वंभर विश्वेन मा भरसा पाहि (2.16.5)

22. अग्ने यत्ते हरः तेन संप्रति हर (2.19.2)

23. अग्ने यत्ते अर्चि ......प्रत्यर्च (2.19.2)

24. अग्ने यत्ते शोचिः .... प्रतिशोच (2.19.2)

25. प्र ते शृङ्गामि शृङ्गे (2.32.6)

26. ग्राहिर्जग्राह (3.11.1)

27. यददः संप्रतीयतीरहाव नदता हते ।

तस्मादानद्यो नामस्थ ता वो नामानि सिन्धवः (3.13.1)

28. तद्वाप्नोदिन्द्रो यतीस्तस्मादापो अनुष्ठन (3.13.2)

29. अप कामं स्यन्दमाना अवीवरत् वोहिकम् ।

इन्द्रो वः शक्तिभिर्देवीः तस्माद् वार्नाम ते हिनम् (3.13.3)

30. उदानिषुर्महारिति तस्मादुदकमुच्यते (3.13.4)

Out of these, the words *pavitra, tāpas, viṣṇu, indriya, paridhi, veda, ketapū, gātha, vartani, rajanī, satrasadas, vāsaḥ, viśvambhara, haras,* and *grāhi* (15 words) are *avagata-saṁskāra* words, and hence *Pratyakṣavṛtti*. The rest are *parokṣavṛtti*. Some of them may be noted here.

(i) *Dhūḥ* : is derived from *dhurv* meaning *hiṁsā*. Pāṇini also derives as *dhurv+kvip*.

(ii) *Dhānya* - from '*dhinoti*'. The *Ṛgveda* derives it from *dhā* (धत्ते धान्यं पत्यते वसव्यै - ऋ. 6.13.4) The *Uṇādi-sūtra* 293 derives it from *dhā*. *Yāska* has derived *dhānā* from *dhā*.

(iii) *Iḍa* - derived from *iḍ*

(iv) *Varīyas* - (comparative of '*uru*) derived from '*vṛ*'

(v) *Jātavedas* - it is a compound of *jāta* and *vedas*. The word *jāta* is related to *jan*. But, *vedas* has been differently shown in the *mantras*. For example -

(a) जन्मन् जन्मन् निहितो जातवेदाः (3.1.21)

(b) विश्वा वेद जनिमा जातवेदाः (6.15.13)

(c) जात आपृणो भुवनानि रोदसी (3.3.10)

(d) जातो यदग्ने भुवना व्यख्यः(7.13.3)

In (a) it is related to *Vid* - to be. In (b) it is from *Vid* - to know. In (c) it is from *Vid* - to obtain, and in (d) it is from *vid* - to know.

(vi) *Rājan* - In the above example, it is related to राज = दीप्तौ, but, it is found related to राज शासनैश्वर्ययो: See e.g.

विश्वस्यहि प्रचेतसा वरुण मित्र राजथ: ।

ईशाना पिप्यतं धिय: (ऋ.5-71-2)

(vii) *Śṛṅga* - from *śṛ* in the sense of *hiṁsā*.

(viii) *Marut* - derived from *mṛ*. This root has been found in relation to *Indra* and *Agni* in the *Ṛgveda* 7.10.23, 10.84.2, 10.87.19. but, not so found with *Maruts*.

(ix) *Nadī* is from *nad*; *Āp* from *āp; Vār* from *vṛ; Udaka* from *ud+an*. In these cases, the action is said to be a *hetu* for the names. This style of derivation was later on developed by the *Brāhmaṇa* works.

It will be evident from what has gone that the derivations in the *saṁhitā*-s are in keeping with the scientific notions. The natural mode of *Nirvacana* is more apparent in the *Ṛgveda* and then comes *Atharva Veda*. The *Vājasaneyī* and the *Sāma Saṁhitā*s also follow the order. The style of the *Nirvacana* found in the *Brāhmaṇa* works is first found in the words like *Nadī, Āpaḥ, Udakam* in the *Atharva Veda*. It is also evident that in the later *Saṁhitās* the *Nirvacana* is proceeding from natural mode to type.

The *Taittirīya Saṁhitā* is a mixture of the *Mantra* and the *Brāhmaṇa* styles. We find in it the *nirvacanas* of the *parokṣa-vṛtti* type in the *mantra* portion and of the style of the *Brāhmaṇa* in the *Brāhmaṇa* portions. For example -

(i) वह्निरसि हव्यवाहन: (1-3-3-10)

(ii) त्रयस्त्रिंशत् तन्तवो मे वितन्विरे (1.5.10.13)

(iii) आजङ्घन्ति सान्वेषां जघना उपजिघ्नते (4-6-6-13)

(iv) यच्च घासिं जघास (4.6.9.3)

These are the *mantras* in the *Saṁhitā* and represent the *nirvacana* of the *parokṣa-vṛtti* of the type of other *Saṁhitās*. They relate the names to the *ākhyāta*. Thus we have *Vahni-vah*; *tantu-tan; jaghana-han; ghāsi-ghas*. But see the examples from the *Brāhmaṇa* portions:

(i) यदरोदीत् तद्रुद्रस्य रुद्रत्वम् (1.5.1.1)

(ii) वेदेन वै देवा असुराणां वित्तं वेद्यमन्वविन्दत, तद् वेदस्य वेदत्वम् (1-7-4-13)

(iii) यन्नवमैत् तन्नवनीतमभवत्, यदसर्पत् तत् सर्पिरभवत्, यदध्रियत तद् घृतमभवत् (2-3-10.1).

Here the *nirvacana* is given by indicating the action as the *hetu* behind the name, and the relation between the name and the action is made clear.

It is in the *Brāhmaṇa* works that we get direct reference to the *Parokṣa-vṛtti* as distinct from the *Pratyakṣa-vṛtti*. Thus we have:

(a) यदब्रुवन् मेदो प्रजापते रेतो दुषत् इति तत् मादुषमभवत् । तन्मादुषस्य मादुषत्वम् । मादुष ह वै नाम एतत् यन्मादुषं सन्मानुषमित्याचक्षते परोक्षेण । (ऐ.ब्रा. - 3.43)

(b) स वा एषोऽग्निरेव यदग्निष्टोमः । ते यदस्तुवन् तस्माद् अग्निस्तोमः । तमग्निस्तोमं सन्तम् अग्निष्टोम इत्याचक्षते परोक्षेण । (ऐ.ब्रा. 3.43)

(c) ते यद् न्यञ्चोऽरोहन् तस्मान्नङ् रोहति न्यग्रोहः । न्यग्रोहो वै नाम तत् । न्यग्रोहं सन्तं न्यग्रोधमाचक्षते परोक्षेण । (ऐ.ब्रा. 7.30)

(d) स होवाच इन्धो ह वै नाम एष योऽयं दक्षिणे अक्षन् पुरुषः । तं वा एतमिन्धं सन्तमिन्द्रमित्याचक्षते परोक्षेण (श.ब्रा. 14.6.11.2)

(e) स उ एष मखः । स विष्णुः । तत इन्द्रो मखवानभवत् । मखवान् ह वै तं मघवान् इत्याचक्षते परोक्षेण । (श.ब्रा. 14.1.1.2)

In these examples we find two stages in the *nirvacana*. '*Ni+ruh*' = *Nyagroha*. This is the first step. This is the *Pratyakṣavṛtti*. From this we get *Nyagrodha*. This is the *Parokṣavṛtti*. *Agnistoma* is the *Pratykṣa-vṛtti*, *Agniṣṭoma* is *Parokṣavṛtti*. *Māduṣa* is *Pratyakṣa*, while *Mānuṣa* is *Parokṣa*. Same is the relation of *Indha* and *Indra*, and the same is the case in *Makhavān* and *Maghavān*. That it is *Parokṣa-vṛtti* has been clearly stated as तमाचक्षते परोक्षेण.

There is no *Ati-parokṣa-vṛtti* in the *Brāhmaṇas*. As a matter of fact, it is not found in Yāska's *Nirukta* also. It has been conceived by the commentators only.

We find that in the *Saṁhitā* the name and the action are put together and there is a suggestion at the *nirvacana*. In the *Brāhmaṇa, however,* this relation is expressly stated by asking a question in the form of 'Why that name ?' कस्मात् तँ होतेति आचक्षते (ऐ.ब्रा. 1.2). This style we find descending in *Nirukta* also. For example निघण्टव: कस्मात् (1.1), व्रज: कस्मात् (3.11).

There are three types of *nirvacana* in the *Brāhmaṇas*. They are:-

(i) To explain the name by referring to a myth. e.g. देवान् ह वै यज्ञेन यजमानान् असुर रक्षांसि ररक्षु: न यक्ष्यध्वमिति, तद् यद् अरक्षन् तस्माद् रक्षांसि (श.ब्रा. 1.1.1.16) Here the name *Rākṣas* is explained by reference to a legend that the *Asuras* prohibited (ररक्षु:) the *Devas* from performing sacrifice, or: वृत्रो ह वा इदं सर्वं वृत्वा शिश्ये यदिदमन्तरेण द्यावापृथिवी । स यदिदं सर्वं वृत्वा शिश्ये, तस्माद् वृत्रो नाम । (श.ब्रा. 1.1.3.4) Here the name Vṛtra is explained by reference to the legend that he covered the whole universe while he slept.

(ii) To explain the myth and bring out the *ākhyāta* and then state it as a *hetu* for the name and express it by adding *tva* to the name-word, e.g. यदरोदीत् तत् रुद्रस्य रुद्रत्वम् ।

(iii) To state the myth, to state the reason and then state the *loka-rūḍhi*. This is found in the *Parokṣa-vṛtti* words such as

Mānuṣa, Nyagrodha, Agniṣṭoma, Indra, Maghavān, etc.

Certain tendencies of the *Nirvacana* in the *Brāhmaṇa* works should be noted here. (i) First, they ignore the original sense of the word and they derive the word so as to suit the subject under discussion; for example, see the etymology of *Veda* in *Taittirīya-saṁhitā,* and that of *Maghavan* in *Śat. Br.* This tendency has both its merits and defects. The merit is to explain the word in new context where it is so used. The words which go from one field to another often change their import; for example, the word *lavaṇa* is originally developed from *lū* = to cut. But now it is used in the sense of a particular taste. We cannot ignore this change. The defect is that while doing this, the comparative method is altogether ignored and the derivation is much stretched artificially, e.g., *Mānuṣa* from *Māduṣa*. On the other hand it would be easy and natural to derive it from Man. Yāska has derived it from Man or Manu, even though occasionally he also falls prey to the old Brāhmaṇical tendency. See मनोरपत्यं मनुषो वा (3.7.2), मनुर्मननात् (12.32). But मत्वा कर्माणि सीव्यति (3.7). This last one is of Brāhmanical type.

(ii) Secondly, the *Brāhmaṇa* works at times explain the principal word as well as the equivalent given in explaining that word, e.g. the nine verses known as *Mahānāmnī Ṛks* are also known as *Simā*. The *Aitareya Br. 5.7.* while explaining the word *Mahānāmnī* has also explained the word *Simā*. This appears to be the general tendency of the time and has come down to Yāska also.

(iii) The *Brāhmaṇa* discussions appear to be of three types, viz., *Adhyātma, Adhibhūta* and *Adhideva*. A word which comes in the *Brāhmaṇa* in its original sense is explained in all these senses, for example, the word *Yajus* is generally derived from *Yaj,* and means a *mantra* in the prose form. But in *Śat. Br,* 10.5.1 - 7. it has been variously interpreted. Thus, in *Adhibhūta* it is *Anna* and in *Adhideva* it is *prāṇa* and is derived as यत् + जु

= यत् + जू (वायु); यत् + जन् = यत् + जू (प्राण); यत् + जन् + यत् + जू (अन्न).

(iv) The *Artha-nirvacana* in the *Brāhmaṇas* is mechanical and has no linguistic basis. Being under the influence of rituals and *Sṛṣṭividyā*, they simply ignored the linguistic aspect. The straightforwardness and the simplicity found in the *Ṛgvedic nirvacanas* is simply absent in the *Brāhmaṇa* words.

(v) We are not able to appreciate the etymologies in the *Brāhmaṇas* firstly because of the style of the *Brāhmaṇas*, and secondly because we are not thoroughly acquainted with the background of those works. It is likely that the word appears to be the same in form, but its import is totally different, and is changed in the course of time. For example सोऽकामयत मेध्यं म इदं स्यात् । आत्मन्वी अनेन स्यामिति । ततोऽश्वः समभवत् । यदश्वत् तन्मेध्यमभूदिति । तदेवाश्वामेधस्याश्वमेधत्वम् । (श. ब्रा. 10.5.7)

Here the word *aśva* is derived from the root '*śvi*' = to swell while we know that the '*aśva*' forms a principal item in the *Aśvamedha*.

The same tendency is found in the derivations in the *Āraṇyakas* and the *Upaniṣads*. They also derive the word in the fashion to suit their purpose. Even though they throw the linguistic aspect of the derivation to winds, it is, however, certain that the *Nirvacana* has secured an important place in them.

NAIRUKTAS BEFORE YĀSKA

The system of *nirvacana* suggested in the *Saṁhitās* and built up in the *Brāhmaṇas*, had attained widespread use in Yāska's time. This can be judged from the names of the predecessors referred to by Yāska and the various discussions found in *Nirukta* from time to time. This method of finding out the hidden meaning of a word attained so much importance that the *Nirukta* was reckoned as a *Vedāṅga* side by side with *Vyākaraṇa*.

It must, however, be noted here that these scholars were not linguists pure and simple. They were first Vedic scholars and then the *Nairuktas*. Their etymologies, therefore, are to be understood in that context and not purely on linguistic grounds. They have all been influenced by Vedic notions, Vedic mythology and rituals and all such factors in which these scholars lived and thought. Today we get tired with all such discussions, and while as a matter of fact we are not able to appreciate them fully due to our ignorance of the things in which they were written, we stamp them as primitive etymologists ! (See Rajwade, pp. XLI-XLII).

It must, however, be remembered that the language for them is not and was not a dead thing. It was a flowing and developing organism and grew under certain circumstances which influenced the *Śāstra* also. This does not mean that we must agree with everything that they have written. We only hope that today we do not outright condemn them as not knowing anything of the science.

It is for this reason that we do not find pure *nirvacana* in the *Nirukta*, but *nirvacana* which sets a word in its original context. The same was the case with the predecessors of Yāska. They also were Vedic scholars first and then everything else. Yāska mentions 22 such authors and discusses their views. We note them here in alphabetical order.

1. **ĀGRĀYAṆA:** He relates the word Indra to *idam karaṇa* and that to the word *idam+kṛ.* (इन्द्रः) इदंकरणादिति आग्रयण: (10.8.).

2. **ĀGRĀYAṆA:** (i) He derives the word *karṇa* from *kha+ṛccha*. Even though Siddheśvara Verma does not accept this derivation, still it does not appear to be baseless for the root in *ṛcchati* is *ṛ* and the word *karṇa* can be related to *kha+ṛ.* (ii) He derives *akṣi* from *añj*. In both these cases *Yāska* refers to some *Brāhmaṇa* which cannot be traced. (iii) He explains the word *Nāsatyau* as सत्यस्य प्रणेतारौ (6-13). This means *Nā+satya*, where *Nā* is *praṇetā*.

3. **AUDUMBARĀYAṆA:** He holds that the word is *anitya* इन्द्रियनित्यं वचनमौदुम्बरायण: (1.1). This shows that the controversy about the nature of *śabda* is very old.

4. **AUPAMANYAVA:** He has been mentioned by Yāska twelve times and once by Śaunaka with Yāska. Yāska mentions him while writing on *Nighaṇṭavaḥ* (1.1), *Daṇḍa* (22.2), *Paruṣa* (26), *Ṛṣi* (2.11), *Kutsaḥ* (3.11), *Indra* (10.8), and also in *Pañcajanāḥ* (3.8), *Yajña* (3.19), *Śipiviṣṭa* (5.7), *Kāṇa* (6.3), *Vikaṭa* (6.30). and *Kāka* (3.18).

His opinions can be stated as follows. He holds that there are stages in the development of the word-form. The original form of a word is clear, but, owing to certain habits of pronunciation, that form becomes somewhat changed and then totally changed, e.g. गम् - निगन्तु - निघण्टु, पर्वस - परुष, दम् - दम्दम्- दम् द - दण्ड, दृशि - ऋषि.

This shows that Aupamanyava was well acquainted with the theory of cerebralisation (मूर्धन्यभाव). He appears to be acquainted with the influence of the *Lokabhāṣā* on the *Sāhityabhāṣā*. In case of *Pañcajana* he holds the sociological view as he says that the word means निषादसहिता चत्वारो वर्णा:. In the case of *Kāka* he does not support the theory of *Śabdānukaraṇa* but, says काकोऽपकालयितव्यो भवति, which shows that he has leanings towards the *Ākhyātaja* theory. Pt. Śiva Nārāyaṇa Śāstrī says that might belong it to *Kṛṣna Yajurveda* (*Nirukta Mīmāṁsā* p. 224)

5. **AURṆANĀBHA:** Yāska mentions him five times and once he is mentioned by Śaunaka. He derives *Urvī* from *vṛṇoti*, *Nāsatyau* from *Na+asatyau*, and *Hotṛ* from *juhoti*. According to him, the term *hotṛ* when applied to *Agni* has a *laukika* sense and in the *laukika* sense it is derived from *hu*. His derivation of the word *Aśvina* is based on अश्वैभिरश्विना (ऋ.8.57). His comment on त्रेधा निदधे पदम् (ऋ.1-22-17) refers to some *rūḍhi*. He appears to be a great Vedic scholar.

6. **KĀTHAKYA**: Yāska quotes his opinion in *Devatākāṇḍa*. By the word *Tanūnapāt* he understands *'Ājya'* while Śakapūṇi takes it to be *Agni*. Yāska appears to agree with Śākapūṇi.

7. **KAUTSA**: He does not believe in the use of the *Nirukta*. According to him, *mantras* have no meaning and hence there is no use in interpreting them.

8. **KRAUṢṬUKI**: He appears to be both a *nairukta* and a Vedic scholar. He takes *Draviṇodas* to be a *paryāya* of Indra (8.2). According to some scholars he is the same as Bhāguri, the known figure in grammar.

9. **GĀRGYA**: Yāska refers to the views of Gārgya at three places, 1.3, 1.12, and 3.13. He held that the *upasargas* have meaning of their own. उच्चावचा पदार्था भवन्ति इति गार्ग्यः । तद्य एषु पदार्थः प्राहुरिमे तन्नामाख्यातयोरर्थविकरणम् (1.3).

He is also said to have prepared a *padapāṭha* of the *Sāmaveda* which is in keeping with his notion of *Upasarga* e.g., वि-प्रासः, सु-नृता. It is to be noted here that Śākalya does not separate the *Upasarga* at such places. He does not subscribe to the view of the *Nairuktas* that all the names relate to the *ākhyāta* (न सर्वाणीति गार्ग्यः वैयाकरणानां चैके । (1.12). In this respect he agrees with the section of *Vaiyākaraṇas*. Pāṇini is also of the same opinion. Yāska quotes his definition of Upamā as यदेतत् तत्सदृशमिति गार्ग्यः (3.13).

10. **GĀLAVA**: He is quoted by Yāska at 4.3. while dealing with the word *Śitāmataḥ* (Vaj. Saṁ. 27.43). According to the *Bṛhaddevatā* 1.24,25, he is one of those who hold that there are nine causes in naming a thing. He is thus opposed to the *Ākhyātaja* theory of the *Nairuktas*.

11. **CARMAŚIRĀH**: He is referred to while dealing with the word *vidhavā* (3.15). He holds that the word is from *vi + dhāvā* meaning one who wanders.

12. **TAIṬĪKI**: Referred to in the discussion of the words *'Śitāmataḥ'* and *'Birī-ṭam'*. He takes *Śitāmataḥ* to mean *Śyāma* from *Śyai* (*śyā*) and *Biriṭam* from vi+ir, i.e. *Viriṭa* and then *Biriṭa*. Thus he refers to the process of cerebralisation in this case.

13. **NAIDĀNĀḤ**: These were according to Durga the scholars of the *Nidāna-grantha* निदानमिति ग्रन्थः । तद्विदो नैदानाः - दुर्ग on 7-12). They have been referred to in the context of *Śyāla* (6.9), and *Sāman* (7.12). According to the *Naidānas* he is called *Śyāla* because he is brought nearer by relation. This is *artha-nirvacana*. The *Śabda-nirvacana* would be *si* + *āla* (*si* = to bind). *Sāman* is *sam + man*. The *Naidānas* perhaps think that there is first *samman* and then *Sāman*, just like *Karṇa - kaṇṇa Karma - kamma - kāma*.

14. **NAIRUKTAS**: They are the teachers of the *Nirukta*. They have been mentioned by Yāska 22 times. Some important references are:

1. नामान्याख्यातजानि इति शाकटायनो नैरुक्तसमयश्च (1.12)

2. पृश्निः = प्र+अश् (प्रश्नुत एनं वर्णः) in the sense of *Āditya* (2.14)

3. तत्र को वृत्रः ? मेघ इति नैरुक्ताः (2.16)

4. निषाद = नि+सद् (निषण्णमस्मिन् पापकम्) (3.14)

5. तस्करः = तत्करः (तस्करः तत्करः भवति, करोति यत् पापकम्) - 3.14)

6. यज्ञः - from यज् (यज्ञः प्रख्यातं यजतिकर्म इति नैरुक्ताः) 3.11

7. स्तेन - from स्त्यै (संस्त्यानमस्मिन् पापकाय इति नैरुक्ताः) (3.19). So also तायु from स्त्यै (4.24)

8. शुचि from शुच्. निषिक्तमस्मात् पापकम् (6.1). This is अर्थनिर्वचन

9. सललूक from सम्+लुभ् (6.3)

10. क्रव्य from विकृत्त. This is अर्थनिर्वचन

11. त्वष्टा = तूर्ण+अश् = तू + अष्टा (8.14)

12. मङ्गल - from मज्जि प्रेरणार्थे (9.4)

In all these, we find संप्रसारण, वर्णविकार, आदिलोप, पूर्वपदविकार etc. These are some important trends of explanation.

15. **VĀRṢYĀYAṆI**: He has been referred to in the context of षड्भावविकाराः (1.1). He appears to be a grammarian of respect for the *Mahābhāṣya* calls him Bhagavān Vārṣyāyaṇi.

16. **VAIYĀKARAṆĀḤ**: They have been referred to thrice. They do not subscribe to the *Ākhyātaja* theory (1.12), *Maṇḍūka* is derived from *Maṇḍa* according to them (9.5). In 13.9 they have been referred to in the interpretation of चत्वारि वाक्परिमिता पदानि। *Ṛv.* I. 164. 45.

17. **ŚATABALĀKṢA MAUDGALYA**: He derived the word मृत्यु as मृतं च्यावयति (11.6). See also *Br. Dev.* 2.60 यत्तु प्रच्यावयन्नेति घोषेण महता मृतम्। तेन मृत्युमिमं सन्तं सौति मृत्युरिति स्वयम्।

18. **ŚĀKAṬĀYANA**: He has been referred to thrice. He held that the *Upasargas* are *dyotaka* (1.3), that the names are *Ākhyātaja* (1.2), and in the *nirvacana* of *satya* (1.13). He was a grammarian of great influence (अनुशाकटायनं वैयाकरणाः। काशिका 1.4.84). His *dyotakatā* theory in the case of the *Upasargas* has been even today upheld by grammarians. His theory of the *Ākhyātaja nāma* has been responsible for the *Uṇādi-sūtras*. The authorship of the *Uṇādi sūtras* is traditionally ascribed to him. He held that the words *Śrat, accha* and *antar* are *upasargas* and that has been held up by such writers as Yāska and Pāṇini. He was a great Vedic scholar and has been referred to in the *Br. Dev.* many times. The authorship of *Ṛk-tantra* is ascribed to him.

19. **ŚĀKAPŪṆI**: He has been referred to 25 times, eleven times in *Deva Śāstra,* three times in the interpretation of verses, and in the case of the *Padapāṭha* once (4.15). In the context of *Nirvacana* he is referred to in the following nine cases:

तळित् from ताड् (3.11); महान् from मान + हा (3.13); ऋत्विज् from ऋग् + यज् (3.19); शिताम् (योनि) विषित from सि (4.3); अक्षा: from क्षि (5.3); अप्सरा: = अप्स: from स्पश् (स्पष्टं दर्शनाय 5.13); अच्छ (उपसर्ग) from आप् (5.28); अग्नि = अ + ग् + नि from अ (इ) + अज्ज or दह् (ग) + नी 7.14; नराशंस = नर + शंस् (8.6); (नराशंस: अग्निरिति शाकपूणि:, नरै: प्रशस्यो भवति - 8.6).

In these derivations he refers to *varṇa-vikāra* (*ṛtvij*) and also *varṇāgama* (in the same); in *Apsa-accha,* there appears 's' as the *nāmakaraṇa*. If so he might be familiar with the influence of *Prākrit*.

Śākapūṇi was well versed in the *Deva-vidyā* (शाकपूणि: संकल्पयांचक्रे सर्वा देवता जानामीति 1.8). There were two classes of the scholars of *Deva-vidyā*, those who referred every deity to Sūrya, and those who referred it to Agni. Śākapūṇi probably belonged to the second class of the scholars (cf. 7.23, 28; 8.2, 5, 6, 7, 10, 14, 17, 18). He held that every terrestrial (पृथ्वीस्थानीय) deity was a form of Agni. He was also a grammarian and held that the *padas* *vidraghe* and *drupade* were in *saptamī* (4.15). The *Purāṇas* call him *Rathītara*. He is said to have written on the three *Saṁhitās* and his fourth work was *Nighaṇṭu* and *Nirukta*. That he has prepared his own *Nighaṇṭu* and had written his *Nirukta* on it has been shown by Pt. Bhagavaddatta and Pt. Śiva Nārāyaṇa Śāstrī.

20. **ŚĀKAPŪṆIPUTRA**: He is referred to in 13.11. as कथमेतदक्षरम् ... आदित्य इति पुत्र: शाकपूणे: I This is the *vyākhyā* of the type of Adhideva - view.

21. **ŚĀKALYA**: He is referred to in 5.21 and 6.28.

22. **STHAULĀṢṬHĪVI** : He is referred to in 7.14 in respect of *varṇopajana* in the words *Agni* and *Vāyu*.

We may, therefore, say that the science of *Nirvacana* had considerably developed before Yāska and many peculiarities in respect of the words were noted down by the scholars on which Yāska built up his science of *Nirvacana*.

YĀSKA'S THEORY OF *NIRVACANA*

At the beginning of the second chapter, Yāska has given an idea of the methods which he is applying in the science of *Nirvacana* (अथ निर्वचनम्). They are as follows:

1. तद्येषु पदेषु स्वरसंस्कारौ समर्थौ, प्रादेशिकगुणेनान्वितौ स्याताम्, तानि तथा निर्ब्रूयात् । Nir 2.1.2

Where it is found that the accent and the grammatical operations are in keeping with the meaning of the words and there are also proper changes in the body of the root, such words should be explained in that manner. Such words are of the *avagata-saṁskāra* type. They should be explained according to the grammatical rules.

2. अथानन्वितेऽर्थे, अप्रादेशिके विकारे, अर्थनित्यः परीक्षेत केनचिद् वृत्तिसामान्येन । Nir. 1.4.

But, when the grammatical operation is not in keeping with the sense of the word, and the modification in the body of the root does not also appear to be proper, then taking the meaning of the word as basis, the word should be explained with the help of some *vṛtti* like *kṛt, taddhita* or *samāsa* (वर्तते तत्र अर्थः इति वृत्तिः = अर्थः। - स्कन्दस्वामी).

3. अथाविद्यमाने सामान्येऽपि, अक्षरवर्णसाम्यात् निर्ब्रूयात् । नत्वेव न निर्ब्रूयात् । न संस्कारमाद्रियेत । विशयवत्यो हि वृत्तयो भवन्ति । यथार्थविभक्तीः संनमयेत् । *Nir.* 1.1.5-13.; 2.2.1-2.

If there is no similarity between the meaning of the word and the *vṛtti,* then, on the basis of the similarity between any syllable or letter in that word, and some other word containing that syllable or letter, the word should be explained. If need be, the grammatical operation may be ignored; the *vṛttis,* after all, are always doubtful; and not final. Keeping the meaning in view the case forms should be changed according to the sense.

4. प्रवत्तम् अवत्तमिति धात्वादी एव शिष्यते । अथाप्यस्तेः निवृत्तिस्थानेषु आदिलोपो भवति । ... अथाप्यन्तलोपः । ....अथाप्युपधाविकारः ...अथापि वर्णलोपः ...अथापि द्विवर्णलोपः ...अथापि आदिविपर्ययः ...अथापि अन्तव्यापत्तिः .... अथापि वर्णोपजनः ।

Yāska then notes different types of the changes that are seen in the body of the word, They are:

(i) In some words only the letter in the beginning of the *dhātu* is seen e.g. प्रत्तम्, अवत्तम् (in these the letter द् or दा is seen in the changed form as त्).

(ii) *A* or *As* is dropped when the *Nivṛtti-sthāna* affix follows, e.g., स्तः, सन्ति (निवृत्तिस्थान affixes are the कित्, ङित् affixes of Pāṇini).

(iii) In certain words, the last letter of the *dhātu* is dropped, e.g., गत्वा, गतम् ।

(iv) Penultimate (उपधा) vowel of the *dhātu* is dropped in certain words, e.g., जग्मतुः, जग्मुः ।

(v) The penultimate vowel is modified in certain words, e.g., राजा, दण्डी.

(vi) In certain words, there is elision of letter, e.g., तत्त्वायामि (याचामि).

(vii) In some words change in the first letter is seen, e.g., (हनः) घनः; (भिंदुः) बिन्दुः (द्योतिः) ज्योतिः; (भाट्यः) बाट्यः.

(viii) In certain words two letters are drop ed, e.g. त्रि + ऋच् = तृचम् (र् and ई are dropped).

(ix) Exchange of the first and the last letter is seen in certain words e.g. स्तोकाः (श्चोताः); रज्जूः (सर्जूः); सिकता (कसिता); तर्कु (कर्तु).

(x) There is seen a change in the last letter of the word in certain cases, e.g. ओघः (ओहः - √ वह्); मेघः (मेहः √ मिह्); नाधः (नाहः √ नह्), गाधः (गाहः √ गाह्).

(xi) In certain words an additional letter is seen inserted, e.g. आस्थत् (अस् + लुङ्; थ् inserted); द्वारः (वारः √ वृ; द् added).

5. तद् यत्र स्वरान्तरा अन्तस्था अन्तर्धातु भवति, तद् द्विप्रकृतीनां स्थानमिति व्यपदिशन्ति । तत्र सिद्धयामनुपपद्यमानाया इतस्या उपपादयिषेत् । तत्राप्येके अल्पनिष्पत्तयो भवन्ति । तद्यथैतत् - ऊतिः, मृदुः, पृथुः पृषतः, कुणारु । *Nir.* 2.2.3-5.

The roots which have an *antastha* letter immediately preceding or following a vowel are known as *Dviprakṛti* i.e. the bases of the words having double tendencies, e.g., in the root *Yaj* there is *'y'* immediately preceding the vowel *A*. From this we get the words like *yajña, yāga, yajamāna, yaṣṭa* etc., and also the words *iṣṭa, iṣṭi, ije,* by *samprasāraṇa*, and also *iyāja* in which both *i* and *y* are seen. In such cases if it is not possible to explain the word by one method, we should resort to the other method. Take for example the word *iṣṭi*. It is related to the root *iṣ* and also to *yaj*. If the context does not justify it being related to *iṣ*, we should try to explain it by reference to *yaj* undergoing *samprasāraṇa*.

Out of these *Dviprakṛtika* words there are a few words which show only one tendency, e.g., *ūti* from *av*; *mṛdu* from *mrad*; *pṛthu* from *prath*; *pṛṣat* from *pruṣ*, and *kuṇaru* from *kvan*. In all these cases the *antasstha-prakṛtika* words are more in use than the *samprasāraṇa-prakṛtika* ones.

6. अथापि भाषिकेभ्यो धातुभ्यो नैगमाः कृतो भाष्यन्ते । दमूनाः, क्षेत्रसाधाः इति ।

Many times the *Vaidika kṛdantas* have to be derived from the *Bhāṣika* roots, e.g. *Damūnas* from *dam* and *Kṣetrasādhas* from *Sādh*. This means that the *tiṅanta* forms of those roots are in vogue in the *Bhāṣā*, while the *kṛdanta* forms are seen used in the *Veda*.

7. अथापि नैगमेभ्यो भाषिकाः । उष्णम्, घृतम् । *Nir.* 2.2.7.

There are certain *Bhāṣika kṛdantas* which are etymologically connected with the *vaidika* roots, e.g. *Uṣṇa* from *uṣ, dāha* and *ghṛta* from *ghṛ* meaning *kṣaraṇa* and *dyotana*. This means that the *kṛdantas uṣṇa* and *ghṛta* have come down to *Bhāṣā* also, but the *tiṅantas* from *uṣ* and *ghṛ* are found in the Veda only.

8. अथापि प्रकृतय एव एकेषु भाष्यन्ते विकृतय एकेषु । Nir. 2.2.8.

It is also found that while the *tiṅantas* are used in one part of the country, the *kṛdantas* are found used in another part, e.g. *Śav-Śavati* is found used in the *Bhāṣā* in the Kamboja territory, but *'Śava'* is used in the Āryan territory. The *tiṅanta dāti* is used by the easterners while *dātra* is used by the northerners.

These are the various ways of explaining a single word.

9. अथ तद्धितसमासेषु एकपर्वसु अनेकपर्वसु च पूर्वं पूर्वमपरमपरं प्रविभज्य निर्ब्रूयात् । Nir. 2.2.10.

In the case of the words which are formed by the *taddhita vṛtti* or the *samāsa vṛtti* or by both, use the following method. In case of *samāsa* the first member should be explained first and then the second. In the *Taddhita* the first part, i.e. *Prakṛti* should be first explained and then the second, i.e. *Pratyaya*. Yāska has given two cases of *Taddhita vṛtti* and three cases of *samāsa vṛtti* as examples.

i. दण्ड्यः पुरुषः In this sentence the word *daṇḍya* is to be explained as *Daṇḍam arhati* or *Daṇḍena sampadyate*. Here, the *prakṛti* is *daṇḍa* and the affix *'ya'* has come in the sense of *Tadarhati* or *Tena sampadyate*. The word *daṇḍa* has come from *dada-dhāraṇe*, for we get the use of that root in अक्रूरो ददते मणिम् in the common parlance. Aupamanyava, however, derives it from *dam* to punish, for we find its use in दण्ड्यस्य आकर्षत to denote censure.

ii. कक्ष्या-अश्वस्य रज्जुः The word *kakṣyā* is drawn from *kakṣa + ya* in the sense of belonging to, for it always remains with the *kakṣa*. The word *Kakṣa* is from *gāh* and *kṣa* is the *Nāmakaraṇa*, or it may be from *kṣā*, an alternative of *khyā*, and the process of reduplication (*abhyāsa*) suggesting the intent 'What is to be seen there?', or it may be from *kaṣ* with the process of reduplication (without intent). Because of its similarity with the *Kakṣa* of the horse, the man's armpit is also called *kakṣā*.

These are the two examples of the *Taddhita vṛtti*.

In the case of the *Samāsa vṛtti* Yāska gives three examples:

i. राजपुरुषः, राज्ञः पुरुषः *Rājā* is from the root *Rāj*. *Puruṣa* is from *pur + sad* or *Pur + si*, or it may be from *pūrayati*. This last derivation is meant only in the case of *Āntara Puruṣa*,

e.g. यस्मात्परं नापरमस्ति किंचित्, यस्मादणीयोनज्यायोऽस्ति किंचित् ।,

वृक्ष इव स्तब्धो दिवि तिष्ठत्येकः, तेनेदं पूर्णं पुरुषेण सर्वम् ॥

ii. विश्वकद्राकर्ष: This is a compound of many words (अनेकपदसमासः) *Vi + cakdra* is said about the gait of a dog. *Dra* is used to denote bad gait and *ka + dra* is still worse gait. *Kadra* becomes *Cakadra* by force of *abhyāsa* having no special meaning. Hence, *Viścakadra* means one who has such a gait. This word is used for *Cāṇḍāla* who uses dogs for hunting, the affix is *matvarthīya*.

iii. कल्याणवर्णरूप: *Kalyāṇa* is from *Kam; Varṇa* is from *Vṛ* and *Rūpa* is from *Ruc*.

These three are the examples of the *Samāsa-vṛtti*.

10. नैकपदानि निर्ब्रूयात् Nir. 2.3.4. - The words should not be explained out of context.

11. एवमन्येषामपि सत्त्वानां सन्देहा विद्यन्ते । तानि चेत् समानकर्माणिसमान

निर्वचनानि, नानाकर्माणि चेत् नानानिर्वचनानि । यथार्थं निर्वक्तव्यानि ।

Yāska has given this rule in 2.2.3. There are words which are used in different meanings in different contexts. They are to be explained after taking their context and meaning into consideration. The words having common meanings should be explained by reference to the common action, and those with different meanings should be explained by reference to different actions, e.g. the word *Nirṛti* has two meanings, viz. *Pṛthivī* and *Durgati*. The first meaning is to be explained by reference to the action denoted by *Ni + ram* and the second meaning by reference to *Ni + ṛcch*.

12. न अवैयाकरणाय न अनुपसन्नाय निर्ब्रूयात् । Nir. 2.3.5-6.

Here Yāska has given the qualifications of the student of the science of *Nirvacana*. One who has not studied grammar and who is not serious about the studies should not be accepted as a student. This clearly shows that according to Yāska *Nirvacana* is a study which leads the science of grammar to its completion.

From what has been said above we now may be able to understand the general notions of Yāska in respect of the science of Etymology i. e. *Nirvacana*.

1. Yāska first divides the words in two classes. The first he calls *Avagata-saṁskāra* and the other he calls *Anavagata-saṁskāra*. This second class has in it two sub-divisions: (1) such words in respect of which the grammatical operation is not in keeping with the meaning of the word, and (2) such words which do not show any relation whatsoever with grammatical operation and the meaning. The *Avagata-saṁskāra* words of Yāska are termed as *Pratyakṣa-vṛtti* words by later writers; the first sub-division of the *Anavagata-saṁskāra* words is termed as *Parokṣa-vṛtti* words; and the second subdivision is termed as *Ati-Parokṣa-vṛtti* words by the later writers. These three types of words are to be explained in the following three ways:

(i) The *Pratyakṣa-vṛtti* words are to be explained according to the grammatical operations. In these words the explanation of the *Taddhita* and the *Samāsa* is more difficult than the *Kṛdanta* words. One has first to determine whether in a particular case the *Taddhita-vṛtti* or the *Samāsa-vṛtti* has operated; then explain the meaning of that word and lastly explain the *antarvarti-padas* in that *vṛtti*.

(ii) In the case of the *Parokṣa-vṛtti* words whatever grammatical operation is suitable, taking into consideration the meaning of the word, that should be used.

(iii) In the case of the *Atiparokṣa-vṛtti* words, one should keep the meaning of the word in mind and whatever letters or words appear to be similar in other words, they should be taken as guide for explanation. In such cases the word to be explained, and the original word conceived should have some element of similarity in respect of letters and meaning. In such cases the grammatical operations may be ignored if so required. We may say in general that the *Pratyakṣa-vṛtti* words of *Nirukta* are the subject-matter of *Pāṇinian* rules, the *Parokṣa-vṛtti* words, that of the *Uṇādi sūtras* and the *Atiparokṣa-vṛtti*, the subject of the *Nipātanas*.

2. In respect of the words of all the three classes, Yāska has noted the phonetic tendencies in the language, as well as the unrestrained flow of the language. Certain phonetic changes noted by Yāska are: *lopa*, modifications of letter, *Samprasāraṇa*, *Varṇa-viparyaya*, and *Āgama*. All these tendencies have been put together by the later writers in the following *Kārikās*:

वर्णागमो वर्णविपर्ययश्च द्वौ चापरौ वर्णविकारनाशौ ।
धातोस्तदर्थातिशयेन योगः, तदुच्यते पञ्चविधं निरुक्तम् ॥ Durga, on *Nir.* 1.1.5.

आदिमध्यान्तलुप्तानि प्रच्छन्नापिहितानि च ।
ब्रह्मणः परिगुप्त्यर्थं वेदे व्यवहितानि च ॥ Durga on *Nir.* 1.9.3.

(These verses are noticed in other works too.)

Regarding the unrestrained flow of the language, Yāska holds that the student must take into consideration the fact of the language that while some forms of the words are found in use in one part of the territory, others are found in the other part. In the same way, while some forms are seen in the old language of the *Veda*, other forms have come down to *Bhāṣā*. His observations अथापि भाषिकेभ्यो धातुभ्यो नैगमा: कृतो भाष्यन्ते .... अथापि नैगमेभ्यो भाषिका .... । अथापि प्रकृतय एवैकेषु भाष्यन्ते विकृतय एकेषु । *Nir.* 2.2.6. - 8. are very significant. This shows that according to Yāska a *Nairukta* should be conversant with the state of language in different parts as well as in different times.

3. A *Nairukta* should be well-versed in Grammar, but should not be its slave. The words are not slaves of rules. They are there not because of Grammar, but, because of the local use (*Lokapravṛtti*). This is true in the case of the words which belong to *Parokṣa-vṛtti* and *Atiparokṣa-vṛtti*.

4. The words should not be derived unless the meaning is grasped. This is the import of नैकपदानि निर्ब्रूयात्. The meaning of a word changes according to the context in which it is used.
In such cases, he differently derived the words in different contexts. Yāska has pointed out the case of the words *Nirṛti* and *Puruṣa*.

5. A word is used in one sense and the same may be used in another sense under different circumstances. The formal derivation, therefore, may not be in keeping with the sense. This is expressed by the maxim अन्यच्च व्युत्पत्तिनिमितमन्यच्च प्रवृत्तिनिमित्तम् । Even though Yāska has not expressed this in clear terms, still he has exemplified it in the case of *Kakṣyā* and *Parva*. In such cases, the principle of Analogy operates, and this appears to be the implication of the rule of *Sāmānya* (which includes both अर्थसामान्य and वर्णसामान्य) stated by Yāska.

ŚAUNAKA'S THEORY OF *NIRVACANA*

Śaunaka has led further the enquiry founded by Yāska. According to him the *Nirvacana* is necessary to understand the nature of a deity. (*Br. Dev.* 1.91-95; 2.24.69). Like Yāska, Śaunaka attaches greater importance to *Artha* than to the form of the word. He holds the *Ākhyātaja* theory of the words.

cf. प्रधानमर्थः शब्दो हि तद्गुणायत्त इष्यते ।

तस्मान्नानान्वयोपायैः शब्दानर्थवशं नयेत् (2.99)

also सर्वाण्येतानि नामानि कर्मणस्त्वाह शौनकः (1.29)

As many *dhātus* as can be traced in a word and also its meaning, so many of them should be used for *Nirvacana* यावतामेव धातूनां लिंगं रूढिगतं भवेत् । अर्थश्चाप्यभिधेयः स्यात्तावद्भिर्गुणविग्रहः ॥ (2.10).

The words are seen to have come from roots, two roots or even from the *Upasargas.* धातूपसर्गावयवगुणशब्दं द्विधातुजं बह्वेकधातुजं वापि पदं निर्वाच्यलक्षणम् (2.103). The words are of five types, viz. धातुज (कृदन्त), धातुजाज्जातम् (तद्धित), समस्तार्थज, वाक्यज (e.g. इतिहास) and व्यतिकीर्ण. The *Taddhita* and the *Samāsa* should be explained through *Vigraha.* धातुज धातुजाजाज्जातं समासार्थजमेव च । वाक्यज व्यतिकीर्णं च निर्वाच्यं पंचधा पदम् ॥ (2.101); विग्रहान्निर्वचः कार्यं समासेष्वपि तद्धिते (2.106).

In the case of *Nirvacana,* the following five points should be kept in view, viz, *Śabdarūpa*, Meaning, *Vyutpatti, Ādhāra* i.e. *Dhātu,* and *Vikāra.* But, all these things may also point to different meanings. Hence, they cannot be said to be capable of bringing out the inner meaning of every case, and the *Nirvacana* cannot be said to be complete if the meaning is not made clear. (शब्दरूपं पदार्थश्च व्युत्पत्तिः प्रकृतिर्गुणः । सर्वमेतदनेकार्थम् ... (2-109)

The importance of the *Nirvacana* lies in bringing out the meaning of difficult words. Why do the words become difficult? Śaunaka has noted reasons for this in 2.109 - 116. They are:-

(i) The words either denote *Sāmānya* or *Viśeṣa*. When in course of time the word denoting *Sāmānya* comes to denote *Viśeṣa*, it becomes *Anavagata*, e.g., the word *Mṛga* means in the *Veda* any forest animal, but in *Bhāṣā* it means deer. Here the Vedic word *Mṛga* has become *Anavagata*.

(ii) When a word denoting *Viśeṣa* in course of time denotes *Sāmānya*, it becomes *Anavagata*, e.g., the Vedic word *Hima* means frozen water, while *Udaka* means ordinary water. Now if *Hima* is understood as water only, the Vedic word *Hima* has become *Anavagata*.

(iii) To understand one word as combination of two words makes that word *Anavagata*, e.g., the word *'Puruṣāda'* is taken by Yāska as *'Puruṣān Adanāya'*.

(iv) To take many words as one word makes those words *Anavagata*, e.g., *'Mā sakṛt'* are taken by Yāska as one word. He explains them as *Māsa-kṛt*.

(v) To treat the separate words as *Samāsa* makes the words *Anavagata*, e.g., while explaining the line 'चकार गर्भं सवितुर्निधानम् (3.31.1)' Yāska says 'चकार एनां गर्भनिधानीं सवितुः हस्तग्राहस्य (नि. 3.6).

(vi) Not to be able to determine the class of words makes them *Anavagata* e.g. we find from the *Nirukta* that some took the word *tva* as *nipāta* while others as *Sarvanāma*.

(vii) The loss of meaning of a word makes it *Anavagata*, e.g., the word '*Sitāman*'. This word must have had meaning in the original stage, but now it is lost.

(viii) The accent has to be taken into consideration. See the discussion of Yāska while explaining the line = वने न वायो न्यधायि चाकन् (*नि.* 6.29).

(ix) To understand the correct order of words helps in arriving at proper meaning, e.g., द्यावा नः पृथिवी, निरुस्वसारमस्कृत (*ऋ.* 1.127.3)

(x) Many times there occurs *Varṇa-lopa*, e.g., अत्-याणि = अत्याणि becomes अत्राणि. कपि is originally कम्पि; यामि = याचामि; अघासु = मघासु.

All these points are to be kept in mind at the time of the *Nirvacana*. While writing on 4.3. Durga also has brought out these points.

THE STAGES OF GRAMMAR AS SEEN IN YĀSKA'S *NIRUKTA*

There are two branches of language study: *Nirukta* and Grammar. The *Nirukta* is a *Sāmānya-śāstra* of language study, while the *Vyākaraṇa* is the *Viśeṣa-śāstra*. From Yāska's *Nirukta* it is clear that both these branches were fully developed in Yāska's time, and their students were known as *Nairuktas* and *Vaiyākaraṇas* respectively.

There are many grammatical terms found in *Nirukta*. Some of them have the same import as in Pāṇini, while others are different in form and sense. A study of these terms will give us an idea of the position of grammar in Yāska's time.

1. *Vyākaraṇa* is the general name of grammar (i.15) but the word *Śāstra* is also used to denote grammar (cf. शास्त्रकृतो योगश्च 1.2) meaning the rule formed by the *Śāstrakṛt* i.e. grammarian. The term *Vaiyākaraṇa* is used many times to denote a scholar of Grammar (1.12, 2.3, 9.5, 13.1).

2. The term *Akṣara* denotes a vowel or a consonant with a vowel (2.1, 11.41, 13.10). *Prātiśākhyas* also use it in the same sense. Yāska interprets the terms *Akṣara* as न क्षरति, न क्षीयते or वाक्क्षय i.e. permanent abode of language.

3. Yāska mentions that the *Vaiyākaraṇas* held the *pada* to be of four types, viz. *Nāma, Ākhyāta, Upasarga* and *Nipāta*. While writing on चत्वारि वाक् परिमिता पदानि he remarks नामाख्याते च उपसर्गनिपाताश्च इति वैयाकरणाः (13.9).

4. Yāska uses the term *Bhāva* in the sense of *Vyāpāra* (1.1). The *Bhāvas* are of two types: those in *siddhāvasthā*, and those in *Sāddhyāvasthā*. In later *Vyākaraṇa*, the term *Bhāva* refers to *Siddhāvasthā* only. This indicates that the discussion on the *Bhāva* was not fully settled in Yāska's time.
5. In the case of *Upasargas* there was a controversy between those who held that the *Upasargas* were *Vācaka*, and those who held that they were *Dyotaka* (1.3).
6. The grammatical operation was termed as *Saṁskāra*, *Vikāra* or *Yoga* (1.2, 1.12, 1.13, 2.1). The words which could be explained according to grammatical operation were termed as *Avagata-saṁskāra* words, while others were *Anavagata-saṁskāra*. In case the word was fully derived the process was called *Siddhi* or *Niṣpatti* (1.2).
7. The *Ākhyāta* was the principal factor in a sentence and therefore in the language. The word denoting action was termed *Ākhyāta* (1.2, 12; 6.28; 7.1,14). The element in the *Ākhyāta* which indicated action, was termed *Dhātu* (1.20; 2.1,). The same was termed *Pradeśa* also. Thus the change that takes place in the *Dhātu* is termed as *Prādeśika guṇa* or *Prādeśika-vikāra* (1.12, 14; 2.1). The *Ākhyāta* form of the *Dhātu* is called *Prakṛti* and the *Nāmarūpa* of *Dhātu* is called *Vikṛti* (2.2). The meaning of the root is termed as *karma or artha* (i.20).
8. The *Dhātus* are not mentioned in the root form as *Bhū*, *Edh*, etc. but in their tip form as *Gateḥ*, *Bhavateḥ*, etc.
9. The *Dhātus* were known as *Sakarmaka* and *Akarmaka*. (5.23).
10. While Pāṇini uses the terms *Prathama*, *Madhyama* and *Uttama Puruṣa*, Yāska uses *Viśeṣya puruṣa* with it (7.2).
11. Yāska has rendered the Vedic word *Āsasrāṇāsaḥ* by

Asasṛvāṁsaḥ (10.3). This shows that the use of *Ātamanepada* and *Parasmaipada* in respect of the *Dhātus* had come in vogue by that time.

12. Pāṇini uses the names *Kit, Git, Ṅit* in cases where the *Guṇa* and *Vṛddhi* operations are prohibited. In such cases Yāska uses the term *Nivṛttisthāna*.

13. The *Abhyāsa* has a technical meaning in *Pāṇini* (cf. पूर्वोऽभ्यास: P. 6.1.4.) But Yāska uses it in the sense of *Āvṛtti* of any type (2.2,3; 10.42). However, the technical sense is also found (in 2.12; 4.23, 25; 6.3) and in the sense of *guṇita* in 3.10. At places, e.g. 2.2,3 he has said 'निष्प्रयोजनोऽभ्यास:' which suggests that *abhyāsa* might be denoting difference in meaning. That way *Adhikārtha-pratīti* has been mentioned in 10.42.

14. *Pratyaya*: The word *Pratyaya* is derived from *prati + i*. It is a technical term in the Pāṇinian system. But Yāska does not appear to use it in that sense. He uses it in the sense of *Jñāna*, e.g. अथापीदमन्तरेण मन्त्रेष्वर्थप्रत्ययो न विद्यते ... यदि ... मन्त्रार्थप्रत्ययाय (1.15).

In the place of *Pratyaya*, Yāska uses the term *Nāmakaraṇa*. This suggests that it was used in the cases of *Kṛt* and *Taddhita* affixes only. In the case of the words *Avasa* (1.17), *Kakṣa* (2.2). *Go* (2.5), *Kṣīra* (2.5). *Uśīra* (2.5), *Mithuna* (7.29), *Śiva-Śeva* (10.17) the term *Nāmakaraṇa* is used in the sense of *Kṛt-pratyaya*, while in Aṇu (6.22) it is used in the sense of *Taddhita-pratyaya*. Yāska uses the word *Upabandha* for *Pratyaya* in *Simataḥ* (1.7), *Adhvaryu* (1.8) and *Agriya* (6.16). In 1.13 the word *antakaraṇa* is used and Skanda takes it in the sense of *Pratyaya* (अन्तकरणं प्रत्यय: । तेन हि साधुत्वाख्यानवेलायां च शब्दस्य अन्त: क्रियते) while Durga, Dr. Sarup and Rajwade take it in the sense of the letter placed at the end.

Yāska does not use *anubandhas* like Pāṇini, but shows the

affixes in their real form, e.g., *asa* (1.17), ira (2.5), O (2.5) *kṣa* (2.2), *tha-thu* (7.29), *tha* (3.16), *yu* (1.8), *va* (19.17) and *Vat* (3.16).

The letters which are not pronounced as *Pratyayas* but which function as *Pratyayas* are: *lya* (6.16), *tya* (8.15), *thā* (3.16, 5.5), *vi* (2.3) and *vin* (4.19). The affix *vi* in the *matvarthīya* sense is applied at the beginning of the word as in *Viścakadra* (विश्वकद्राकर्ष: - चक्रद्राति कद्रातीति सत:, अन्वर्थकोऽभ्यास: । तदस्मिन् इति विश्वकद्र: । On this Durga: विइत्युभयोरर्थयो: मत्त्वर्थ:)

This means that the affixes were at times applied at the beginning of the word. This is against Pāṇini who says: प्रत्यय: । परश्च (3.1.1,2) except सुपो बहुच् पुरस्तात्तु (5.3.69) and अव्यय सर्वनाम्नामकच् प्राक् टे: (5.3.71).

The meanings of the *Pratyayas* given by Yāska are as follows: इदं कामयमान: (1.9; 6.31), तत्र जात: (9.8), तत्र शृतम् (11.39), तदर्हति (2.3), तद्वान् (3.7, 4.19, 6.31), तस्मै हितम् (3.7, 11.36), तस्यापत्यम् (*Ibid*), तस्य समूह: (4.2), तेन संपद्यते (2.2), तेन संस्कृतम् (11.39), सोऽस्य निवास: (10.44) and in the sense of विभक्ति (1.7). There is no division as *Kṛt* and the *Kṛtya-pratyayas*. The *Kṛtya* affixes were called *Arhārthīya*. e.g. प्रस्नेया स्नानार्हा: (1.10).

15. *Vṛtti*: Yāska has used this word in the technical sense. The *Vṛtti*s were *Kṛt, Taddhita*, and *Samāsa* (2.2), *Kārita* (*Hetumaṇ-Ṇijanta*) (1.13), *Cikīrṣita-Icchā Sannanta* (6.1). *Carkarīta-Yaṅ* and *Yaṅluṅanta* (2.28). The parts of a word were called *Parvas* (2.2). The *Taddhita* was *ekaparva* and the *Samāsa* was *anekaparva*. We do not find the word *Vigraha* in the *Nirukta*; in its place '*Pravibhaj* was perhaps used (2.2). The forms without *nic, san*, etc., were called *Śuddha* (1.13).

The *Nāma* was of two types: *Satva-vācaka-Nāma* and *Sarvanāma* (1.7.8; 7.2). *Sarvanāma* is not defined in *Nirukta*, it was perhaps so commonly known. Names were either *Dṛṣṭa-vyaya* or *Adṛṣṭavyaya Nāma*, had *Vibhakti* known as *Nāmavibhakti*

(7.1), which suggests the existence of *Ākhyātavibhakti* also. Pāṇini has actually called them so in 1.4.104. There are four causes for *Nāma* to come into existence as mentioned before. Yāska calls the *Nāma* as *'ākhyātaja'* but as a matter of fact the *Nairuktas* treat all the words as *Ākhyātaja*. While Śākapūṇi derives *accha* from *'Āp'* (5.28), Yāska derives *avis* from *Ā+vid*.

16. *Other grammatical terms found in the Nirukta*: *Lopa* (2.1), *Upadhā* (2.1, 5.12), *Pratiṣedha* (1.4, 5, 8; 3.5; 11.18), *Anvādeśa* (4.25; 6.13, 31; 7.9), *Saṁhitā* (1.17), *Udātta* (4.15; 5.5; 6.28), *Anudātta* (1.7; 4.25; 5.5, 22, 23), *hrasva* (3.13), *Hrasita* (2.17; 6.11), *Guṇa* (10.17). All these terms are found used in later grammar also.

17. *Accent*: There is *tīvratā* in the *Udātta* speech and *'alpatā'* in the *Anudātta* speech (4.15). *Yāska* has referred to *Svara* while giving derivations in 1.12, 14, 15; 2.1. He has given more importance to *Svara* than to *Saṁskāra*. The whole *Nirukta* was *Sasvara* originally.

THE STATE OF LANGUAGE AS FOUND IN YĀSKA'S *NIRUKTA*

Yāska's *Nirukta* shows a state of language which is far prior to that in the days of Pāṇini. This may be inferred from the following facts:

1. Yāska explains the word *Pṛthuṣṭuka* as *Pṛthukeśastuke Pṛthuṣṭute vā* (11.32). The *sandhis* in *Pṛthuṣṭute* was not current in the days of Pāṇini (*cf.* Pāṇini, 8.3.105). It is Vedic. There are many *sandhis* in Yāska's *Nirukta* which cannot be justified according to *Pāṇinian* rules e.g. अभीषाद् = अभिषहमाण: (3.3), तेभिष्ट्वा = तैष्ट्वा (6.30).

2. *Daghna* is a *pratyaya* in Pāṇini but Yāska derives it from *Dagh* (1.9). *Pravataḥ*, *Nivataḥ* and *Udavataḥ* are explained by Pāṇini by उपसर्गाच्छन्दसि धात्वर्थे - (5.1, 118). But Yāska derives it from *Av-gatyarthe* (10.20). *Ṛjūyata*, *Nīcāyamānaḥ*, are *Nāmadhātus* according to Pāṇini. But for Yāska it is *Nīcaiḥ*

ayamānaḥ (4.24) and *ṛju-gāminaḥ* or *ṛtu-gāminaḥ* respectively (12.39). This shows that he takes them as *Nāma* and *yat* is the *Śatranta nāmapada* from i. *Apatya = Apa + tya, Satya = Sat + tya.* So *tya* appears to be treated as *pratyaya* by him. It is from *'tan - tata'* e.g. अपततंभवति (3.1), सत्सुतायते, सत्प्रभवं भवति इति वा (3.13).

It appears that many *pratyayas* of Pāṇini were words in the days of Yāska.

3. Yāska explains the word *Adhvaryu* as अधीयान (अध्वर्युः अध्वरयुः, अध्वरं कामयते इति वा । अपि वा अधी याने युः उपबंधः) and the word *'idamyu'* as ' इदं कामयमानः, अथापि तद्वदर्थे भाष्यते । वसूयुरिन्द्रो वसुमानित्यर्थः ।

This means that the affix *yu* was used in these senses of *adhīyāna, kāmayamāna* and *tadvā'.* It was used in the sense of *tadvān* in the *Bhāṣā* even though the senses of *adhiyāna* and *kāmayamāna* were becoming rare. Secondly, the field of the affix *yu* was not restricted. Pāṇini restricts its use only in the case of five words, viz. *Ūrṇāyu, Kamyu, Śamyu, Ahamyu, and Śubhamyu.* The *Kāśikā* says that according to some, even *Ūrṇāyu* is also Vedic. *Kāśika* on 1.5.2. 123/1929. This shows that the state of language is very old in the *Nirukta.*

4. The affix *tya* (*tyak, tyap*) has been ordained by Pāṇini in the *Śaiṣika* senses such as *tatra jātaḥ* (4.3.25), after the words *dakṣiṇā, paścāt, puras* and *avyaya* (4.2.98, 104). In the later period such *avyayas* were also enumerated to be *amā, iha, kva, ni, nis, and āvis.* But in the *Nirukta,* we find in the explanation of *Āviṣṭya* as आविरावेदनात्, तत्त्यः (8.15). Now, here *tya* is added to *tat.* In *satya* also which is explained as सत्सु तायते and सत्प्रभवं भवतीति (3.13). It appears that the affix would be *tya.*

5. In Pāṇini, the roots *Cakṣiṅ* and Khyāñ are not quite independent in respect of all the forms. We have चक्षिङःख्याञ् and वा लिटि (2.4, 54, 55). But, in the *Nirukta,* we find both the roots

having similar meaning, but, independent existence e.g. चक्षुः ख्यातेर्वा चष्टेर्वा (4.3). घोरचक्षसे - घोरख्यानाय (4.3).

6. In Pāṇini, the standard root is *hṛ* and *bhṛ* is its Vedic alternative (हृग्रहोर्भश्छन्दसि - 1.8.232). But, in the *Nirukta,* we find both being used in the *Bhāṣā* भर इति संग्रामनाम भरतेर्वा हरतेर्वा (4.24), भ्राता भरतेर्हरति कर्मणः (4.26).

The word *Garbha* has been derived by Yāska from *Grabh* not from *Grah*. This indicates that Yāska lived in the state of language when *Grabh* was in use.

7. Pāṇini derives *Ayam* from *Idam* by substituting *ay* for id. But, in Yāska we find *Ayam* derived from *i* (3.16). In the Veda we get such forms as *īm, ayā,* etc. Yāska derives *Asau* from as (3.16). He does not reduce it from *Adas*.

8. Pāṇini gives option in the matter of *y-v-lopa* (लोपः शाकल्यस्य). P. 8.3.19. Now, we find in the *Padapāṭha* of Śākalya that this *lopa* is observed in all cases. Now Yāska has followed Śākalya in this respect. This shows that Yāska was nearer to Śākalya than to Pāṇini.

Chapter Five

PRE-PĀṆINIAN GRAMMARIANS

We have mentioned some names of the scholars of language while writing on the *Prātiśākhyas.* The *Nairuktas* were also scholars of Grammar. The names mentioned by Śaunaka are also enumerated. This shows that there have been a number of scholars before Pāṇini who worked on the science of language. Pāṇini mentions only ten names of his predecessors in his *Aṣṭādhyāyī.* But there are references to other writers on Grammar also found in various works. Pt. Yudhiṣṭhira Mīmāṁsaka has done yeoman's work in collecting all these references and in giving a connected account of all the Grammarians in his *'History of Sanskrit Vyākaraṇa Śāstra'* (संस्कृत व्याकरण शास्त्र का इतिहास, 3 vols.). In this chapter, I am attempting to give a gist of Pt. Yudhiṣṭhira's account about the writers who came before Pāṇini. This has been based on chapters III and IV from his *'History of Sanskrit Vyākaraṇa Sāstra'*, Vol. I. For the convenience of treatment, I have divided this chapter into two sections. The first section deals with the grammarians who are not mentioned by Pāṇini and the second deals with the grammarians who have been mentioned by Pāṇini.

The science of *Vyākaraṇa* is very old. The extant *Padapāṭha* shows acquaintance with *Prakṛti, Pratyaya, Dhātu, Upasarga,* the splitting of the *Samāsa*, etc. These things have been so uniformly shown in the *Padapāṭha* that we have to assume some uniform theory behind it. The original work of *Vyākaraṇa* must have had the purpose more of splitting:- splitting the *saṁhitā* into *padas*, the *padas* into *padyas*, etc., rather than building of the *padas* as we see in the *Siddhānta Kaumudī.* There is a reference to this activity in *Mahābhārata, Udyoga Parva* 43.61.

सर्वार्थानां व्याकरणात् वैयाकरण उच्यते । तन्मूलतो व्याकरणं व्याकरोतीति तद्यथा ॥

We find direct reference to grammatical terms in the *Maitrāyaṇī Saṁhitā* as तस्मात् षड् विभक्तय: (1.7.3). That this has a reference to grammar is evident from the fact that it comes in the context of *Prayājas* in *Punarādheya*, and we have Patañjali saying in the *Mahābhāṣya*. 1.1.1, प्रयाजा: सविभक्तिका: कार्या: । We have *Aitareya Brāhmaṇa* saying सप्तधा वै वागवदत् (7.7), which has been explained by Bhaṭṭa Bhāskara as सप्त विभक्तय: । In the *Gopatha Brāhmaṇa* we have direct mention of the grammatical terms about which there cannot be two opinions. It is:

ओंकारं पृच्छाम: । को धातु:, किं प्रातिपदिकम्, किं नामाख्यातं, किं लिङ्गम्, किं वचनं, का विभक्ति:, क: प्रत्यय:, क: स्वर: उपसर्गो, निपात:, किं वै व्याकरणम्, को विकार:, को विकारी, कतिमात्र:, कतिवर्ण:, कत्यक्षर:, कतिपद:, क: संयोग:, किं स्थानानुप्रदानानुकरणम् (*Gopatha Br.* 1.24)

This shows that the grammatical activity is as old as the *Brāhmaṇa* works. That Indra split the word into two parts has been mentioned in the *Taittirīya Saṁhitā* 6.4.7.

Tradition refers to two schools of Grammar, viz., the *Aindra Sampradāya* and the *Māheśvara Sampradāya*. The *Kātantra Vyākaraṇa* is said to belong to the *Aindra* school, while Pāṇini's work belongs to the *Māheśvara* school.

AINDRA SAMPRADĀYA

The *Aindra* school was started by Indra. Indra learnt from Bṛhaspati and Bṛhaspati got Vedic speech from Brahmā. Brahmā was the first promulgator of speech which was reduced to analysis by his student. This, we get in the *Ṛk-tantra*.

ब्रह्मा बृहस्पतये प्रोवाच, बृहस्पतिरिन्द्राय, इन्द्रो भरद्वाजाय, भरद्वाज ऋषिभ्य:, ऋषयो ब्राह्मणेभ्य : । (*Ṛk-tantra*, I.4).

It is particularly interesting to note that this is said in respect of *Akṣara-samāmnāya* which has formed the basis of the grammatical aphorisms in various schools of Grammar.

The science of Grammar is termed as *Śabdānuśāsana*. The word *Anuśāsana* presupposes *Śāsana*. So, whatever Brahmā said was *Śāsana* and it was followed by *Anuśāsana*. Thus Brahmā was the first *pravaktṛ* of Language (*Vāk*).

The second *pravaktṛ* was Bṛhaspati. According to *Ṛk-tantra* and also *Mahābhāṣya* he taught *Vyākaraṇa* to Indra. cf. बृहस्पतिः इन्द्राय दिव्यं वर्षसहस्रं प्रतिपदोक्तानां शब्दानां शब्दपारायणं प्रोवाच (म.भा. I.1). *Śabdapārāyaṇa* was the name of his *Śāstra*, as explained by Bhartṛhari रूढिशब्दोऽयं कस्यचित् ग्रंथस्य (म. टी. p. 24); also Kaiyaṭa शब्दपारायणशब्दः योगरूढः शास्त्रविशेषस्य (म.प्र.).

Another reference to Bṛhaspati's *Vyākaraṇa* is from the *Auśanasas*. According to them *Vyākaraṇa* was a *Maraṇānta vyādhi*. c.f. तथा च बृहस्पतिः ह्लह्ल प्रतिपदमशक्यत्वात्, लक्षणस्य अव्यवस्थितत्वात्, तत्रापि स्खलितदर्शनात्, अनवस्थाप्रसङ्गाच्च, मरणान्तव्याधिर्व्याकरणम् इति औशनसाः (जयन्तभट्ट, न्यायमंजरी, 1.418).

What was the nature of Bṛhaspati's *Vyākaraṇa*? Nothing can be definitely said. But it was a *Pratipadapāṭha*, i.e., the enumeration of *padas* having similar forms. This similarity of course must have been in respect of form (*rūpa*) only. We have seen while dealing with the *Prātiśākhyas* that there must have been a stage in the study, where the lists of such words which undergo similar modifications in the *saṁhitā* were prepared. We may, therefore, hazard a surmise that it was of the nature of preparing the lists of words showing similar forms and similar operations. Indra, the pupil of Bṛhaspati, broke these *akhaṇḍa padas* (अखण्डा वाक्) into *prakṛti* and *pratyaya*, the process which was later on followed by his pupils. This came to be known as the *Aindra* School.

Pāṇinian *saṁjñās* generally consist of one letter such as *ṭi*, *ghu, it,* etc. If there is a bigger *saṁjñā* it is said to be *anvarthaka*. But we find that the *Nadī-saṁjñā* though a big one, is not *anvarthaka*. Now we have similar *saṁjñā*s in the *Kātantra Vyākaraṇa*, such as *Agni, Śṛddhā* and the like (*Kātantra* 2.1.8, 10). Agni stands for masculine nouns ending in i, *Śṛddhā* means feminine nouns ending in ā, and so on. The *Nadī-saṁjñā* of Pāṇini appears to be of that type. *Kātantra* is said to belong to Aindra tradition. We may therefore suggest that the lists of similar words prepared earlier were headed by these words and that later on they were treated by grammarians as *saṁjñā*s.

This suggestion may throw light on one peculiar *sūtra* in Pāṇinian grammar. Pāṇini says गोतो णित् (7.1.90). In this *sūtra* the word *gotah* is *go+tas*. We do not find *Pāṇini* using *tas* with any other word in the *Aṣṭādhyāyī*. Some scholars say that it is not *tas* but *taparakaraṇa*, but we do not find *taparakaraṇa* in Pānini in respect of words; it is found in respect of letters only. Now if we take the word *Gotaḥ* to mean after the word *Go*, then we have to make an *upasaṅkhyāna* for *Dyo*. But if we understand *Gotaḥ* as 'after the words ending in O', by taking the word गो to stand at the head of the list of words of that sort, then we need not make an *Upasaṅkhyāna* (cf. केचिदोतो विदिति पठन्ति । यो शब्दादपि यत् सर्वनामस्थानं विद्यते तदर्थम् (काशिका 7.1.90) also. ओतो णिदिति वाच्यम् विहितविशेषणं च (सि.कौ.).

The *Taittirīya Saṁhitā*, 6.4.7, says: वाग्वै पराचि अव्याकृता अवदत्। ते देवा इन्द्रमब्रुवन् इमां नो वाचं व्याकुरु इति । ... तामिन्द्रो मध्यतोऽवक्रम्य व्याकरोत् (also मै. सं. 4.5.8 अहं वा एतां वाचं व्यावर्तयिष्यामि, स वै वाचैव वाचं व्यावर्तयत् ।).

On this Sāyaṇa writes: तामखण्डां वाचं मध्ये विच्छिद्य प्रकृतिप्रत्ययविभागं सर्वत्र अकरोत् ।

This shows that Indra was the first grammarian proper.

The *Aindra* grammar is not available to us at present. But many writers refer to it. For example,

(i) 'जराया इन्द्रस्याचि' - जैनशाकटायन (1.2.37)

(ii) इन्द्रो महामते अनेकशास्त्रविदग्धबुद्धिः स्वशास्त्रप्रणेता । (Quotation from लंकावतारसूत्र given in *Technical Terms of Skt. Grammar*, p. 280.)

(iii) ऐन्देशानादिषु च अज्झलादिरूपसिद्धेः (हैमवृत्त्यवचूर्णि, P. 10).

(iv) यान्युज्जहार माहेन्द्रात् व्यासो व्याकरणार्णवात् ।
पदरत्नानि किं तानि सन्ति पाणिनिगोष्पदे ॥ - देवबोध.

So the existence of *Aindra Vyākaraṇa* cannot be doubted. It must have been very big as has been suggested by Devabodha in his couplet given above.

Even though the *Aindra Vyākaraṇa* is not available to us at present, still, we can get some idea of certain concepts from various references of other writers. The references are:

(1) शास्त्रेष्वपि - 'अथ वर्णसमूहः' इति ऐन्द्रव्याकरणस्य.

(quoted by Bhaṭṭāraka Haricandra in his *Carakanyāsa* (1.58). This shows that there was a *Varṇa-samāmnāya* in the *Aindra Vyākaraṇa.*)

(2) Durga writes in his commentary on the *Nirukta*: 'नैकं पदजातम् यथा 'अर्थः पदम्' ऐन्द्राणाम् । Suṣeṇa Vidyābhūṣaṇa writes in *Kālāpa Candra Sandhi* 20,

'अर्थः पदम्' आहुरैन्द्राः, विभक्त्यन्तं पदमिति आपिशलीयाः सुप्तिङन्तं पदमिति पाणिनीयाः'

A group of letters having meaning was, according to *Aindra*, a पद. We cannot say whether the classification of *Padas* into *Nāma, Ākhyāta, Upasarga,* and *Nipāta* was mentioned in the *Aindra Vyākaraṇa.*

(3) 'संप्रयोगप्रयोजनमैन्द्रेऽभिहितम्'

said by Abhinavagupta in *Abhinavabhāratī* on 14.32.

(4) तथा चोक्तमिन्द्रेण अन्त्यवर्णसमुद्भूता धातवः परिकीर्तिताः । - उपमन्यु in his gloss on नंदिकेश्वरकारिका.

Paribhaṣenduśekhara, Ed. Ānandāśram Sanskrit Granthāvali, Granthānka 72., Pune., 1913.

(5) While writing on प्राचीनवैयाकरणनये वाचनिकानि (परिभाषेन्दुशेखर), Vaidyanātha Pāyaguṇḍe writes प्राचीनेति इन्द्रादि इत्यर्थ : । (com. on first verse)

It appears from *Taittirīya Saṁhitā* 6.4.7. that Indra had taken assistance from Vāyu in writing his grammar. cf. वाग्वै पराचि अव्याकृता अवदत् । ते देवा इन्द्रमब्रुवन् इमां नो वाचं व्याकुरु इति । सोऽब्रवीद् - वरं वृणे, मह्यं चैव वायवे च सह गृह्याता इति । मै. सं. 4.5.8 says "वाग्वै ऐन्द्रवायव :।"

Vāyu Purāṇa 2.44 calls Vāyu *Śabdaśāstraviśārada*. It is also to be noted that Hanūmān, the son of Vāyu, was well-versed in grammar. cf.

नूनं व्याकरणं कृत्स्नमनेन बहुधा श्रुतम् ।
बहु व्याहरताऽनेन न किंचिदपशब्दितम् ॥ (रा. कि. 3-29)

According to *Ṛk-tantra,* Bharadvāja was the pupil of Indra. Bharadvāja was a man of great longevity. He lived for a span of three human lives. cf.भरद्वाजो ह वै त्रिभिरायुभिः ब्रह्मचर्यमुवास । तं जीर्णिं स्थविरं शयानं इन्द्र उपव्रज्य उवाच यत्ते चतुर्थमायुर्दद्याम् - किं तेन कुर्याः ।

This has been referred to by ऐ. ब्रा. - 15. 5 also.

There are references to Bharadvāja which have grammatical import. They are:

(1) तस्य यानि व्यञ्जनानि तत् शरीरम्, स घोषः, स आत्मा, य ऊष्माणः स प्राणः, एतदुवाह इन्द्रो भरद्वाजाय प्रोवाच (ऐ.आ. 2.2.4)

This means that Indra taught him the nature of *Ghoṣavat* and *Ūṣman* letters.

(2) The *Śukla Yajuḥ Prātiśākhya* says: "भारद्वाजकमाख्यातम्.

1.8.58. On this Uvaṭa writes, भारद्वाजेन दृष्टमाख्यातम् । It may be that Bharadvāja specially wrote on *Ākhyāta*. It is also to be noted here that Bhaṭṭoji refers to some *Bharadvājīya Dhātus* in the *Siddhānta-kaumudī*. P.7.2.13, or P. 7.2.66.

MĀHEŚVARA SAMPRADĀYA

We may proceed to another school of *Vyākaraṇa* which is said to have culminated into the Pāṇinian System. It was started by Maheśvara Śiva. The following are some quotations which indicate that Maheśvara Śiva had introduced a school of grammar:

(1) वेदात् षडङ्गानुद्धृत्य (म.भा.शां.प. 284-92). Śiva took out *Vedāṅgas* from the Veda. The *Vedāṅgas* include *Vyākaraṇa*.

(2) येनाक्षरसमाम्नायमधिगम्य महेश्वरात् ।
कृत्स्नं व्याकरणं प्रोक्तं तस्मै पाणिनये नम : ॥

(3) ब्राह्ममैशानमैन्द्रं च प्राजापत्यं बृहस्पतिम् ।
त्वाष्ट्रमापिशलं चेति पाणिनीयमथाष्टमम् ॥ - हैमबृहद्वृत्तिचूर्णि

(4) समुद्रवद् व्याकरणं महेश्वरे
तदर्धं कुम्भोद्धरणं बृहस्पतौ ।
तद् भागभागाच्च गतं पुरन्दरे
कुशाग्रबिन्दूत्पतितं हि पाणिनौ ।

Thus far about the two schools prominently known in the field of Sanskrit Grammar. We now proceed to individual grammarians known so far. The first among them is Bhāguri.

1. **BHĀGURI** : There is no mention of Bhāguri in Pāṇini. But the following verse noting the opinion of Bhāguri is very famous among the Sanskrit Grammarians:-

वष्टि भागुरिरल्लोपमवाप्योरुपसर्गयो: ।
आपं चैव हलन्तानां यथा वाचा दिशा निशा ॥

This shows that Bhāguri was a grammarian. The following opinions have been referred to as of Bhāguri by various writers:-

(i) नप्तेति भागुरिः in *Bhāṣāvṛtti* on 4.1.10

(ii) मुण्डादेस्तत्करोत्यर्थे गृह्णात्यर्थे कृतादिनः ।
वक्तीत्यर्थे च सत्यादेः, अङ्गादेस्तन्निरस्यति ।

(iii) तूस्ताद्विघाते संछादेर्वस्त्रात् पुच्छादिवत्तथा ।
उत्प्रेक्षादौ कर्मणोवाणिस्तदव्यय पूर्वतः ॥

(iv) वीणात उपमाने स्यात् हस्तितोतिक्रमे तथा ।
सेनातश्चाभियाने णिः श्लोकादेरप्युपस्तुतौ ॥

(v) गुपूधूपविच्छिपणि पणेरायः कोस्तु णिङ् ।
ऋतेरियङ् चतुर्लेषु नित्यं स्वार्थे परत्र वा ॥

(vi) गुपो वधोश्च निन्दायां क्षमायां तथा तिजः ।
प्रतीकाराद्यर्थकाच्च कित : स्वार्थे सनो विधिः ॥

(vii) अपादानसंप्रदानकरणाधारकर्मणाम् ।
कर्तुश्चान्योन्यसंदेहे परमेकं प्रवर्तते ॥

Out of the above six verses, the first five are quoted in *Śabdaśaktiprakāśikā* of Jagadīśa Tarkālaṃkāra as "*iti Bhāgurismṛteḥ*", and about the seventh it is said 'इति भागुरिवचनमेव शरणम्' in *Bhāṣā Vyākhyāprapañca* of Puruṣottama's परिभाषावृत्ति.

If these verses are actually from *Bhāguri's* work, then it must have been a metrical work like *Ṛk-Prātiśākhya*.

The following three verses refer to the opinion of Bhāguri, though they are not in his own words.

1. वष्टि भागुरिरल्लोपमवाप्योरुपसर्गयोः ।
आपं चैव हलन्तानां यथा वाचा दिशा निशा ॥

2. हन्तेः कर्मण्युपष्टम्भात् प्रासुमर्थे तु सप्तमीम् ।
चतुर्थीं बाधिकामाहुः चूर्णिभागुरिवाग्भटाः ॥

3. स्यान्मतम् करोतीति कारणम् । यथोक्तम्-ष्टिव सिव्योर्लिट्परयोः दीर्घत्वं वष्टि भागुरिः । करोतेः कर्तृभावे च सौनागाः प्रतिचक्षते ॥ दिकृत नयचक्त (मल्लवादिकृत द्वादशार- नयचक्रटीका भा. १ पृ. ४१)

There are two more references to the *Chāndasa* words being permitted by Bhāguri in the *Bhāṣā* as per the *Bhāṣāvṛtti* of Puruṣottamadeva. cf.

(i) शिवतातिः शंतातिः, अरिष्टतातिः, अमी शब्दाः छान्दसा अपि कदाचित् भाषायां प्रयुज्यन्ते इति त्रिकाण्डे भागुरिनिबन्धनात् वा अव्युत्पन्नसंज्ञाशब्दत्वात् वा सर्वथा भाषायां साधु । (4.4.143).

(ii) तथा भागुरिरपि ह्रस्वान्तं मन्यते, यथाह च भार्या भेकस्य वर्षाभ्वी, शृंगी स्याद्मद्गुरस्य च । शिली गण्डूपदस्यापि, कच्छपस्य डुलिः स्मृता ॥ - (धातुवृत्ति on भू)

Bhāguri must have been a very ancient writer, for in the *Saṅkṣiptasārasūtra, Taddhita* 454 अयाज्ञवल्क्यादेर्ब्राह्मणे a *Bhāguri Brāhmaṇa* has been mentioned along with Śāṭyāyanī, and Aitareyī. Even, according to Pāṇini, the *Bhāguri Brāhmaṇa* must belong to *Purāṇa-prokta* works.

2. **PAUṢKARASĀDI**: He has been mentioned in the *vārtika* चयो द्वितीयाः शरि पौष्करसादेरितिवाच्यम्. P. 8.3.28. Many opinions of Pauṣkarasādi have been mentioned in the *Taittirīya Prātiśākhya*. In the *Dhātupāṭhaṭīkā* of Cannavīra, Pauṣkara has been mentioned along with Indra, Candra, Āpiśali, Gārgya and Gālava. cf. (सद्भिः इन्द्रचन्द्रापिशलिगार्ग्यगालवपौष्करैः)

From his name, it appears that he must have been the son of Puṣkarasad. Pāṇini has mentioned him in *Taulvalyādigaṇa*. According to Haradatta he must have been an Easterner (*Puṣkarasādeḥ prācyatvāt*) and according to Pāṇini also he must have been a *Prācya*, for he comes under an exception to *Iñaḥ prācām* (2.4.60). He has also been mentioned in *Śāṅkhāyana Āraṇyaka* 7.8; *Hiraṇyakeśīya Gṛhyasūtra* 1.6.8; *Agniveśya Gṛhyasūtra* 1.1; *Āpastamba Dharmasūtra* 1.19.7; 1.28.1. According to Māhiṣeya on *Taittirīya Prātiśākhya* he was a promoter of a *śākhā* (cf. शैत्यायनादीनां कोहलीपुत्र-भरद्वाज-स्थविर-कौण्डिन्य-पौष्करसादीनां शाखिनाम् ।

3. **CĀRĀYAṆA**: Devapāla quotes in his gloss on *Laugākṣi*

Gṛhya. 5.1 as follows: तथा च चारायणीयं सूत्रम् - "पुरुकृतेच्छ्रयोः इति । पुरुच्छदनं पुच्छम् । कृतस्य छ्रदनं विनाशनं कृच्छ्रम् ।"

This appears to be a grammatical *sūtra*. The *Mahābhāṣya* on 1.1.73 refers to Cārāyaṇa when he says: कम्बलचारायणीयाः, ओदनपाणिनीयाः घृतरौढीयाः meaning the students of Cārāyaṇa who study under him not for learning grammar, but, because they get blankets there.

He was a promoter of a *Śākhā* of *Yajurveda* and his *Cārāyaṇīya Mantrārṣādhyāya* is available. There is also *Cārāyaṇīya Śikṣā*. He holds an opinion on *Nāṭaka* also.

4. **ŚANTANU**: Śantanu (and not Śāntanava) is the author of the *Phiṭ-sūtra*s स पुनः शन्तनुप्रणीतः 'फिष्' इत्यादिकम् । - पदमञ्जरी; also शन्तनुराचार्यः प्रणेता इति 'द्वारादीनां च' इति सूत्रे कैयटः । - नागेश, बृहच्छब्देन्दुशेखर. The *Phiṭ-sūtras* belong to the school which holds the theory of *Avyutpanna Prātipadika*. These *sūtras* are very old and appear to be pre-Pāṇinian. They have been recognised by Patañjali (प्रत्ययस्वरस्यावकाशो यत्रानुदात्ता प्रकृतिः - समत्वं सिमत्वम्, (म.भा. on p. 6-1-158). The अनुदात्तत्व of सम and सिम can be known only from फिट् सूत्र-त्वसमसिमेत्यनुच्चानि and from nowhere else.

(ii) प्रातिपदिकस्वरस्यावकाशः, आम्रः, शालः (p. 6.1.9) Here the महाभाष्य refers to 'फिषः'.

(iii) स्वरितकरणान्न भविष्यति - 'न्यङ्स्वरौ स्वरितौ' इति । (1.2.3). Here *Patañjali* quotes the *Phiṭ-sūtras*.

They are earlier than Kātyāyana (प्रकृतिप्रत्यययोः स्वरस्य सावकाशत्वादसिद्धिः (वार्तिक on p. 1.6.158). On this Patañjali writes प्रत्ययस्वरस्यावकाशो यत्रानुदात्ता प्रकृतिः समत्वम्, सिमत्वम् । This shows that the *Vārtikakāra* had in mind the फिट्सूत्र - त्व समसिमेत्यनुच्चानि). The *Phiṭ-sūtras* appear to be older than Pāṇini also. Even though Nāgeśa in his *Udyota* on 6.1.158 says : यद्वा फिट्सूत्राणि पाणिन्यपेक्षया आधुनिककर्तृकाणि, still, they appear to be older than Pāṇini for the following reason:

Candragmin states in his *vṛtti* on the *Pratyāhāra-sūtras* एष प्रत्याहार: पूर्वव्याकरणेऽपि स्थित एव । अयं तु विशेष: 'ऐ औष्' यदासीत् तत् 'ऐ औच्' इति कृतम् । तथा हि - लघावन्ते द्वयोश्च बह्वषो गुरु:' (फि. २१९) तृणधान्यानां च द्व्यषाम् (ऋ.) इति पठ्यते ।

This means that the earlier *Pratyāhāra* was ऐ औष् and Pāṇini changed it to ऐ औच्. Now, in the Āpiśala grammar also, the *pratyāhāra* is अच् (स्वर) and not अष्. This means that the अष् *pratyāhāra* was earlier than even Āpiśali. The *pratyāhāra* is found in the *Phiṭ-sūtras*.

The group of the *sūtras* consisting of the four *pāda*s and dealing with the accent of the *prātipadika* is known as *Phiṭ-sūtra* because the first *sūtra* therein is *Phiṣaḥ* (and not *Phiṣo'nta udāttaḥ*). This collection of the *sūtras* appears to be a section of a bigger work, for, in this, there are many *saṁjñās* used without their explanation; they might have been explained in the earlier portion of the work of which the present four *pādas* once formed a part. Such *saṁjñās* are: फिष् = प्रातिपदिक (सू - 1); नप् = नपुंसक (सू. 23, 61); यमन्वा = वृद्ध (41); शिट् = सर्वनाम (21); स्फिग् = लुक् (29). Likewise there are certain *pratyāhāras* used which require explanation e.g. अष् = अच् (स्वर) (27, 42, 49), खय् = खय् = वर्ग= प्रथमद्वितीय (31); हय् = हल् = व्यंजन (46, 66) (हय इति हलां संज्ञा - लघुशब्देन्दुशेखर).

The reading of the first *sūtra* in this collection as given in the *Siddhānta-kaumudī* is फिष: (27,8). But in a manuscript in the Adyar Manuscript Library, it is फिट् (and not फिष:), followed by the *vṛtti* स्वरविधौ अन्त उदात्त: इति प्रक्रान्तम् । This means that the words अन्त उदात्त: are to be carried over by *anuvṛtti*. It appears that when these *sūtras* were carried over into the Pāṇinian system, the word फिट् which was in the nominative, was changed to फिष: in genitive, to fit into the system. Pāṇini mentions the *Kāryin* by genitive. But, in the earlier grammars, nominative was used to mention the *Kāryin* cf. पूर्वसूत्रनिर्देशश्च 'चित्वान् चित:' इति । पूर्वाचार्या: कार्यभाजान् षष्ठ्या न निरदिक्षन् (म.भा.). In the same manuscript, there are two more statements which are relevant in this connection. They are: शान्तनवाचार्य: 'फिष्' इति प्रातिपदिकसंज्ञां कृतवान् । अर्थवदधातुरप्रत्यय: फिट्, कृत्तद्धितसमासाश्च इति ।

Jinendrabuddhi in his *Nyāsa* on *Kāśikā* 1.2.30 writes:-

त्व-समसिमेत्यनुच्चानि इति सर्वादिष्वेव पठ्यन्ते । This means that the words त्व, सम etc. had been read in the *Sarvādi-gaṇa* itself, as a *gaṇasūtra* and also as a *Phiṭ-sūtra*. We know that in Pāṇini's *sarvādi-gaṇa* there are three *gaṇa-sūtras* which are also read in the *Aṣṭādhyāyī*. But, this *sūtra* is not found there. So, we have to conclude that the remark of Jinendrabuddhi refers to some *sarvādi-gaṇa* which included that *sūtra*. It might be the *sarvādi-gaṇa* of Śantanu and the *sūtra* under consideration might have been given under the *sūtra* which was perhaps "सर्वादीनि शिट्".

We may, therefore, say that Śantanu had written a bigger grammatical work of which the present *Phiṭ-sūtra* was a section.

5. **VAIYĀGHRAPADYA**: There is a line in the *Kāśikā* 7.1.94. 'गुणं त्विगन्ते नपुंसके व्याघ्रपदां वरिष्ठ:' explained by Haradatta as व्याघ्रपादपत्यानां मध्ये वरिष्ठ: वैयाघ्रपद्य आचार्य:। This word is a *gotrapratyayānta*. Hence, the original word from which this word has come into being must be Vyāghrapat. Vyāghrapat is mentioned in the *Mahābhārata* as one of the sons of Vasiṣṭha (cf. व्याघ्रयोन्यां ततो जाता वसिष्ठस्य महात्मन: । एकोनविंशति: पुत्रा: ख्याता व्याघ्रपदादय: ॥ (अनु. 53-30). Pāṇini mentions Vyāghrapat in *Gargādi-gaṇa* (p. 4.1.105) from which the word Vaiyāghrapadya is derived by adding *yañ*. Vaiyāghrapadya is mentioned in the *Śatapatha Brāhmaṇa* 10.6.1.7,8; *Jaiminīya Upaniṣad Brāhmaṇa* 3.7.3.2; 4.9.1.1; *Śānkhāyana Āraṇyaka* 9.7.

The verse शुष्किका शुष्कजङ्घा च etc. quoted in the *Kāśikā* on P. 8.2.1 has been treated by Bhaṭṭoji as *Vaiyāghrapadya-vārtika* (अत एव शुष्किका... इति वैयाघ्रपद्यवार्तिके जि शब्द एव पठ्यते । शब्दकौस्तुभ I.1.) But, it might be a *Kārikā* from the grammar belonging to

Vaiyāghrapadīya school. It is not found in the *Mahābhāṣya*. *Kāśikā* on p. 4.2.65. gives an illustration as दशका वैयाघ्रपदीयाः and on p. 5.1.58 as दशकं वैयाघ्रपदीयम्. It may be that his grammar might have ten *adhyāyas*.

6. **MĀDHYANDINI**: The *Kāśikā* says - संबोधने तूशनसस्त्रिरूपं सान्तं तथा नान्तमथाप्यदन्तम् । माध्यंदिनिर्वष्टि गुणंत्विगन्ते नपुंसके व्याघ्रपदां वरिष्ठः ॥

According to Mādhyandini, the word Uśanas has three forms in the vocative, viz. हे उशनः, हे उशनन्, हे उशन. Vimala Sarasvatī gives in the *Rūpamāla* an opinion of Mādhyandini as इकः षष्ठेऽपि संबुद्धौ गुणो माध्यंदिनेर्मते । This is quoted in the *Bhūmikā* of the *Prakriyā-kaumudī*, p. 32. This shows the existence of Mādhyandini's Grammar.

The word *Mādhyandini* is *Apatyapratyayānta* and is derived as मध्यंदिनस्यापत्यं माध्यंदिनिराचार्यः । This is by treating the *Bāhvādi-gaṇa* (p. 4.1.96) as *Ākṛtigaṇa*. Pāṇini mentions Madhyandina in the *Utsādi-gaṇa* (4.1.86). This Madhyandina was *Padakāra* of the *Śukla Yajuḥ Saṁhitā* and was the direct pupil of Vājasaneya Yajñavalkya (c.f. याज्ञवल्क्यस्य शिष्यास्ते कण्व-वैधेय - शालिनः । मध्यंदिनश्च शापेयी विदग्धश्चाप्युद्दालकः ॥ (वायुपुराण 61.24, 25).

7. **RAUḌHI**: We read in *Kāśikā* 6.2.37 आपिशलपाणिनीयाः, पाणिनीयरौढीयाः रौढीयकाशकृत्स्नाः. Of these Pānini, Āpiśali and Kāśakṛtsna are grammarians. We may, therefore, say that Rauḍhi also was a grammarian.

The word *Rauḍhi* is an *Apatyapratyayānta* derived from *Rūḍha*. Vardhamāna in his *Gaṇaratnamahodadhi* reads Rauḍhi in *Krauḍyādi gaṇa*. Accordingly the sister of Rauḍhi would be Rauḍhyā. This is not mentioned in Pāṇini but is indicated in the *Bhāṣya* on 4.1.69. It says "सिद्धं तु रौढ्यादिषूपसंख्यानात् । सिद्धमेतत् । कथम् । रौढ्यादिषूपसंख्यानात् । के पुनः रौढ्यादयः ? ये क्रौड्यादयः । This shows that the *sūtra* क्रौड्यादिभ्यश्च in Pāṇini was read by elders as रौढ्यादिभ्यश्च. This shows that Rauḍhi was a predecessor of Pāṇini. Pālyakīrti reads the *sūtra* as रूढादिभ्यश्च (2.3.4).

Rauḍhi must have been a very well-to-do scholar. We get in the *Kāśikā* 1.1.73, the word घृतरौढीया: for those students who joined Rauḍhi's school not for learning, but, because they were supplied ghee in their meals घृतप्रधानो रौढि:, घृतरौढि: । तस्य छात्रा: घृतरौढीया: । Rauḍhi was so well-placed that he could afford to serve ghee to his students.

8. **ŚAUNAKI**: Jajjhaṭa in his commentary on the *Caraka* : *Cikitsā-sthāna* 2.27, says: कारणशब्दस्तु व्युत्पादित: करोतेरपि कर्तृत्वे दीर्घत्वं शास्ति शौनकि: ॥ We find the following statement in the commentary of Siṁhasūrigaṇi on Mallavādin's statement:- स्यान्मत्तम् - करोतिरिति कारणम् यथोक्तम् - ष्ठिवसीव्योर्ल्युट्परयो: दीर्घत्वं वष्टि भागुरि: । करोते: कर्तृभावे च सौनागा: प्रतिचक्षते (also compare कुञ: कर्तरि । - चन्द्र 1.1.99)

It is likely that Śaunakas were originally Śaunakāḥ. *Jayamaṅgalā* on Bhaṭṭi 3.47 says धाञ् कृञोस्तनिहयोश्च बहुलत्वेन शौनकि: meaning that *api* and *ava* drop their *a* when followed by *Dhāñ, Kṛñ, Tanu,* and *Naḥ* optionally according to the opinion of Śaunaki. These instances show that Śaunaki was a grammarian. He evidently must have been the son of Śaunaka and this Śaunaka might be the same who wrote various treatises on the *Ṛgveda*.

9. **GAUTAMA**: We get reference to Gautama in the *Mahābhāṣya* as आपिशल-पाणिनीय-व्याडीय-गौतमीया: (6.2.36). This shows that Gautama was a grammarian of the status as could be mentioned along with Āpiśali and Pāṇini. The *Taittirīya Prātiśākhya* 5.38 and *Maitrāyaṇī Prātiśākhya* 5.40 refer to the opinion of Gautama as प्रथमपूर्वो हकार: चतुर्थं तस्य स्थानम् प्लाक्षि-कौण्डन्य-गौतम-पौष्करसादीनाम् । We have *Gautamī Śikṣā* also.

10. **VYĀḌI**: We find Vyāḍi mentioned in the *Ṛk-Prātiśākhya* at 2.23, 28; 6.43; 13.31, 37. Puruṣottamadeva mentions Vyāḍi along with Gālava. Gālava has been mentioned by Pāṇini at four places. The *Mahābhāṣya* mentions Vyāḍi along with other grammarians. There is no doubt that Vyāḍi was a grammarian. Vyāḍi has been referred to as Dākṣāyaṇa in the *Mahābhāṣya*

(P. 2.3.6). The *Kāśikā* refers to him as Dākṣi in Kumārīdākṣāḥ (P. 6.2.69). Jayāditya on P. 2.2.39 says व्याड्युपज्ञं दुष्करणम् । The *Nyāsa* says व्याड्युपज्ञं दशहुष्करणम् and explains as व्याडिरप्यत्र युगपत्कालभाविनां मध्ये दशहुष्करणानि कृत्वा परिभाषितवान् पूर्वं पूर्वं कालमिति । On this, Maitreyarakṣita says: प्रथमतरं दशहुष्करणानि कृत्वा कालमनद्यतनादिकं परिभाषितवान् । The *Padamañjarī* says: 'दुष्' इत्ययं संकेतशब्दो यत्र क्रियते यथा पाणिनीये 'वृत्' इति । तद् दुष्करणं व्याकरणम् । कामशास्त्रमित्यन्ये । All these references show that Vyāḍi must have been a reputed scholar of grammar.

Vyāḍi is said to be a maternal uncle of Pāṇini. He wrote the work known as the *Saṅgraha*. The *Saṅgraha* was a philosophical work like the *Vākyapadīya*. It had influenced the scholars to a great extent. The work is now lost. We get the following references to that work in the writings of later writers:

1. शोभना खलु दाक्षायणस्य सङ्ग्रहस्य कृतिः (म.भा. *Mbh.* on P. 2.3.66)

2. पञ्चकः सङ्ग्रहः (चांद्रवृत्ति 4.1.62). This suggests that it had five chapters. (compare अष्टकं पाणिनीयम्).

3. इह पुरा पाणिनीयेऽस्मिन् व्याकरणे व्याड्युपरचितं लक्षग्रंथपरिमाणं सङ्ग्रहाभिधानं निबंधनमासीत् (पुण्यराज in वाक्यपदीयटीका).

4. सङ्ग्रहो व्याडिकृतो लक्षश्लोकसंख्यो ग्रंथ इति प्रसिद्धिः । (नागेश, महाभाष्य, उद्योत)

5. The *Mahābhāṣya* on 4.2.66 gives an example as साङ्ग्रहसूत्रिकः This shows that सङ्ग्रह consisted of *sūtras*.

6. सङ्ग्रहे तावत् प्राधान्येन परीक्षितम् -नित्यो वा स्यात् कार्यो वा । तत्रोक्ता दोषाः, प्रयोजनान्यप्युक्तानि । तत्र त्वेष निर्णयः यद्यप्येष नित्यो तथापि कार्यः । उभयथापि लक्षणं प्रवर्त्यम् । (म.भा. पस्पशा). *Mbh.Paspaśā*. Vol. I. P. 6.

7. सङ्ग्रहे पुनः कार्यप्रतिद्वन्द्विभावात् मन्यामहे नित्यपर्यायवाचिनो ग्रहणम् । (म.भा. पस्पशा). *Mbh.Paspaśā*. Vol. I. P. 6.

References 6 & 7 indicate that संग्रह was a work of philosophical contents.

8. एवं च संग्रहादिषु तदुदाहरणदानमसंगतं स्यात् । (नागेश on P. 4.3.37). This shows that the संग्रह contained examples of Pāṇini.

9. श्वोभूतिव्याडिप्रभृतयः 'श्युकः किति' इत्यत्र द्विककारनिर्देशेन हेतुना चर्त्वभूतो गकारः प्रश्लिष्ट इत्येवमाचक्षते । (न्यास on P. 7.2.11).

Perhaps Vyāḍi wrote an explanation of the *sūtras* of Pāṇini. This has also been mentioned in कृष्णचरित ascribed to Samudra Gupta as "दाक्षीपुत्रवचोव्याख्यापटुमीमांसकाग्रणिः ।"

10. Bhartṛhari while commenting on the statement, सङ्ग्रहे तावत् प्राधान्येन परीक्षितम् which appears in the *Mahābhāṣya* writes: चतुर्दशसहस्राणि वस्तूनि अस्मिन् संग्रहग्रन्थे (परीक्षितानि) । This indicates that there were about fourteen thousand topics considered by Vyāḍi in *Saṅgraha*.

That *Saṅgraha* wielded great influence in the field of grammar is evident from the example Kumāridākṣāḥ (*Kāśika* p. 6.2.69); and the various statements of Patañjali given above. The following verse appearing in the *Mahābhāṣya* on p. 7.4.93 also indicates the same.

किरतिं चर्करीतान्तं पचतीत्यत्र यो नयेत् ।

प्राप्तिज्ञं तमहं मन्ये प्रारब्धस्तेन संग्रहः ॥

The following verses from the *Vākyapadīya* show that the study of the *Saṅgraha* had gone out of vogue long before Bhartṛhari.

प्रायेण संक्षेपरुचीन् अल्पविद्यापरिग्रहान् ।
संप्राप्य वैयाकरणान् संग्रहेऽस्तमुपागते ॥ 4.84
कृतेऽथ पतञ्जलिना गुरुणा तीर्थदर्शिना ।
सर्वेषां न्यायबीजानां महाभाष्ये निबन्धने ॥4.85

We give below the quotations which the later writers cited in their works. From these, we may get some idea of the work of Vyāḍi and the Philosophy of Grammar.

1. न हि किंचित् पदं नामरूपेण नियतं क्वचित् ।
पदानां रूपमर्थो वा वाक्यार्थादेव जायते ॥

2. अर्थात् पदं साभिधेयं पदात् वाक्यार्थनिर्णयः ।
पदसङ्घातजं वाक्यं वर्णसङ्घातजं पदम् ॥

3. शब्दार्थयोरसंभेदे व्यवहारे पृथक् क्रिया ।
यतः शब्दार्थयोस्तत्त्वमेकं तत् समवस्थितम् ॥

4. संबन्धस्य न कर्तास्ति शब्दानां लोकवेदयोः ।
शब्दैरेव हि शब्दानां संबन्धः स्यात् कृतः कथम् ॥

5. वाचकोपादानस्वरूपवान् अव्युत्पत्तिपक्षे । व्युत्पत्तिपक्षे तु अर्थावहितं समाश्रितं निमित्तं शब्दव्युत्पत्तिकर्मणि प्रयोजकम् । उपादानोद्योतक इत्येके । सोऽयमिति व्यपदेशेन संबन्धोपयोगस्य शक्यत्वात् ॥

6. नहि स्वरूपं शब्दानां गोपिण्डादिवत् करणे सन्निविशते । तत्तु नित्यमभिधेयमेव अभिधानसन्निवेशे सति तुल्यरूपत्वात् असन्निविष्टमपि समुच्चार्यमाणत्वे नावसीयते।

7. शब्दस्य ग्रहणे हेतुः प्राकृतो ध्वनिरिष्यते ।
स्थितिभेदे निमित्तत्वं वैकृतं प्रतिपद्यते ॥

8. असतश्चान्तराले यान् शब्दानस्तीति मन्यते ।
प्रतिपत्तुरशक्तिः सा ग्रहणोपाय एव सः ॥

9. यथाद्य संख्याग्रहणमुपायः प्रतिपत्तये ।
सङ्ख्यान्तराणां भेदेऽपि तथा शब्दान्तरश्रुतिः ॥

10. शब्दप्रकृतिरपभ्रंशः ।

11. शुद्धस्योच्चारणे स्वार्थः प्रसिद्धो यस्य गम्यते ।
स मुख्य इति विज्ञेयो रूपमात्रनिबन्धनः ॥

12. संस्त्यानं संहननं तमोनिवृत्तिरशक्तिरुपरतिः प्रवृत्तिप्रतिबन्धतिरोभावः स्त्रीत्वम् । प्रसवो विष्वग्भावो वृद्धिशक्तिलाभोऽभ्युद्रेकः प्रवृत्तिराविर्भावः पुंस्त्वम् । अविवक्षातः साम्यस्थितिः औत्सुक्यनिवृत्तिः अपदार्थत्वमङ्गाङ्गीभावनिवृत्तिः कैवल्यमिति नपुंसकत्वमिति ॥

13. इकां यणभिर्व्यवधानमेकेषामिति संग्रहः ।

14. जाज्वलीति संग्रहे ।

15. यस्त्वन्यस्य प्रयोगेण यत्नादिव नियुज्यते ।
तमप्रसिद्धं मन्यन्ते गौणार्थाभिनिवेशिनम् ॥

16. शब्दे तां जातिं शब्दमेवार्थजातौ जातिः, शुक्लादौ द्रव्यशब्दे गुणं, कृत्तत्संयोगं योगित्वाभिन्नरूपं वाच्यं वाच्येषु त्वादयो बोधयन्ति ।

17. किं कार्यशब्दोऽथ नित्यः इति ।

18. असति प्रत्यक्षाभिधाने -

19. काश्यपस्तु आत्वपक्षे दिदासते इत्येके इत्युक्त्वा संग्रह इत्वव्यतिरिक्तस्य द्युकार्यस्य उक्तत्वात् इस्भावः उपदित्सते इत्याह ।

20. ज्ञानं द्विविधम् सम्यक्, असम्यक् च ।

21. ओंकारश्चाथशब्दश्च द्वावेतौ ब्रह्मणः पुरा ।
कण्ठं भित्त्वा विनिर्यातौ तस्मान्माङ्लिकावुभौ ॥

One *Paribhāṣā* work called *Paribhāṣāsūcanam* is ascribed to *Vyāḍi* (published in the collection of *Paribhāṣā* works by MM K.V. Abhyankar, BORI, Poona, 1967, called *Paribhāṣāsaṅgraha*.

11. **KĀŚAKṚTSNA**: There is no reference to Kāśakṛtsna in Pāṇinian grammar but he has been mentioned by various writers in their works. Some important references to him are as follows:

(i) Bopadeva in his Kavikalpadruma says: इन्द्रश्चन्द्रः काशकृत्स्नापिशली शाकटायनः । पाणिन्यमरजैनेन्द्रा जयन्त्यष्टादिशाब्दिकाः ॥ In this couplet Kāśakṛtsna has been mentioned along with other grammarians of repute.

(ii) Kṣīrasvāmin says in his *Taraṅgiṇī*: काशकृत्स्नाः अस्य निष्ठायामनिदत्वमाहुः । आश्वस्तः, विश्वस्तः ।

(iii) Kaiyaṭa refers to him at two places in his *Pradīpa* on the *Mahābhāṣya*:

(a) काशकृत्स्नस्य 'प्रत्ययोत्तरपदयोः' सूत्रे तद् विचारयति । (P. 2-1-50)

(b) आपिशलकाशकृत्स्नयोस्तु 'अग्रन्थे' इति वचनात् (P. 5-1-21)

(iv) Bhartṛhari in his *Svopajña-ṭīkā* on the *Vākyapadīya Brahmakāṇḍa* quotes two *sūtras* as (i) धातुसाधने दिशि पुरुषे चिति तदाख्यातम् and लिङ्गं किमिति विभक्तावेतन्नाम ।

Vṛṣabhadeva while writing on these says: धातुरिति काशकृत्स्नानां सूत्रम् - लिङ्गमिति ।

(v) The *Vākyapadīya, Prakīrṇakāṇḍa* says तदर्हमिति नारब्धं सूत्रं व्याकरणान्तरे ।' (*Vākyapadīya* 3.14.56) On this, Helārāja writes आपिशला:काशकृत्स्नाश्च सूत्रमेतन्नाधीयते ।

(vi) The *Mahābhāṣya* mentions the grammar of Kāśakṛtsana along with those of Pāṇini and Āpiśali as "प्रोक्तादयश्च तद्धिता नोत्पद्यन्ते । पाणिनिना प्रोक्तं पाणिनीयम्, आपिशलम्, काशकृत्स्नम् । न हि पाणिनिना शब्दा: प्रोक्ता:, किं तर्हि, सूत्रम् । *Mbh. Paspaśā*, Vol. I. P. 12. (पस्पशा). These references conclusively prove the existence of the grammar of Kāśakṛtsna and that he was of such a status as could be mentioned along with Pāṇini and Āpiśali.

Kāśakṛtsna flourished in the Pre-Pāṇinian period. Kshitish Chandra Chatterji had suggested in his *"Technical Terms and Technique of Sanskrit Grammar"* that Kāśakṛtsna came after Pāṇini. But Pt. Yudhiṣṭhira Mīmāṁsaka has conclusively shown that he came before Pāṇini (See काशकृत्स्न व्याकरण तथा उनके उपलब्ध सूत्र- युधिष्ठिर मीमांसक). Some of the references given by him are the following:

(i) In the *Upakādi-gaṇa* (p. 2.4.69) Pāṇini mentions the name of Kaśakṛtsna, (कशकृत्स्न) and in the *Arīhaṇadi-gaṇa* (P. 4.2.80) he mentions Kāśakṛtsna (काशकृत्स्न).

(ii) The *Dhātupāṭha* of Kāśakṛtsna along with the *ṭīkā* in Kannada written by Cannavira Kavi has been published by A.N. Narasimhayyar in 1952. That *Dhātupāṭha* contains some 450 roots more than those in the Pāṇinian *Dhātupāṭha*. In that, many roots exhibit double forms, e.g. *īḍ, īḷ*, and so on. In Pāṇini, we get only one form as *īḍ*. This shows that Kāśakṛtsna's *Dhātupāṭha* represents that state of the language when both the forms *id* and *iḷ* were in use. In the time of Pāṇini the form *iḷ* had gone out of vogue. Again, the roots *vas, vad, svi,* etc. which are *parasmaipadī* only in Pāṇini are shown *Ubhayapadī* in *Kāśakṛtsna's Dhātupāṭha*. This means that the stage of this *Dhātupāṭha* is prior to that of Pāṇini.

(iii) In the *Āpiśala* grammar there was a *sūtra* शताच्च ठन्यतावग्रन्थे । This was improved by *Pāṇini* as शताच्च ठन्यतावशते (5-1-21). Now Kāśakṛtsna also reads this *sūtra* as ठन्यतावग्रन्थे. If he had been later than Pāṇini he would have adopted the improved version of the *sūtra* as given by Pāṇini rather than the old one of Āpiśali.

(iv) Both Āpiśali and Kāśakṛtsna did not have the *sūtra* तदर्हम् (तदर्हमिति नारब्धं सूत्रं व्याकरणान्तरे) - Pāṇini had newly introduced it. It was perhaps for this reason that Patañjali was required to justify the necessity of that *sūtra*. Had Kāśakṛtsna been later than Pāṇini he would have followed Pāṇini rather than Āpisåali in this respect.

(v) The *Kātantra* is practically a summary of Kāśakṛtsna. It deals with the forms in the *Laukika Bhāṣā* and not the *Chāndasa* शर्ववर्मणस्तु वचनात् भाषायामप्यवसीयते । नह्ययं (कातन्त्रकार:) छान्दसान् शब्दान् व्युत्पादयति । - कातंत्रवृत्ति)

Now, this *Kātantra* has a *sūtra* भिस ऐसु वा । It is to be noted that this *sūtra* has reference in the *Kātantra* in the field of *Bhāṣā* and not the Vedic usage. Hence it points to that state of *Bhāṣā* in which the forms देवेभि: as well as देवै: were freely used in the *Bhāṣā* also. This state of things was definitely earlier than Pāṇini. Now the *Kātantra* must necessarily have borrowed this *sūtra* from *Kāśakṛtsna* of which it was a summary. Hence it is clear that the state of grammar in the work of Kāśakṛtsna was prior to that of Pāṇini. The view that the *Kātantra* is an abridged version of the *Kāśakṛtsna* is not accepted by all scholars.

Kāśakṛtsna's grammar was termed as the *'Śabdakalāpa'* or *'Kalāpa'*. The *Kātantra*, which was the summary of the

Śabdakalāpa was, therefore, termed as *'Kalāpaka'* i.e. *mini-kalāpa* (अल्पार्थे कन्), *Kātantra*, i.e. *mini-Tantra*, or the *Kaumāra Vyākaraṇa*. The expression 'त्रिकं काशकृत्स्नम्' indicates that it consisted of three chapters. The expression काशकृत्स्नं गुरुलाघवम् indicates, as suggested by Pt. Yudhiṣṭhira Mīmāṁsaka, that in his grammar the words which had gone out of vogue (अप्रयुक्तशब्द) were not considered. The work was probably metrical. The *Kāśakṛtsna-sūtras* which are available now, when compared with the *Kātantra-sūtras*, point to this conclusion. The fact that the *Kātantra* is a summary of the *Kāśakṛtsna* has been convincingly proved by Pt. Mīmāṁsaka.

The Kannada-*ṭīkā* of Cannavīra Kavi on the *Dhātupāṭha* of Kāśakṛtsna quotes many *sūtras* from his grammar. All such *sūtras* as well as the *sūtras* quoted by Bhartṛhari have been collected together by Pt. Mīmāṁsaka in his essay mentioned above. He has also written their explanation in Hindi. We give below those *sūtras* here for the information of our readers:-

1. धातौ साधने दिशि पुरुषे चितिं तदाख्यातम् ।
2. लिङ्गे किमि (चिति) विभक्तौ एतन्नाम ।
3. प्रत्ययोत्तरपदयोः ।
4. शताच्च ठन्यतावग्रन्थे ।
5. क्विप् or धातोः क्विप् or क्विब्विणौ सर्वधातुभ्यः ।
6. अनुनासिकोऽनुषङ्गः ।
7. अनुषङ्गस्य लोपः ।
8. धात्वादेः षः सः ।
9. नो णः ।
10. गमां वः । गमो गच्छ । गमादेश्छः ।
11. लोपोऽनुनासिकानां कानुबन्धे ।
12. उदनुबन्धादिड् वा ।
13. दिवादेर्यन् ।
14. चजयोः कगौ कानुबन्धे ।
15. चुषादेर्दीर्घः ।
16. हो ढः ।
17. सतवर्गयोः शचवर्गयोगे शचवर्गौ ।

18. षटवर्गयोः योगे षटवर्गौ ।
19. ढोढे लोपः; पूर्वस्य समानस्य दीर्घः ।
20. नामिनो गुणः सार्वधातुकार्धधातुकयोः ।
21. सेर्डा ।
22. अनुबन्धे स्तनादेर्लोपः ।
23. बर्हेरु रो मनि ।
24. सन्ध्यक्षराणामाकारः ।
25. आतो युः ।
26. ईद् आतः कानुबन्धे ।
27. धेरोऽयः ।
28. पाः पिबः ।
29. घ्रो जिघ्रः ।
30. ध्मो धमः ।
31. स्थः तिष्ठः ।
32. म्नो मनः ।
33. दाणो यच्छः ।
34. ऱ्हस्वस्य तोऽन्तः पानुबन्धे ।
35. ऋ ऋच्छः ।
36. चजोः कगौ ।
37. दृशेः पश्य ।
38. दृशादीनां स्वृणां यवरा अ(का)नुबन्धे ।
39. छशषराजादीनां षोऽघोषे ।
40. दिशादीनां कः ।
41. कशेर्यप इपुश्च ।
42. अनुषङ्गलोपोऽनुनासिकानाम् ।
43. भूते भव्ये वर्तमाने भावे कर्तरि कर्मणि ।
    प्रयोजके गुणे योग्ये धातुभ्यः स्युः क्लिबादयः ॥
44. पुल्यगिभ्यामस्त्योऽस्तिश्च ।
45. स्फायः स्फी ।
46. प्यायः पी ।
47. नान्तः क्षुण्णादीनाम् ।
48. इक्तिपौ धातुस्वरूपे ।
49. कृपो रो लः ।
50. मानुबन्धान्मा ।
51. आतो युरिनि ।

52. आतो पुरिनि ।
53. ज्ञाजनोर्जाः ।
54. क्र्यादेर्ना ।
55. स्वार्थे यिन् ।
56. सदेः सीदः ।
57. शदेः शीयः ।
58. गतौ नलोपः ।
59. खनेः खाः ।
60. गुहोर्दीर्घः ।
61. दानादीनां सन् सार्वधातुके ।
62. द्विः सनि ।
63. अदादीनामनो रुक् ।
64. हनो धा ।
65. दूव्यादीनां वृद्धिस्तिसिमिषु ।
66. रुदादेरिः सार्वधातुके ।
67. स्वरवद् यः कृत् ।
68. ह्रस्वपूर्वयोर्हकारचवर्गयोः कवर्गः ।
69. तनादेरुः । or तनादेरुविकरणः ।
70. ब्रुजादेरी तिसिमिषु ।
71. ह्वादे द्विः ।
72. कवर्गहकारयोश्चवर्गः ।
73. पूर्वोऽभ्यासः ।
74. द्वयमभ्यस्तम् ।
75. अभ्यस्तस्य धुटः तृतीयाः प्रथमाः ।
76. ह्रस्वोऽभ्यासस्य ।
77. अभ्यासस्य ऋवर्णस्य इकारम् ।
78. अभ्यासाद् युः अभ्यस्ते ।
79. यनि दीर्घश्च ।
80. क्रृ ईर् यनि कृति च ।
81. ओ लोपो यनि ।
82. शमादेर्दीर्घो यनि ।
83. अनुदात्तङानुबन्ध आत्मनेपदम् ।
84. स्वरितानुबन्ध उभयपदम् ।
85. उदात्तानुबन्ध परस्मैपदम् ।
86. स्वादेर्नुविकरणः ।

87. ऋननुबन्धात् ईः ।
88. तुदादेरगृविकरणः ।
89. सकृद्बाधितो विधिर्बाधित एव ।
90. लृदनुबन्धान्नुः ।
91. इरनुबन्धान्नुः ।
92. ईदनुबन्धान्नुः ।
93. स्वरितानुबन्धान्नुः । (नुः) ।
94. यजां यवराणां खृतः संप्रसारणं कानुबन्धे च । यवराणां खृतः ।
95. खृणां यवरास्तृचि । खृणां यवराः ।
96. ऊदनुबन्धादिड् वा ।
97. ऋ इर् ।
98. इरुरो रीरूरौ ।
99. ऋत ईर् ।
100. ऋत ऊर् ।
101. खोर्धातोरियुवौ स्वरे ।
102. रधादेर्नम् ।
103. चतुर्थात् तथयोर्धः ।
104. अपृक्त एकवर्णः प्रत्ययः ।
105. न आ ई आत्मने पदे ।
106. क्तक्तवतू निष्ठा ।
107. निष्ठायास्तो नः ।
108. प्वादेर्ह्रस्वः ।
109. ग्रहादे रीट् ।
110. गृहाः पुंसि च भूम्न्येव ।
111. श्रादेर्वः ।
112. क्षिप्नादीनां न नो णः ।
113. चुरादेः इन् स्वार्थे ।
114. सर्वे हिंसार्थाश्चुरादौ परस्मैपदिनो ज्ञेयाः ।
115. लक्षेर्मीमन्मनाः ।
116. नथादेरिनि दीर्घः ।
117. निरः परो यतिः प्रतिदानधनधान्यविषयव्यतिहारार्थे चुरादौ वर्तते ।
118. चरादन्तिन् ।
119. नादन्तात् सन् ।
120. महादेरन्तः ।
121. प्रशस्तस्य श्रा ।

122. वृद्धस्य च ज्या ।
123. अन्तिकबाढयोर्नेदसाधौ ।
124. युवाल्पयोः कन् वा ।
125. स्थूलदूरयुवक्षिप्रक्षुद्राणामन्त्यस्वरादेर्लोपे गुणश्च नामिनाम् ।
126. बहोरियादि भू च ।
127. प्रियस्थिरस्फिरोरुगुरुबहुलतृ प्रदीर्घह्रस्ववृद्धवृन्दारकाणां प्र स्था स्फा वरागराबृंहा त्रप् द्राघ ह्रस वर्ष वृन्दाः ।
128. तद्वद् इष्ठेमेयस्सु बहुलम् ।
129. गुणवचनात् ।
130. अनाकौ णानुबन्धवत् ।
131. इन् णानुबन्धवत् ।
132. वृद्धिरादौ सणे ।
133. दाराः पुंसि भूम्न्येव ।
134. प्रयोज्य कर्तरि णिच् ।
135. नाम्न उपमानादाचारे आयङीयौ ।
136. आयङीययोर्लुक् ।
137. अकर्मकेभ्यो धातुभ्यो भावे कर्मणि यङ् स्मृतः ।

Out of these 137 *sūtras* the first two are quoted by Bhartṛhari in the *Svopajña-ṭīkā* of the *Vākyapadīya - Brahmakāṇḍa*. The third and the fourth *sūtras* are quoted by *Kaiyaṭa* in his *Mahābhāṣya-pradipa*. The remaining 133 have been collected by Pt. Yudhiṣṭhira Mīmāṁsaka from the *Kannada-ṭīkā* of Cannavīra on the *Dhātupāṭha* of Kāśakṛtsna. All of these *sūtras* may not be in the original form in which they were written by Kāśakṛtsna; some of them may be in the form of statements of the commentator bringing out the meaning of the original *sūtras*. Again, there might be at places errors and slips at the hand of the scribe as noted by Pt. Mīmāṁsaka. Still they contain much of the original material as can be seen from their comparison with the *Kātantra-sūtra*s. The students of Sanskrit Grammar would be grateful to Pt. Yudhiṣṭhira Mīmāṁsaka for the strenuous work he has carried out in bringing these *sūtras* of the Pre-Pāṇinian grammarians to light, for it is bound to throw much fresh light on the Pāṇinian *sūtras* themselves. It will also reveal some points and spots in the background against which Pāṇini wrote his famous *Aṣṭādhyāyī*. All these points we shall take notice of in the concluding chapter of this part.

THE GRAMMARIANS MENTIONED BY PĀṆINI

Ten grammarians have been mentioned by Pāṇini in his *Aṣṭādhyāyī*. We shall note them here in alphabetical order.

1. **ĀPI ALI**: Pāṇini mentions Āpiśali in 6.1.92. - 'वा सुप्यापिशलेः'. He is mentioned in the *Mahābhāṣya* also in 4.2.45 as एवं च कृत्वा आपिशलेराचार्यस्य विधिरुपपन्नो भवति । Other mentions about him are *Kāśikā* 7.3.86, *Nyāsa* on 4.2.45, Kaiyaṭa's *Mahābhāṣya-pradipa* 5.1.21.

The word Āpiśali has been derived in *Kāśikā* as अपिशलस्यापत्यमापिशलिराचार्यः, अत इञ् । Pālyakirti has derived it as अपिशलस्यापत्यम्, अत् इञ् । Then from आपिशल we get आपिशल्या (रुढादिगण P. 1.3.4). Vardhamāna in *Gaṇaratnamahodadhi* says : पिंशति इत्यौपादिक-कलप्रत्यये पिशलः, न पिशलः अपिशलः, तस्यापत्यम् ।

The word पिशल means क्षुद्र; hence अपिशल means महान्. Vardhamāna calls him कुलप्रधान. He is also known as Āpiśala, e.g. शिक्षा आपिशलीयादिका (काव्यमीमांसा, पृ. ३), तथेत्यापिशलीयशिक्षादर्शनम् (वृषभदेव वा. प. 105)

This shows that the original word taken here is *Āpiśala* and *cha* added to it. His sister is Āpiśalyā and is mentioned in *Kraudyadi-gaṇa* (4.1.80). Āpiśali-śāla is mentioned in *'Chatrādi-gaṇa'* (6.2.46).

Yudhiṣthira Mīmāṁsaka has noted at one place the *sūtras* of Āpiśali which have been quoted by various writers. They are:

1. उभस्योभयोऽद्विवचनटापोः ।
2. विभक्त्यन्तं पदम् ।
3. मन्यकर्मण्यनादरे उपमाने विभाषा प्राणिषु ।
4. चिरसाययोः मश्च प्रगप्राह्वयोरेच्च ।
5. धेनोरञः ।

6. शताच्च ठन्यतावग्रन्थे ।
7. शब् विकरणे गुण: ।
8. करोतेश्च ।
9. मिदेश्च ।
10. तुरुस्तुशम्यम: सार्वधातुकासु च्छन्दसि ।
11. ञमङणनम् ।

The *Pañcapādi Uṇādi* belongs to Āpiśali. We get there a *sūtra* ञमन्ताड्ड: (1.107). In this *sūtra ñam* is a *pratyāhāra*. In the *Āpiśala-Śikṣā*, we have ञमङणना: स्वस्थानानासिकास्थानाश्च । From these two references, Pt. Yudhiṣṭhira Mīmāṁsaka has surmised that the eleventh *sūtra* noted above must be a *Pratyāhāra-sūtra*.

There is a *kārikā* of Bhartṛhari as तदर्हमिति नारब्धं सूत्रं व्याकरणान्तरे । On this line Helārāja writes आपिशला: काशकृत्स्नाश्च सूत्रमेतन्नाधीयते (वा. प. 3). From this we can say that Āpiśali did not have the *sūtra* 'तदर्हम् ।'

Āpiśali did not have the *sūtra* नाज्झलौ, for, he took the *Ūṣmavarṇas* as having *Īṣadvivṛta-prayatna*. He says in his *Śikṣā* ईषद्विवृतकरणा ऊष्माण: । विवृतकरणा वा (3.7,8) Pāṇini on the other hand, took them as having *Vivṛta-prayatna*. Hence, he required the *sūtra* नाज्झलौ ।

The following are the views of Āpiśali noted in various works:

1. यथा आपिशलिना उक्तम् ऌऌ ऋॡवर्णयोर्दीर्घा (न) भवन्ति इति । quoted by अनन्तदेव in his भाषिक सूत्र व्याख्या.

2. एकवर्णकार्यं विकार:, अनेकवर्णकार्यमादेश: इत्यापिशलीयं मतम्, said by कविराज in his कातन्त्रटीका 2.3.37. Compare विकारो नाम वर्णात्मक आदेश: (शब्दकौस्तुभ)

3. तथा च आपिशलीय: श्लोक:
आगमोऽनुपघातेन, विकारश्चोपमर्दनात् ।
आदेशस्तु प्रसंगेन, लोप: सर्वापकर्षणात् ॥ - Durga in कातन्त्रवृत्ति

4. तथा चापिशलिः -
दन्त्योष्ठत्वाद्वकारस्य वहवृधव्यधां न भष् ।
उदूढौ भवन्ते यत्र यो वा प्रत्ययसन्धिजः ।
अन्तस्थं तं विजानीयात् शेषो वर्गीय उच्यते ॥
quoted by Sṛṣṭidhara in his commentary on Bhāṣāvṛtti.

5. सदृशत्वं तृणादीनां मन्यकर्मण्यनुक्तके ।
द्वितीयावच्चचतुर्थ्यापि बोध्यते बाधितं यदि ॥ - इत्यापिशलेर्मतम् । quoted by चतुर्थ्यापि Jagadīśa Tarkālaṁkāra in his *Śabdaśakti-prakāśikā*.

6. आपिशलिस्तु न्यङ्कोर्नैच् भावं शास्ति । न्याङ्कवं चर्म ।

7. स्वधा पितृतृप्तिरित्यापिशलिः ।
6th & 7th quoted by Ujjvaladatta in his *Uṇādisūtra-vṛtti*.

8. शश्वदभीक्ष्णं नित्यं सदा सततमिति सातत्ये इति अव्ययप्रकरणे आपिशलिः ।
quoted by Bhānuji Dīkṣita in his *Amarakośaṭīkā*.

9. आपिशलीयं मतं तु -
पादस्त्वर्थसमाप्तिर्वा ज्ञेयो वृत्तस्य वा पुनः ।
मात्रिकस्य चतुर्भागः पाद इत्यभिधीयते ॥ quoted by Durga in his commentary on *Kātantra-vṛtti*.

Out of the nine quotations given above the first and the sixth appear to be from Āpiśali's grammar and the second, third, fourth and fifth, though belonging to Āpiśali, are not his *sūtras* but, his opinions given by others. The last two appear to be from his *Kośa*.

From the above information, it becomes evident that there was a close relation between Pāṇini's grammar and the grammar of Āpiśali. Many *Saṁjñās*, *Pratyāhāras* and *Pratyayas* appear common to both, e.g. - We get in the above *sūtras* the *Saṁjñās* like *Dvivacana, Vibhāṣā, Guṇa* and *Sārvadhātukā*. These *saṁjñās* are found in Pāṇini also except that he has *Sārvadhātukam* instead of *Sārvadhātukā*. The *Pratyayas* mentioned in the above *sūtras* are *Ṭāp*, Than, and *Śap*. They are in Pāṇini also. Āpiśali's *Pratyāhāra* भष् (वहव्यधवृधां न भष्) as quoted by Sṛṣṭidhara) is the same in Pāṇini. The same can be said about the *Pratyāhāra* ञम्.

It appears that like Pāṇini, Āpiśali had a *Dhātupāṭha*, a *Gaṇapāṭha*, and an *Uṇādipāṭha* as appendices to his *Sūtrapāṭha*. These works are not available, but, there are the following references to those works.

(i) *Dhātupāṭha*: (a) In the *Mahābhāṣya* (P. 1.3.22) we get the following statement. अस्ति सकारमातिष्ठते । आगमौ गुणवृद्धी आतिष्ठते । The same statement is founc in the *Kāśikā* (P. 1.3.22). also, which has been explained by the *Nyāsa* as follows: सकारमात्रमस्ति धातुमापिशलिराचार्यः प्रतिजानीते । तथा हि न तस्य पाणिनेरिव 'अस् भुवि' इति गणपाठः । किं तर्हि ? 'स भुवि' इति सः पठति । आगमौ गुणवृद्धी आतिष्ठते एवं स प्रतिजानीते इत्यर्थः । This means that while Pāṇini reads अस् भुवि Āpiśali reads स भुवि. In the forms *asti*, *āsīt*, Āpiśali takes *guṇa* (अट्) as *āgama* in *asti*, while *vṛddhi* (आट्) as *āgama* in *āsīt*. Haradatta also writes: स्तः सन्ति इति सकारमात्रस्य दर्शनात् 'स भुवि' इत्येव धातुः पाठ्यः । अस्तीत्यादौ पिति सार्वधातुके गुणो विधेयः। आस्तामासन्न इत्यादौ आडागमः स्यादिति आपिशला मन्यन्ते । (P. 1.3.22)

(b) Skandasvāmī writes on the *Nirukta* 2.2: उषि जिघर्ति छान्दसौ धातू व्याकरणस्य शाखान्तरे आपिशलादौ स्मरणम् ।

(c) Vāmana writes in the *Kāśikā* इतरौ (रिहि लिहि) तु धातुषु न पठ्येते । कैश्चिदभ्युपगम्येते । (कैश्चिदिति आपिशलिप्रभृतिभिः - न्यास). Again तत्रान्तरे चत्वारो अपरे पठ्यन्ते - सहिमुहिरिहिलिहादयः । and तथा च तन्त्रान्तरे-निजिविजिष्वज् जिवर्गम), here also the *Nyāsa* writes तत्रान्तरे इति आपिशलेर्व्याकरणे ।

(d) Maitreyarakṣita writes about the root *tu* – तु छान्दसोऽयम् इत्यापिशलिः ।

All these references suggest the following points:

1. There was a *Dhātupāṭha* of Āpiśali,

2. The roots in some cases were differently read from those in Pāṇini's *Dhātupāṭha,*

3. This difference resulted in the difference of the *prakriyā,*

4. There were *Chāndasa-dhātus* also read in Āpiśali's *Dhātupāṭha,*

5. In Āpiśali's *Dhātupāṭha,* there were more roots than those in Pāṇini.

(ii) *Gaṇapāṭha*: There is the following statement in the *Mahābhāṣyadīpikā* of Bhartṛhari: इह त्यदादीनि आपिशले: किमादीनि अस्मतूपर्यन्तानि, तत: पूर्वापराधरेति...

Kaiyaṭa also says in the *Pradipa* त्यदादीनि पठित्वा गणे कैश्चित् पूर्वादीनि पठितानि । These references point to the existence of a *Gaṇapāṭha* in Āpisåali's Grammar.

(iii) *Uṇādisūtras*: Pt. Yudhiṣṭhira Mīmāṁsaka is of the opinion that the *Pañcapādī Uṇādisūtras* belong to Āpiśali while the *Daśapādī Uṇādisūtras* belong to Pāṇini. He says that the *Pratyāhāra* ञमङणनम् belongs originally to Āpiśali. The same is found in his *Śikṣā* also as ङमङणना: स्वस्थाना नासिकास्थानाश्च । While *Pāṇinīya Śikṣā* states them as ङञणनमा: स्वस्थाननासिकास्थाना: (शिक्षा-सूत्र 1.24). Āpiśali was required to form this *Pratyāhāra* to get the *saṁjñā* ञम्. This is used in the *Uṇādisūtra* ञमन्ताड्डः (पं.पा. 1.107, द.पा. 5.77). Now the *Pañcapādī* is earlier in time than the *Daśapādī*. Pt. Mīmāṁsaka, therefore, surmises that the *Pañcapādī* may belong to Āpiśali while the *Daśapādī* may be that of Pāṇini.

(iv) *Āpiśali-Śikṣā* : The following references point to the *Āpiśali-Śikṣā* :-

(1) एवमापिशले: पञ्चदशभेदाख्या वर्णधर्मा भवन्ति । (quoted by Y. Mīmāṁsaka as *Pāṇinīya-śikṣā Sūtra* in his *'History of Sanskrit Grammar,'* Part I, p. 143 6.4.5).

(2) 'शेषा: स्थानकरणा:' इत्यापिशलिशिक्षावचनात् । (The

Vaidikābharaṇa on the *Taittirīya Prātiśākhya* 2.46.)

(3) शिक्षा आपिशलीयादिका । - काव्यमीमांसा पृ. ३

(4) तथेत्यापिशलिशिक्षादर्शनम् । वृषभदेव on वाक्यपदीय.

(5) तथा चापिशलिः शिक्षामधीते - 'नाभिप्रदेशात् ... बाह्यप्रयत्नतः' - हैमशब्दानुशासन, स्वोपज्ञवृत्ति, 4.9-10.

Āpiśalīya Śikṣā has been published by Dr. Raghuveera.

2. **KĀŚYAPA**: Pāṇini refers to Kāśyapa in two *sūtras* viz. (1) तृषिमृषि-कृशेः काश्यपस्य (P. 1.2.25) and नोदात्तस्वरितोदयमगार्ग्य - काश्यपगालवानाम् (P. 8.4.67). In the *Vājasaneyī Prātiśākhya*, there is a *sūtra* लोपं काश्यपशाकटायनौ (4.5). Here Kāśyapa has been mentioned along with Śākaṭāyana and there is every likelihood that he may be a grammarian, and in the same way he has been mentioned by Pāṇini.

Pāṇini has a *sūtra* काश्यपकौशिकाभ्यामृषिभ्यां णिनिः । (P. 4.3.103) A *Vārtika* on this says काश्यपकौशिकग्रहणं कल्पे नियमार्थम् (म.भा. 42.16). This means that Kāśyapa was a *Kalpakāra*. The same might have been a grammarian also. No *sūtra* of Kāśyapa is available to us. *Vājasaneyi-Prātiśākhya* mentions that *Nipāta* is termed so by Kāśyapa. (निपातः काश्यपः स्मृतः। 1-8-51).

3. **GĀRGYA**: Pāṇini mentions Gārgya in the following three *sūtras*. अङ्गार्ग्यगालवयोः (P. 7.3.99); ओतो गार्ग्यस्य (P. 8.3.20); and नोदात्तस्वरितोदयमगार्ग्यकाश्यपगालवानाम् (P. 8-4-67).

Gārgya's opinions have been noted in the *Ṛk-Prātiśākhya*, and *Vājasaneyi-Prātiśākhya*. He has been mentioned in the *Nirukta*. Gārgya is credited with the *Padapāṭha* of *Sāmaveda* also. *Bṛhaddevatā* mentions Gārgya along with Yāska and Rathītara.

It appears that Gārgya mentioned by Yāska and Śaunaka is a *Nairukta*, while one mentioned by *Prātiśākhya* and Pāṇini is a *Vaiyākaraṇa*. It cannot be definitely said whether these two are one and the same. However, if they are one and the same then the *Padakāra* Gārgya and the grammarian Gārgya would be the same person. In that case we shall have to suppose that the grammar written by him was of a different nature than that of Pāṇini; for, his division of the Padas is peculiar. e.g. मित्र = मि+त्र; पुत्र = पुत् + त्र etc. According to Pāṇini they would form one *pada* without *avagraha*.

Differences of views between Gārgya and Śākaṭāyana have been mentioned in the *Nirukta*. One peculiarity of the *Padakāra* Gārgya has been noted in the following *Kārikā*.

पुनरुक्तानि लुप्यन्ते पदानीत्याह शौनकः ।
अलोप इति गार्ग्यस्य काण्वस्यार्थवशादिति ॥
Uvaṭabhāṣya on *Vājasaneya Prātiśākhya* 4. 117.

4. **GĀLAVA**: Pāṇini mentions Gālava in the following four *sūtras*. (1) इको ह्रस्वोऽङ्यो गालवस्य (P. 6.3.61), तृतीयादिषु भाषितपुंस्कं पुंवत् गालवस्य (P. 7.1.74), अड् गार्ग्यगालवयोः (P. 7.3.99), and नोदात्तस्व (P. 7.4.67) No work of Gālava on grammar is available. However, his opinion has been noted by Puruṣottamadeva as इकां यण्भिर्व्यवधानं व्याडिगालवयोरिति वक्तव्यम् । The *Mahābhārata, Śānti*, 342, 103, 104 mentions Gālava as the author of the *Kramapāṭha* and a *Śikṣā*., a *Nirukta*, the *Bṛhaddevatā* and the *Aitareya Āraṇyaka* also mention his views. Pt. Bhagavaddatta says that he was a pupil of Śākalya.

5. **CĀKRAVARMAṆA**: Cākravarmaṇa has been mentioned by Pāṇini in the *sūtra* ई चाक्रवर्मणस्य (P. 6-1-130) and also in the *Uṇādisūtra* कपश्चाक्रवर्मणस्य (पं.पा. 3-144 : द.पा. - 7-11). No work from him is available, but, his opinion has been noted in the *Śabdakaustubha* as follows: यस्तु कश्चिदाह चाक्रवर्मणव्याकरणे द्वयपदस्यापि सर्वनामताभ्युपगमात् तद्रीत्यायं प्रयोगः तदपि न । मुनित्रयमतेनेदानीं साधुत्वासाधुत्वविभागः । तस्यैव इदानींतनशिष्टैः वेदाङ्गतया परिगृहीतत्वात् ।

According to Cākravarmaṇa *Dvaya* is a *sarvanāma*. Hence the form द्वयेषाम् used by Māgha in *Śiśupālavadham*, 12.13. is justifiable according to *Cākravarmaṇa*. Pāṇini does not mention *Dvaya* as *sarvanāma* except in *jas*.

6. **BHĀRADVĀJA**: Bhāradvāja has been mentioned by Pāṇini in ऋतो भारद्वाजस्य (P.7.2.63). In P. 4.2.145. also the word Bhāradvāja occurs, but, according to the *Kāśikā*, it is the name of a territory and not a person. The *Taittirīya Prātiśākhya* mentions his opinion as अनुस्वारे अण्विति भारद्वाजः (17.3) and the *Vājasaneyi Prātiśākhya* says that *Ākhyāta* is *Bhāradvājaka* (भारद्वाजकमाख्यातम्).

We cannot form any idea of Bhāradvāja's grammar. However, we have in the *Mahābhāṣya* his *Vārtikas* as also *Bhāradvājīya Dhātus* in the *Siddhānta-kaumudī*. If those *vārtikas* are on the *sūtras* of Pāṇini, then their author must be later than Pāṇini and they cannot belong to Bhāradvāja mentioned by Pāṇini. These *vārtikas* are more extensive than those of Kātyāyana e.g. कात्यायन - घुसंज्ञायां प्रकृतिग्रहणं शिदर्थम् (P. 1.1.,20.56); भारद्वाज - घुसंज्ञायां प्रकृतिग्रहणं शिद्विकृतार्थम् । कात्या - युक्चिणोः प्रतिषेधे हेतुमण्णिश्रिब्रुआमुपसंख्यानम् । भार-युक्चिणोः प्रतिषेधे णिश्रिश्रन्थिग्रन्थिब्रुजा-मात्मनेपदाकर्मकमुपसंख्यानम् । (Also see P. 6.4.47; P..1.20; P. 3.1.89.) But if these *Vārtikas* are on the Bhāradvāja *Vyākaraṇa* then we have to say that there was a great similarity between Pāṇini's grammar and that of Bhāradvāja.

7. **ŚĀKAṬĀYANA**: Pāṇini mentions Śākaṭāyana in the following three *sūtras*:- (लङः शाकटायनस्यैव (P. 3.4.111), व्योर्लघुप्रयत्नतरः शाकटायनस्य (P. 8-3-18), त्रिप्रभृतिषुशाकटायनस्य (P. 8.4.50).

He is also mentioned at various points in the *Ṛk-Prātiśākhya* and the *Vājasaneyī Prātiśākhya*. Yāska has given his opinions at various places in the *Nirukta* and Patañjali mentions him as a grammarian. (cf. नाम च धातुजमाह निरुक्ते व्याकरणे शकटस्य च तोकम् (P. 3.3.1), अथ भवति कश्चिज्जाग्रदपि वर्तमानकाले नोपलभते । तद्यथा - वैयाकरणानां शाकटायनः रथमार्ग आसीनः शकटसार्थं यन्तं नोपलेभे । (P. 3.2.115)

That he is a grammarian of repute can be seen from the *Kāśikā* 1.4.83, 87 where it says अनुशाकटायनं वैयाकरणा: and उपशाकटायनं वैयाकरणा:

We know from the *Nirukta* that Śākaṭāyana, though a grammarian, held the theory of नामान्याख्यातजानि. It was perhaps for this reason that he was held in great esteem. Some of his theories have become controversial. Yāska, however, has many times defended Śākaṭāyana.

cf. अथानन्विते अप्रादेशिके विकारे पदेभ्य: पदेतराभ्यां संचस्कार शाकटायन:। एते: कारितं च यकारादिं च अन्तकरणमस्ते: शुद्धं च सकारादिं च । (नि. 1-13)

Śākaṭāyana's opinions have been found in the *Ṛk-Prātiśākhya, Vājasaneyī-Prātiśākhya, Ṛk-Tantra* and *Śaunakīya Caturadhyāyī* which says: समासावग्रहविग्रहान् पदे, यथोवाच छन्दसि शाकटायन:, तथा प्रवक्ष्यामि चतुष्टयं पदम् ।

Śākaṭāyana has been termed as *Ādiśābdika* (cf. शाकटायनसूरिस्तु व्याचष्टे स्मादिशाब्दिक:) (Keśava in नानार्थार्णवसंक्षेप)

Śākaṭāyana's grammar is not available, but, there is no doubt that he dealt with both the *Vaidika* and the *Laukika* words. According to Dr. Sūryakānta, *Ṛk-Tantra* is the work of Śākaṭāyana. The *Uṇādisūtras* also are ascribed to him. Pt. Y. Mīmāṁsaka, however, does not agree with this view.

One of the modes of the *Nirvacana* in case of Śākaṭāyana is that he derives words from many *Dhātus* (cf. शाकटायनाचार्यो अनेकै: धातुभि: एकमभिधानमनुविहितवान् । एकेन चैकम् । -) - (Durga, 1.13)

That this was the earlier mode of derivation can be seen from the *Brāhmaṇa* works, e.g. *Śatapatha* 14.8.41, *Maitrāyaṇāraṇyaka* 6.8.

Śākaṭāyana held the theory of त्रयी शब्दानां प्रवृत्ति:, as is said by the author of the *Nyāsa* at 3.3.1 तदेवं निरुक्तकारशाकटायनदर्शनेन त्रयी शब्दानां प्रवृत्ति:, जातिशब्दा; गुणशब्दा:, क्रियाशब्दा: इति ।

Almost all the grammarians count the *Upasargas* as twenty but, Śakaṭāyana adds *Accha, sárat,* and *antar* to them. (cf. अच्छ - श्रद् - अन्तरित्येतानाचार्यः शाकटायनः । उपसर्गान् क्रियायोगान् मेने ते तु त्रयोऽधिकाः (बृ.दे- 2.95). Pāṇini takes them as *'gati'* only, but, Kātyāyana treats them as *Upasargas* also. (cf. श्रत् - शब्दस्योपसंख्यानम् (म.भा. P. 1-4-58) अन्तःशब्दस्य अङि विधिः समासणत्वेषूपसंख्यानम् । (म.भा. P. 1.4.64)

8. **ŚĀKALYA**: Śākalya has been mentioned by Pāṇini in the four *sūtras* संबुद्धौ शाकल्यस्येतावनार्षे (P. 1.1.16); इकोऽसवर्णे शाकल्यस्य ऱ्हस्वश्च (P. 6-1-127); लोपः शाकल्यस्य (P. 8.3.19); सर्वत्र शाकल्यस्य (P. 8.4.51).

The *Ṛk-Prātiśākhya* and the *Vājasaneyī Prātiśākhya* also give his views. Śākalya and Śaunaka were perhaps closely related. In the *Kārtakaujapādi gaṇa* (P. 6.2.37) Pāṇini gives the word शाकल–शुनकाः । According to the *Kāśikā* it is a *Dvandva* of *Śākalyaśiṣya* and *Śaunaka-putra*. It is perhaps for this reason that we find Śaunaka basing all his ten *Anukramaṇīs* on the *Śākala Caraṇa*.

We get in the *Aitareya Brāhmaṇa* the following statement: यदस्य पूर्वमपरं, यद्वास्यांपरं तदेवास्य पूर्वम् । अहेरिव सर्पणं शाकल्यस्य न विजानन्ति (ऐ.ब्रा. 14.5). This shows that Śākalya was a very ancient writer.

Śākalya's work on grammar is not available. It is likely that he might have written both on *Vaidika* and *Laukika* words. Some hold that the rules which Pāṇini has mentioned as of Śākalya were based on Śākalya's *Padapāṭha* only. But that is not correct. The rule इकोऽसवर्णे शाकल्यस्य ह्रस्वश्च is based on the *Laukika- saṁhitā* and not the *Padapāṭha*. There is a reference to a certain rule of Śākalya in the following statement of Lakṣmīdhara. On the *Hārita-sūtra* जातपुत्रायाधानम् Lakṣmīdhara writes: जातपुत्रायाधानमित्यत्र जातपुत्रशब्दः प्रथमाबहुवचनान्तः । शाकल्यमताश्रयेण यकारपाठः । i.e. In the *sandhi* जातपुत्राः and आधानम् the *visarga* is changed to *yakāra* according to the Śākalya rule. This applies to the *laukika* field only.

9. **SENAKA**: This grammarian has been mentioned by Pāṇini in the *sūtra* गिरेश्च सेनकस्य (P. 5.4.11). We know nothing about him.

10. **SPHOṬĀYANA**: He has been mentioned by Pāṇini in the *sūtra* अवङ् स्फोटायनस्य (P. 6.1.123). On this the *Padamañjarī* writes: स्फोटो अयनं परायणं यस्य सः स्फोटायनः । स्फोटप्रतिपादनपरो वैयाकरणाचार्यः । ये त्वौकारं पठन्ति ते नडादिषु अश्वादिषु वा स्फोटशब्दस्य पाठं मन्यन्ते ।

If this be correct, then the theory of *Sphoṭa* which is of great importance to the grammarians goes to the pre-Pāṇinian period. *Hemacandra* says in the *Abhidhānacintāmaṇi* स्फोटायनस्तु कक्षीवान् । Keśava also states similarly in the *Nānārthārṇa-vasamkṣepa*. It seems that the real name of the grammarian was Kakṣīvān, Sphoṭāyana being his pen-name or nick-name.

According to Yudhiṣṭhira Mīmāṁsaka the name Sphoṭāyana is connected with the *Sphoṭa* in the *Vimāna-vidyā*. He bases his argument on the *Sūtra* चित्रिण्येवेति स्फोटायनः from Bhāradvāja's *Yantrasarvasva*. This *sūtra* has been commented upon as follows:- तदुक्तं शक्तिसर्वस्वे वैमानिकगतिवैचित्र्यादिद्वात्रिंशतिक्रियायोगे एकैव चित्रिणी शक्तिरलम् इति शास्त्रे निर्णीतं भवति इत्यनुभवतः शास्त्राच्च मन्यते स्फोटायनाचार्यः।

Chapter Six

FROM PADAPĀṬHA TO PĀṆINI

We shall now have a look at Pāṇini's *Aṣṭādhyāyī* against the background described in the last five chapters. Pāṇini's *Aṣṭādhyāyī* has been honoured as a *Vedāṅga*. Under the present state of Sanskrit grammar this honour does not go to any other system of Sanskrit grammar. The *Sūtra* वृद्धिरादैच् (अ. 1.1.1) is recited by orthodox Brāhmins when they perform *Brahmayajña* every day. This points to the fact that Pāṇini's grammar is not a grammar of the *Bhāṣā* only but it is equally a grammar of Vedic usage. Perhaps it is first a *Vyākaraṇa* of Vedic usage (hence वेदाङ्ग) and then of *Bhāṣā*. The *Sādhutva* of the Sanskrit words, whether *Vaidika* or *Laukika* has mainly to be determined by reference to Pāṇini's rules in general. It is very rarely that one has to refer to the opinions of other *Śābdikas*. By Pāṇini's grammar is meant his *Aṣṭādhyāyī* along with its appendices, viz, *Dhātupāṭha, Gaṇapāṭha, Uṇādipāṭha* and *Nāmaliṅgānuśāsana*, as interpreted by the *Vārtikas* of Kātyāyana and the *Mahābhāṣya* of Patañjali. These three, viz., Pāṇini, Kātyāyana and Patañjali are termed as *Munitraya*. And it is this *Munitraya* that determines the correctness, or otherwise, of the usage of words, as Bhaṭṭoji Dīkṣita says:-

मुनित्रयमतेन च इदानीं साधुत्वासाधुत्वविभागः । तस्यैव इदानींतनशिष्टैः वेदाङ्गतया परिगृहीतत्वात् ॥

And it is but natural; for it is only the Pāṇinian System of Sanskrit Grammar that deals extensively with both the *Vaidika* and the *Laukika* forms of words.

Patañjali opens his *Mahābhāṣya* with the words stating this fact. He says :

अथ शब्दानुशासनम् । केषां शब्दानाम् ? लौकिकानां वैदिकानां च ॥

Grammarians like Candra and others deal only with the *Laukika* words, while, all others like Bhoja deal with the *Vaidika* words only as appendix, which do not form part of the main body of their works.

The rules in the *Aṣṭādhyāyī* pertain both to the Laukika and *Vaidika* usages. The forms and usages which Pāṇini finds being used only in the *Vaidika* speech and not in the *Laukika* as they have become अप्रयुक्त are noted by him, by using the term *Chandasi*. The words and usages which are found only in the *Laukika* speech and not in the *Chandas* are noted by using the word *Bhāṣāyām*. These are special usages which pertain only to *Chāndasa* or to *Bhāṣā*. The rest of the rules pertain to the words and usages which are common to both. And such rules form the core of *Aṣṭādhyāyī*. It is for this reason that Pāṇini's work is a grammar of both *Vaidika* and *Laukika* speech at one and the same time. This fact is brought out in such statements as य एव वैदिकास्त एव लौकिकास्त एव तेषामर्थाः and the like. We have therefore to note that when Pāṇini framed his *Sūtras* he placed before him the whole language, viz., *Vaidika* and the *Laukika* together as one mass of words and usages.

Today we are accustomed to study Sanskrit grammar from Bhaṭṭoji's *Siddhānta-kaumudī*. There, we get two independent sections - a grammar of *Laukika* words and that of *Vaidika* words. At the end of the first section of *Laukika* words *Bhaṭṭoji* writes -

इत्थं लौकिकशब्दानां दिङ्मात्रमिह दर्शितम् ।
विस्तरस्तु यथान्यायं दर्शितः शब्दकौस्तुभे ॥

and he ends the second section by saying:-

इत्थं वैदिकशब्दानां दिङ्मात्रमिह दर्शितम् ।

This second section of the *Vaidika-prakriyā* includes the subsection of the Vedic words and usages which are found only in the *Veda* and not in the *Laukika* speech and the rules pertaining to *Svara*. This gives an impression that there are two different speeches and that the *Svara* pertains to the *Vaidika* words only and not to the *Laukika* speech. Even though this was the correct position in respect of the language in the days of Bhaṭṭoji, still such was not the case when Pāṇini wrote his *Sūtras*. In Pāṇini's days even the *Laukika* speech had an accent and that has been noted by him. The result has been that the students generally study the *Laukika* portion of the *Kaumudī* only and leave out the *Vaidika* portion. This type of study does not give us the correct idea of Pāṇini's *Aṣṭādhyāyī*. For instance, a student of the *Kaumudī* is under the impression that देवेन देवाभ्याम् देवै: are the only forms of तृतीया. He hardly knows that देवेभि: is also a form in तृतीया unless he studies the second part of the *Kaumudī*. The result has been that the student of today is acquainted not with the *Aṣṭādhyāyī* as Pāṇini has constructed it, but only with a portion of it.

Secondly, such students hardly know that Pāṇini explains to us not only the form of the words but its accent also both in case of the *Vaidika* and the *Laukika* words. We of today hardly know that in the days of Pāṇini even the *Laukika* words had accent. Thus, the students of grammar today do not study the whole of *Aṣṭādhyāyī* but only a portion of it, and hence they are not able to appreciate the work and skill of Pāṇini in framing the *Sūtras* and arranging them. True, that Pāṇini also talks of the *Chāndasa* words and the *Laukika* words, but, when he constructs his *Sūtras*, he takes the whole language as one mass of words and usages and does not deal with them in two different sections. For him the study of स्वरसंस्कार in respect of words is one single study whether the word is *Chāndasa* or *Laukika*.

The point will be clear from a few examples:

(1) Pāṇini says: अतो भिस ऐस् । बहुलं छन्दसि (P. 7.1-9,10). These two *Sūtras* point to the cases where ऐस् is substituted for भिस्. The meaning of the *Sūtras* is "after a nominal stem ending in अ, ऐस्

is substituted for the case-ending भिस्, and in the *Vaidika* speech this substitution takes place diversely." The import of these two *Sūtras* together is that such words as देव, राम, कृष्ण etc. have four forms in तृतीया. They are देवेन, देवाभ्याम्, देवैः, देवेभिः । All these four forms are found in the *Vaidika* speech. In the *Laukika* speech, however, देवेभिः is not found.

Now, if we keep these rules against the rule भिस ऐस् वा which is the rule of Kāśakṛtsna according to Yudhiṣṭhira Mīmāṁsaka we get a position in language when in the *Laukika* speech also both the forms देवैः and देवेभिः were in vogue. Gradually, the word देवेभिः appears to have gone out of use and only देवैः remained in use in the *Bhāṣā* by the days of Pāṇini.

(2) Today, for us the affixes अण् and अञ् which mean अ only do not make any difference. The same is the case with the affixes तव्यत् and तव्य meaning तव्य only. But for Pāṇini they are not the same; they are different affixes indicating different accents, e.g. there is a *Sūtra* उदक् च विपाशः (P. 4.1.74) by which the *Cāturarthika* affix अञ् (and not अण्) is laid down in case of nominal stems while denoting a well situated on the northern bank of the river Vipāśā. But, if we refer to the well situated on the southern bank, the affix अण् will be added. The affix अण् will indicate that the word is अन्त्योदात्त while the affix अञ् will make the word आद्युदात्त. The expression गौप्तः कूपः । will suggest well on the northern bank while गौप्तः कूपः will indicate the same on the southern bank. Likewise, the affix तव्य is आद्युदात्त, e.g. कर्तव्यम्. But, the affix तव्यत् is स्वरित e.g. कर्तव्यंम् ।

Such cases point to the minute distinction noted by Pāṇini and the importance attached by him to the accent as the *Kāśikā* says: महती हि सूक्ष्मेक्षिका सूत्रकारस्य.

(3) Not only in the case of the affixes, words and accents, but, even while framing the *Sūtras*, Pāṇini has treated the *Vaidika* and *Laukika* words and usages as one mass of words, e.g. the *sūtra* न ङिसम्बुद्ध्योः । (8.2.8) prohibits dropping of न् in

the case of the stems ending in न् when followed by the case affix ङि and in case of सम्बुद्धि. An example of सम्बुद्धि is राजन् which is both a *Laukika* and a *Vaidika* word. But, the example of ङि is found only in the *Veda*, such as परमे व्योमन् ।, the word form व्योमन् here being the form of locative, the affix ङि being dropped by सुपां सुलुक् P. 7. 1. 39. etc. Thus, in this *Sūtra,* a *Vaidika* usage and a *Laukika* usage are noted together in one and the same rule.

All these examples indicate that for Pāṇini, there is no *Vaidika* Sanskrit as different from the *Laukika* one as we suppose it to be, but for him it was one language which consisted of both, the *Chāndasa* usages and the *Bhāṣika* usages.

At one end of the grammatical activity there is the *Vaidika Padapāṭha* and at the other end there is Pāṇini's *Aṣṭādhyāyī*, and it is very interesting to note that the *Pada* concept of Pāṇini is intrinsically related to the *Vaidika Padapāṭha*. The Pāṇinian concept of *Pada* is completely based on the *Vaidika Padapāṭha*. We shall study this point in some detail, for that will throw much light on the import of the *Sūtras* and their relation to *Padapāṭha*.

The following *Sūtras* in the *Aṣṭādhyāyī* relate to the *Pada* as conceived by Pāṇini:-

1. सुप्तिङन्तं पदम् ।
2. नः क्ये ।
3. सिति च ।
4. स्वादिष्वसर्वनामस्थाने ।
5. यचि भम् ।
6. तसौ मत्वर्थे ।
7. अयस्मयादीनि छन्दसि (P. 1-4-14 to 20) and
8. प्रत्ययलोपे प्रत्ययलक्षणम् । (P. 1-1-62).

These *Sūtras* fall under the following groups:-

(i) *Pada-saṁjñā* applied to *Subanta* and *Tiṅanta* (P. 1-1-14).

(ii) *Pada-saṁjñā* applied to crude form when certain affixes follow (P. 1-4.15, 16, 17).

(iii) *Bha-saṁjñā* as exception to *Pada-saṁjñā* given under (ii) (P. 1.4.18, 19).

(iv) *Ubhaya-saṁjñā* of the words of *ayasmayādi* class in the *Chāndasa* (P. 1.4.20).

(v) *Pada-saṁjñā* of the *pūrva-pada* of *Samāsa* etc. (P. 1.1.62).

The purposes for which these definitions are framed are not the same in all cases. Thus all the functions for which *Subanta* and *Tiṅanta* are called *pada* cannot be held applicable in the case of words which are termed *pada* under other *Sūtras*. The term *pada* under *Sūtra*s P. 1.4.15, 16 and the term *Bha* under P. 1.4.19 have very limited functions. Certain questions therefore naturally arise. Why has Pāṇini used the same term for all these when the functions are different? He could have well invented other technical terms for each different function. Or, was there any common basis for all these in spite of their different functions on the strength of which he could term all of them as *pada*? Another question arises in respect of the extent of this *Saṁjñā*. It is stated that the *pada Saṁjñā* under P. 1.4.17 extends upto the affix *'kap'* in the *sūtra* उरःप्रभृतिभ्यःकप् । P. 5-4-151. How has this limit been fixed? The Commentators only say अत्र व्याख्यानमेव शरणम् । (the *Bālamanoramā* on P. 1.4.17). This can hardly satisfy an enquiring mind.

It should be noted at the outset that these *pada-saṁjñā*s of Pāṇini relate to two different positions in Sanskrit Grammar. The *Sūtra* सुप्तिङन्तं पदम् । (P. 1-4-14) relates to the *Subantas* and *Tiṅantas* i.e., the finished forms of words capable of being used in a sentence. The other *pada Saṁjñā* that is formed under the rest of the *sūtras* applies to the word-forms (शब्दरूप) undergoing the *Prakriyā*. To distinguish one from the other, the grammarians call the latter by the term 'अन्तर्वर्तिपदसंज्ञा,' though Pāṇini has not used the term himself. By this latter *saṁjñā*, we get what may be called *pada* within a *pada*.

A study of these *sūtras* in relation to *Vaidika-padapāṭha* may help us to get into the matter. The *padapāṭha* consists of an analysis of *Saṁhitā* into *padas* each given separately in the finished form. Each *pada* there is either a *subanta* or a *tiṅanta*. All these *padas* are covered by the *sūtra* सुप्तिङन्तं पदम् (P. 1.4.14). Now among these *padas* a number of them are again split up into two by placing an *avagraha* in between. Thus, we have रत्नऽधातमम् । ऋषिऽभिः । वीरवत्ऽ तमम् । उद्ऽवतः । धूःऽसु । and so on. These separated parts in a *pada* are termed as *padya* in *Ṛk Prātiśākhya*, a term explained by Uvaṭa as '*padāvayava*'. These correspond to the अन्तर्वर्तिपद of later grammarians, i.e. they are *pada* within a *pada*. Thus we find *samāsas* split up into two parts, certain case affixes separated from crude forms, and certain *pratyayas* separated from *prakṛtis*. It is interesting to note that the first of these two parts, i.e. *prakṛti*, in all these cases falls under the *pada-saṁjñā* according to Pāṇini, the *samāsas* by P. 1.1.6 (प्रत्ययलोपे प्रत्ययलक्षणम्), while other by P. 1.4.15 to 17. The *padyas* of the *Ṛk-Prātiśākhya*, therefore, correspond to the *pada* of Pāṇini under *sūtras* P. 1.4.15 to 17 and P. 1.1.61.

But such separation is not found in the case of all the *pratyayas* whatsoever, nor is it found in the case of all the *prakṛtis* where the same *pratyaya* is seen. Thus, we get पितृऽभ्यः with the affix separated, but, we get पितृन् which is not separated, though the *prakṛti* is the same. Likewise, we get ऋषिऽभिः with the affix separated but, we get पूर्वेभिः with the affix not so separated, though the affix is the same. If we study these forms carefully we find that the cases of non-separation do not fall under the category of *pada* as conceived by the *sūtras* P. 1-4-15 to 17.

On the other hand they fall under the category of '*Bha*' which, according to Pāṇini, is an exception to *pada*, or under अङ्गाधिकार which has distinct field from that of पदाधिकार. Thus the *pada saṁjñā* of Pāṇini under the *sūtras* P. 1.4.15 to 17, which is termed as अन्तर्वर्तिपद by later grammarians, and which is the same as *padya* of the *Prātiśākhya*, appears to have been developed from the *Padapāṭha* of the Vedic *Saṁhitās*. Perhaps, it is this concept of the Vedic *pada*, which Pāṇini utilises for explaining the forms of the *Bhāṣā* also, for य एव वैदिकास्त एव लौकिकाः, त एव तेषामर्थाः ।

Earlier than Pāṇini, the *padapāṭha* was subjected to study by the *Prātiśākhya*s of various schools. According to *Ṛk-Prātiśākhya,* the term *pada* is used to denote a *Subanta* or *Tiṅanta*, and the *Sandhi* rules initially relate to the *padasandhis* (*Ṛk. Pt.*II-42). All these rules, thereafter, are extended to *padyas* except those of *nati*, *upācarita, krama* and *svara*: पदवच्च पद्यान् ऋते नतोपाचरितक्रमस्वरान् (ऋ.प्रा. P. 1.61-62). We find in the *Aṣṭādhyāyī* of Pāṇini that all the rules corresponding to *nati*, *upācarita* and *krama* of the *Prātiśākhyas* are collected together under the *Adhikāra* अपदान्तस्य (P. 8.3.55). We may therefore legitimately surmise that the basis on which Pāṇini worked out his *padasaṁjñā* was the same as that of *Prātiśākhya* and was therefore based on the *Padapāṭha* of Vedic *Saṁhitās*.

In Pāṇinian grammar also the *pada-saṁjñā* is first applied to *Subanta* and *Tiṅanta* (P.1.4.14) and then it appears to have been extended to *padāvayavas* by the *sūtras* P. 1.4.15 to 17, for the purpose of *prakriyā*, though this extension has not been clearly stated. The *Prātiśākhyas* state the extension clearly. *Ṛk-Prātiśākhya* says: पदवच्च पद्यान् (1.61), while the *Yajuḥ Prātiśākhya* puts it as अवग्रहः पदान्तवत् (1.153). On both these Uvaṭa gives the following examples ऋषिऽभिः । (from *Ṛgveda*) and भरद्ऽवाजः, तिष्ठद्ऽभ्यः (from *Yajurveda*). It should be noted that Pāṇini also uses the word *avagraha* in the same sense at P. 8.4.26. Considering the similarity between the *sūtras* of Pāṇini and Kātyāyana, we may be allowed to infer that in *Aṣṭādhyāyī* also, in similar cases (and they are covered by *sūtras* P.1.4.15 to 17), the *padasaṁjñā* is an extended one for the purpose of *Prakriyā*.

The purpose of Pāṇini, however, was far more extensive than that of the author of the *Padapāṭha* or the authors of the *Prātiśākhyas*. It covered them and also went beyond them. The *padapāṭha* only stated that the word, e.g., मरुद्भ्य: in the Saṁhitā, should at the stage of *pada* be recited as मरुद्ऽभ्य:, the *Prātiśākhya* stated that you must allow an interval of a *mātrā* at the place of the *avagraha*. But, Pāṇini went beyond both of them. He subjected both the *Saṁhitā* forms and the *pada* forms of the Vedic text to minute study from the point of morphology; he arrived at the fact of जश्त्व etc. in this and other similar cases and finally framed the rule झलां जशोऽन्ते (P. 8.2.39) which was of universal nature. It is of interest to note that all the rules which apply to the formation of the *padas* from the *padyas* of the *Prātiśākhya* come under the topic of *Padādhikāra* of *Aṣṭādhyāyī* and those which are its exceptions are grouped in the *Aṣṭādhyāyī* under the topic of अपदान्तस्य. The *Padapāṭha* supplied the raw material for grammar, the *Prātiśākhyas* sifted and analysed it so far as their own schools were concerned, but Pāṇini constructed a science out of it. And he did it so successfully that not only did it explain the word formation relating to all the Vedic *Śākhās*, but, it also explained the same in popular speech. That is why Patañjali says: सर्वपारिषदं हि इदं शास्त्रम् (P. 6.3.14) and explains its scope saying अथ शब्दानुशासनम् । केषां शब्दानां लौकिकानां वैदिकानां च । *Mbh. Paspaśā*. Vol. I. P. 1.

This may now help us to understand why the expression स्वादिषु in the *sūtra* स्वादिष्वसर्वनामस्थाने (P. 1.4.17) has to be taken to mean from the affix सु of nominative case to the affix कप् in the *sūtra* P. 5.4.151. The point in that *sūtra*, as hinted by the *Tattvabodhinī*, is whether the स्वादि should be taken to mean सु of the nominative case and other case affixes, or it should be taken to mean सुप् of the locative case and other affixes that follow it.

In the first alternative, such Vedic *padas* उद्ऽवत:, मधुमत्ऽतंम: etc. cannot be explained as these affixes fall outside the scope of *Vibhakti pratyayas* and in the second alternative such *padas* as ऋषिऽभि: would not be explained as all the case affixes will not be covered by the expression. The expression स्वादि must be so taken to mean as would cover all the cases of *avagraha* in the *Vedic padapāṭha*, and that is possible only when we take स्वादि to mean the affixes beginning with the affix सु of the nominative case to the affix कप् in the *Sūtra* उर: प्रभृतिभ्य: कप् (P. 5-4-151), (of course with the exception of [illegible]). Taken in this way we are not required to say अत्र व्याख्यानमेव शरणम् ।

Thus it will be clear now as to how the Pāṇinian concept of the *Pada* is integrally related with the Vedic *Padapāṭha*.

Pāṇini, however, was not the first and the only grammarian to subject the *Padapāṭha* to such a scrutiny. On the other hand, his *sūtras* present to us the final result of the long and continuous investigations carried out by generations of earlier grammarians in the field of the Vedic *padas*. The *Aindra* School of Grammar, which is believed to be earlier than Pāṇini, defines *pada* as 'अर्थ: पदम् ।' Mahāmahopādhyāya K.V. Abhyankar has shown in his learned introduction to the Marathi edition of *'Patañjali's Mahābhāṣya'* (p.126), that this *Aindra* definition of the term *pada* was probably to explain the *Padapāṭha* itself, for as we have seen earlier the *pada* construction depended on *Sāmarthya*. This defintiion was lucid. But, Pāṇini rejected it, for it could not stand the scientific test. According to this definition the *padasaṁjñā* could be applied not only to the case-inflected words, the finite verbs and the *prakṛtis* in the *avagṛhīta padas*, but also to the *pratyayas*, as all these possess meaning. To apply *padasaṁjñā* to *pratyaya* was surely an anomaly. Pāṇini therefore, rejected this definition and formed new ones as सुप्तिङन्तं पदम् and स्वादिष्वसर्वनामस्थाने. These new definitions avoided the anomaly of the *pratyaya* being called a *pada*.

Pāṇini's definition of the *pada* is highly technical and is based purely on morphological considerations. It must not, however, be supposed that he ignored the semantic aspect of the *pada* which is present in the *Aindra* definition, simply because he rejected it. He is quite alive to it. Whenever he has to refer to the semantic aspect of the *pada*, he qualifies it by the term समर्थ (See e.g. समर्थः पदविधिः (P. 1.2.1) and समर्थानां प्रथमाद् वा (P. 4.1.82). He was thus able to explain satisfactorily all the aspects of the *pada*, the *pada* as appearing in the *Saṁhitā* text, the one appearing in the *padapāṭha*, and the one in its semantic aspect, without getting into any sort of anomaly. His *sūtra*s, therefore, serve to be most scientific statements of the grammatical investigation in respect of the *pada* as it appears in the Vedic as well as popular speech.

Āpiśali's grammar might have been of great help to Pāṇini in building up his own grammatical system. Pāṇini's indebtedness to Āpiśali has been clearly shown by M.M. K.V. Abhyankar (*op. cit.* pp. 130-133). Āpiśali defines *pada* as विभक्त्यन्तं पदम्. This must have served as a model for Pāṇini while framing his own definition as सुप्तिङन्तं पदम्. It is interesting to note that he names सुप् and तिङ् as विभक्ति (P. 1.4.104).

The *Prātiśākhyas*, the *Nairuktas* and the *Vaiyākaraṇas* all these have the Vedic *padapāṭha* as the basis of their enquiry. But their purposes were different. The aim of the *Prātiśākhya* was only to note the modifications which the *padādi* and the *padānta* letters undergo in the *Saṁhitā* recital. Their study ultimately gave us the *Sandhi* rules in respect of letters and accents. The *Nairukta*s principally concerned themselves with finding out the import of the *mantras*. For that they concerned themselves with the *Nirvacana* and showed us the ways and methods of etymology, for which they were required to acquaint us with what they called *Dhātu*s and *Nāmakaraṇa* better known as *pratyaya* in the later stage. The *Vaiyākaraṇas* in their *prakriyā* utilise the concepts from both these brother-investigators. Hence, they stand in between these two. For the purpose of finding out the import of the *padas*, they broke the *pada* into two viz. *Prakṛti* and *Pratyaya* and tried to explain the process by which the *pada* evolved in the form in which it was seen used in the language. For that they made extensive use of the *sandhi* rules. These *sandhi* rules which the *Prātiśākhyas* evolved in respect of the *padasandhis* were extended by the grammarians in application to the internal *sandhis* seen in the body of a *pada*. The *Pada-sandhi* of the *Prātiśākhyas* thus got turned into *Varṇa-sandhis* at the hands of grammarians and covered the cases of both external and internal *sandhis*. How the *pada-sandhis* ultimately got into *varṇa-sandhis* has been already explained with help of a few examples in the chapter on the *Prātiśākhya*.

The *Prātiśākhya* had nothing to do with the *artha* of the *pada*, but, the *Padakāras*, the *Nairuktas* and the grammarians were concerned also with the basis of their enquiry. The *Aindra* definition of *pada* as अर्थः पदम् is a semantic definition of it. Where we find two *padakāras* constructing *padas* differently, it is an indication of the fact that they understand the meaning differently. This has been hinted at by Skandasvāmin, when he says in connection with the *pada Āditya* as follows:-

विचित्राः पदकाराणामभिप्रायाः । केचिदुपसर्गविषयेऽपि नावगृह्णन्ति । यथा शाकल्येन अधिवासमिति नावगृहीतम् । आत्रेयेण तु अधि - वासम् इत्यवगृहीतम् ।

Now Yāska refers to a controversy between Śākaṭāyana and Gārgya in respect of whether the *Upasargas* have meaning. It is noted in the following words:

न निर्बद्धा उपसर्गा अर्थान् निराहुः इति शाकटायनः । नामाख्यातयोस्तु कर्मोपसंयोगद्योतका भवन्ति । उच्चावचा पदार्था भवन्ति इति गार्ग्यः । तद् य एषु पदार्थः प्राहुः इमे तम् । नामाख्यातयोरर्थविकरणम् ॥ (नि. 1.3).

Śākaṭāyana held that the *Upasargas*, unless they are joined with the nouns and verbs, have no meaning, i.e., they have no meaning of their own. They only add something more to the meaning of the word to which they are attached. Gārgya on the other hand, says that the *Upasargas* are *padas* and as such they have various meanings. Whatever meaning we see in them, the *Upasargas* have that meaning and that meaning of the *Upasarga* changes the meaning of nouns and verbs.

Here, we get an indication that according to Gārgya the *Upasargas* are *padas* and have their own meaning. It is interesting to note in this context that in the *Sāmaveda-padapāṭha* (which is ascribed to Gārgya) we do get *Upasargas* as separate *padas*. A comparative view of the same *padas* as understood by Śākalya and Gārgya will make it clear. See for example :-

Padas found in *Saṁhitā*	*Pada* as treated by Śākalya	*Pada* as treated by Gārgya
परीणसि	परीणसि	परि । नसि
दुरोणे	दुरोणे	दुः । ओने
दूरात्	दूरात्	दुः । आत्
उत्सः	उत्सः	उत् । सः
समुद्रम्	समुद्रम्	सम् । उद्रम्
समत्सु	समत्सु	सम् । अत्सु
समिद्भिः	समित्ऽभिः	सम् । इद्भिः
विषुवतः	विषुऽवतः	वि । सुवतः
सूनृतावती	सूनृतावती	सु । नृतावती
प्राणः	प्राणः	प्र । आनः
दुरोणयुः	दुरोणऽयुः	दुः । ओनयुः

Such a division of *padas* has helped grammarians a lot. We find here that the *padas* समित्ऽभिः, विषुऽवतः, दुरोणऽयुः form the cases of स्वादिष्वसर्वनामस्थाने. If we look at Gārgya's division, we find there that he has treated the *upasarga* as an independent *pada*, but, has nowhere separated the *pratyaya* from the *prakṛti*. The controversy about whether *Upasargas* are वाचक or द्योतक thus has its beginning at the stage of *padapāṭha* itself as is seen hinted at by Śākaṭāyana and Gārgya.

The comparison of certain *padas* of the *Sāmaveda* with Yāska's *Nirvacana* and the Grammarians' derivation clearly shows how those three are integrally related to one another.

The following examples will make the point clear:-

(1) स्वस्ति Gārgya divides the *pada* स्वस्ति as सु । अस्ति । Yāska says स्वस्ति । सु अस्तीति (नि. 3.21). An *Unādi Sūtra* says सावसे: (5.620) - सौ उपपदे अस भुवि इत्यस्मात् ति प्रत्यय:।

(2) चन्द्रमा: According to Gārgya चन्द्र । मा: । According to Yāska - चन्द्रो माता । चन्द्रं मानमस्येति वा (11.5); According to the *Uṇādi* चन्द्रे मो डित् (667) चन्द्रपदात् माङो असि: स्यात्, स च डित् ।

(3) अद्भुतम् According to Gārgya अद् । भुतम् । According to Yāska, इदमपि इतरत् अद्भुतम् । अभूतमिव अन्यस्य । According to *Uṇādi* अदि भुवो डुतच् (679) 'अद्' इत्यव्ययम् आकस्मिकार्थे । अस्मिन्नुपपदे भूधातो: डुतच् स्यात् । डित्त्वात् टिलोप: ।

(4) दूरात् - According to Gārgya दु: । आत् ।, According to Yāska दूरं कस्मात् । द्रुतं भवति । दुरयमिति वा । According to *Uṇādi* दुरीणो लोपश्च (177) - इण् गतौ इत्यस्मात् दुरित्युपपदे रक् स्यात् । धातोर्लोपश्च। रो रि, ढ्रलोपे इति दीर्घ: ।

(5) उच्चा According to Gārgya उद् । चा । According to Yāska उच्चैरुचितं भवति (4.24). According to *Uṇādi* ''उदिचेर्डैसि । (690) उदुपपदे चे: डैसि प्रत्यय: (उच्चै:) ।

(6) सखि According to Gārgya स । खि । According to *Uṇādi* समाने ख्य: । स चोदात्त: (576) - समानशब्दे उपपदे ख्या इत्यस्मात् इण् स्यात्, समानस्य च उदात्त: स इत्यादेश: । स च इण् डित् स्यात् ।

(7) उदरम् According to Gārgya उ । दरम् । According to *Uṇādi* 'उदि दृणातेरजलौ' पूर्वपदान्त्यलोपश्च (697) उदि उपपदे दृ विदारणे इत्यस्मात् अच् अल् इति प्रत्ययौ स्त: । उदो दकारस्य लोपश्च ।

Such examples can be multiplied. The above examples will give us an idea as to how in respect of व्युत्पत्ति also, *Vyākaraṇa* is integrally related to *padapāṭha*. The examples are taken from

Uṇādisūtras which belong to the Pāṇinian system (उणादयो बहुलम्- P.3.3.1).

How did the grammarians analyse the *padas,* how did they arrive at the *Pratyayas* of various types and how did they build up the rules? In the absence of any pre-Pāṇinian work of grammar, we have simply to depend on surmise.

The method of analysing the *pada* into प्रकृति and प्रत्यय had been already hinted at in the *Taittirīya Saṁhitā*. Indra divided the *pada* into प्रकृति and प्रत्यय. This is a grammarian's method of analysing *pada*. He takes the *pada* as used in the *Padapāṭha* and divides it into प्रकृति + प्रत्यय as many times as is necessary till he gets at the root. Let us take the *pada* प्रजाऽवती: for example:

(1) The first division will be of the *Prātipadika* and case affix. Thus we have प्रजावती + अस् (जस्).

(2) The *Prātipadika* प्रजावती can still be divided into प्रातिपदिक and स्त्री प्रत्यय. Thus प्रजावत् + ई (ङीप्).

(3) The *Prātipadika* प्रजावत् can still further be divided into प्रातिपदिक and तद्धित प्रत्यय. Thus प्रजा + वत् (मतुप्).

So, first the *Vibhakti-pratyaya* is separated, then, the *Strī-pratyaya* and then *Taddhita-pratyaya*. It is interesting to note that Pāṇini has given the *pratyaya*s in the 4th and 5th chapters which are attached to *Prātipadika* in this very order, i.e. सुप्, स्त्रियाम् and तद्धिताः ।

(4) The *Prātipadika* प्रजा is a *Kṛdanta*. It is capable of being further divided - प्रजा is a word in feminine gender (i) Hence the first division will be the base प्रज and feminine affix आ (टाप्). (ii) The base प्रज appears to be related in sense with the root जन् with प्र as an *Upasarga*. So the further division will be प्र + जन् + अ (ड). So the complete analysis of the *pada* प्रजावती: will be as follows:- प्र + जन् + अ + आ + वत् + ई + अस्.

Now, at this stage, we have to explain modifications at two places - one, that जन् + अ + आ is modified to जा and second, that ई + अस् is modified to ईः. Pāṇini explains this modification by adding the *anubandha* ड् to अ in the case of अ, and by the rule प्रथमयोः पूर्वसवर्णः p. 6.1.102 in the case of ई + अस्. According to the Pāṇinian method the analysis would be:-

प्र + जन् + ड + टाप् + मतुप् (changed to वत्) + ङीप् + जस्.

This is the analysis of the *pada* प्रजावतीः. By joining these factors according to *Sandhi*-rules, we can rebuild the *pada* प्रजावतीः. Thus Mahidhara says:-

प्रजावतीः । 'उपसर्गे च संज्ञायाम्' (P. 3.2.99) इति जनेर्डप्रत्ययः, ततः टाप् । तेन सह एकादेशेऽपि उदात्तान्तः प्रजाशब्दः। तस्मात् 'तदस्यास्ति आसीत्' इति मतुप् (P. 5.2.94) 'मादुपधायाश्च मतोर्वोऽयवादिभ्यः' (P. 8-2.9) इति मस्य वः । 'उगितश्च' (P. 4.1.6) इति ङीप् । मतुप्ङीपोरनुदात्तत्वात् प्रजाशब्द स्वर एव । 'वा छन्दसि' (P. 6-1-106) इति पूर्वसवर्णदीर्घत्वम् ।

Here, the *pada* प्रजावतीः has been fully explained in respect of the base, the affixes and the modification in respect of स्वरसंस्कार.

This is about the प्रकृतिप्रत्ययविभाग conceived by the grammarian in the study of the *pada* which is actually found being used in the language. This is the morphological aspect of grammar. The other aspect is semantic, pertaining to the breaking of the sentence which is the unit of language into *padas*. The breaking of the sentence into *padas* is based on सामर्थ्य as has been explained in the second chapter dealing with the *Padapāṭha*. Now, let us look at the whole process in the grammatical activity with the help of an example:-

यो जात एव प्रथमो मनस्वान्

देवो देवान् ऋतुना पर्यभूषत् ।

This is a sentence uttered by the *Veda* and it is in the *Saṁhitā* form and as such it is a unit of language. We have now to understand it in its full implication.

(i) The first step will be to divide this sentence into the *padas*. The *padas* will be:

य: । जात: । एव । प्रथम: । मनस्वान् ।
देव: । देवान् । ऋतुना । परिऽअभूषत् ॥

This is done on the basis of सामर्थ्य and will be studied by reference to the case relations (कारकसंबंध) and the *Samāsa-vṛtti*. The modifications of विसर्ग will be explained by rules of पदान्तसन्धि.

(ii) The second step will be that we would take each *pada* independently and break it into parts by the method of प्रकृतिप्रत्ययविभाग, as exemplified above in the case of the *pada* प्रजावती:।

(iii) The third step would be to study modifications that the letters have undergone. This is termed as the *Prakriyā* in grammar. These modifications might be of the nature of लोप, आगम, आदेश etc.

Now let us look at Pāṇini's *Aṣṭādhyāyī*.

(i) The second *Adhyāya* deals with the *pada* as a member of the sentence and its study is based on the principle of *Sāmarthya*. See समर्थ: पदविधि: (2.1.1). This covers the whole of the second chapter.

(ii) The 3rd, 4th and 5th chapters deal with the *pratyayas* of various types. See प्रत्यय:, परश्च, (3.1.1,2). This governs the chapters 3,5 and 6 (अधिकारोऽयं आ पञ्चमाध्यायपरिसमाप्ते: ।). The topic of these three chapters is treatment of प्रकृति - प्रत्ययविभाग. The third chapter deals with the *pratyayas* which are found applied in the case of *Dhātus* and the fourth and the fifth deal with the *pratyayas* in the case of the *prātipadikas*. The order of the *pratyayas* which come after the *prātipadikas* is the same in which we would separate them from the given *pada*, i.e. *vibhaktipratyayas* are given first, then come the *strīpratyayas* and *taddhitapratyayas* come last.

Thus, the order of Pāṇini's *Aṣṭādhyāyī* has close similarity with the order which we would follow in the actual study of the *Vedic Saṁhitā* and the *Padapāṭha*. This fact throws all the more light on the integral relation of Vedic *padapāṭha* and Grammar. It also makes the study of the *sūtras* more interesting and alive.

(iii) The remaining chapters of the *Aṣṭādhyāyī* deal with the प्रक्रिया and treat of लोप, आगम, आदेश, वर्णविकार and स्वर modifications and the rest. This makes the study of words complete. The first chapter deals with *Saṁjñās* and *Paribhāṣās* which are necessary to understand the method and technique of Pāṇinian system. Thus, in about four thousand *sūtras*, Pāṇini explains the nature and structure of the words in Sanskrit language both Vedic and popular.

Today we are generally accustomed to study Pāṇinian Grammar through *Siddhānta-kaumudī*. We first study the *Laukika* section of the *Kaumudī*. Those who are not interested in the Vedic study and are satisfied with the study of the *Laukika* Sanskrit such as *Kāvyas*, dramas etc. complete their study of Grammar with the *Laukika* section of the *Kaumudī* and do not touch the *Vaidika* section consisting of *Vaidika-prakriyā* and the *Svara-prakriyā*. Such students read only part of the *Aṣṭādhyāyī* and leave out about 600 *sūtras*. Hence, they are unable to fully grasp the import of the various *sūtras* and to fully appreciate the skill and genius of Pāṇini. I give here a few examples which will bring out the correctness of my statement:-

(1) Pāṇini explains the word कृषीवल as कृषि + वलच्. The affix वलच् is added to the word कृषि in the sense of मतुप् by the *sūtra* रजःकृष्यासुतिपरिषदो वलच् (P. 5-2-112). When this affix follows, the short vowel at the end of the base is lengthened by the *sūtra* 'वले'

(P. 6-3-118). We get the form as कृषि + वलच् (P. 5-2-112) = कृषी + वलच् (P. 6-3-118) = कृषीवल: । In this form the word is used in the language.

Now, this *sūtra* वले (P. 6-3-118) comes under संहिताधिकार by the *sūtra* संहितायाम् (P. 6-3-114). It, therefore, means that whenever the words कृषि and आसुति occur in the *Saṁhitā*, they will be recited or pronounced as lengthened. This naturally suggests that when not in the *Saṁhitā* these words would not be lengthened, even when followed by the affix वलच्. Such a position can never be obtained in the *Bhāṣa* for the word used there will always be in the form कृषीवल: and आसुतीवल:. They will never be used as कृषि-वल and असुति-वल. But, in the *padapāṭha,* we have such a position. Thus we have in the *Ṛgveda* बह्वन्नामकृषीवलाम् (*Ṛg.* x-146-6) where the *padas* are बहुऽअन्नाम् । अकृषिऽवलाम् । Here the affix वलच् is separated by the *avagraha* and hence the word अकृषि is shortened. The *sūtra,* therefore, relates to the position of the word कृषि in the *Saṁhitā-pāṭha* and the *padapāṭha*. As a matter of fact, this *Saṁhitādhikāra* relates to the words and positions in the Vedic *Saṁhitās*. The *Kāśikā*, while explaining this *sūtra* संहितायाम् (P. 6.3.114) has given the examples from the Vedic *Saṁhitās* and has made the position quite clear. It says:

संहितायाम् (P. 6-3-114) - यदित ऊर्ध्वमनुक्रमिष्याम: संहितायामित्येव तद्वेदितव्यम् । वक्ष्यति द्वचोऽतस्तिङ: इति । विद्मा हित्वा सत्पतिं शूर गोनाम् । संहितायामिति किम् । विद्म । हि । त्वा । सत्पतिम् । शूर । गोनाम् ।

In the *Prakriyāsarvasva,* Nārāyaṇabhaṭṭa also remarks अधिकारोऽयम् छन्दस्येव सफल: इति हर: ।

(2) The *sūtra* अणोऽप्रगृह्यस्यानुनासिक: । (P. 8.4.58) lays down that an अण् vowel, not being a *pragṛhya* and standing at the *avasāna* is optionally nasalised, e.g. दधि-दधिँ, मधु-मधुँ अप्रगृह्यस्याणो अनुनासिको वा, as stated by Bhaṭṭoji. The *Kāśikā* also has a similar note with additional example कुमारी - कुमारीँ. What is the import of this option? Candra (P. 8-4-150) and Puruṣottamadeva, writing

not on the *Vaidika* but on the *Laukika Bhāṣā* also dealt with this rule and after giving the above examples, as are found in the *Kāśikā* and the *Kaumudī* added such ones as कर्म-कर्मं, खट्वा-खट्वाँ. Bhoja also includes this *sūtra* in the *Laukika* section of his grammar (P. 7.6.168). It, therefore, appears that this option is treated by these writers as referring to the *Laukika Bhāṣā*. What does this indicate? Was there in the *Bhāṣā* a tendency of nasalising a vowel standing at the *avasāna*? If so, shall we be allowed to recite the lines as

आसीद्राजा नलो नाम वीरसेनसुतो बलीँ ।

or

याहीति जन्यानवदत् कुमारीँ ।

The examples given by these writers do not give us any guidance regarding the import of this *sūtra* or the usage of that type if any. Both Kātyāyana and Patañjali are silent on this *sūtra*.

We can, however, get a clue to this problem by referring this *sūtra* to the Vedic usage, as recorded by the *Prātiśākhyas*. We have, for example, the following two *sūtras* in the *Ṛk-Prātiśākhya*:-

अष्टावाद्यानवसानेऽप्रगृह्यान्
आचार्या आहुरनुनासिकान् स्वरान्
तत् त्रिमात्रे शाकला दर्शयन्ति
आचार्यशास्त्रापरिलोपहेतवः ॥ (1.26)

The *Ācāryas* maintain that the first eight vowels, where they occur at the *avasāna* and are not *pragṛhya*, are nasalised (63). The followers of Śākalya, however, exhibit that nasalisation only in the case of vowels having three *mātrās* (i.e., *pluta* vowels), in order to prevent the loss of (or the respect for) the teaching of the *Ācāryas*.

Pāṇini's *sūtra* corresponds to the first rule quoted above, except that he does not include ऋ in the vowels to be optionally nasalised. The examples as given by *Uvaṭa* are: ईड्यो नूतनैरुतँ (*Rg.* 1.1.2), इन्दवो वामुशन्ति हिँ (ऋ. 1.2.4) but not in सुतानां वाजिनीवसू 1.2.5) where the ऊ is a *pragṛhya*. The next *Prātiśākhya*-rule says the *Śākala*s do not follow this rule of the *Ācāryas* except in the case of *pluta* vowels standing at the *avasāna*. The example of this type is न त्वा भीरिव विन्दतीइँ (Ṛg. 10.145.1). This indicates that while the *Ācārya*s desired to resort to nasalisation of vowels at the *avasāna*, the *Śākala*s did not universally favour that practice except in the case of the *pluta* vowels. Hence arose an option which Pāṇini has recorded in the *sūtra* under consideration. The *Sūtra*, therefore, has bearing on the Vedic modes of recital. The *Taittirīya Prātiśākhya* also refers to this option in the *Sūtra* अप्रग्रहा समानाक्षराणि अनुनासिकानि एकेषाम् (15.6). It will be of interest to note the *Māhiṣeya-vṛtti* on this, which says: एकेषामाचार्याणां यानि समानाक्षराणि अप्रग्रहाणि, तानि अनुनासिकानि भवन्ति। यथा दधिँ, मधुँ (तै.सं. 2.2.3)। अप्रग्रह इति किम्। वैष्णवी इति (1.3.2) हनू इति। (6.2.11). Here also the reference is to the optional mode of reciting *padas* in the *padapāṭha*.

It is interesting to note that these examples दधिँ and मधुँ are found in the *Kāśikā* and the works of Bhaṭṭoji, Candra and Puruṣottama. Will it be wrong if we say that these had become standard examples (मूर्धाभिषिक्तान्युदाहरणानि) and the commentators used them to illustrate the *sūtra* technically only?

(3) Let us take the case of the *sūtra* लोपः शाकल्यस्य (P. 8.3.19). This *sūtra* is explained in the *Siddhānta-kaumudī* as अवर्णपूर्वयोः पदान्तयोः यवयोः वा लोपोऽशि परे। Here the word शाकल्यस्य has been rendered by वा only. This indicates that according to Bhaṭṭoji this is a simple option. This is all right so far as the *Laukika Bhāṣā* is concerned. But, here, we may naturally ask that if शाकल्यस्य means only वा then why has Pāṇini used the name शाकल्यस्य? He would have better read the *sūtra* as लोपो वा. That would have made the *sūtra* shorter and clearer. We wonder as to why he should read शाकल्यस्य instead of वा if he has to state only an option.

Now, let us read it in reference to the Veda. In the famous पुरुषसूक्त a *mantra* reads in the *Ṛgveda*:

मुखं किमस्य कौ बाहू का ऊरू पादा उच्येते ।

The *Padapāṭha* of the *Saṁhitā* का ऊरू पादा उच्येते is given as कौ । ऊरू । पादौ । उच्येते. In the *Saṁhitā* these *padas* are read as का ऊरू पादा उच्येते. This is explained by the *Ṛk-Prātiśākhya* as उत्तमौ च (2.25) (स्वरोदयौ आकारमापद्येते) meaning that the vowels ऐ and औ at the end of the *pada* when followed by a vowel are recited as आ in *Saṁhitā*, e.g. कौ + ऊरू = का ऊरू; पादौ + उच्येते = पादा उच्येते । The example of ऐ is अन्वेतवा रु, the *padas* there being अन्वेतवै । ऊ इति. This is पदवृत्तिसन्धि of the *Ṛk-prātiśākhya*. It does not give the *prakriyā* but only the final position in *Saṁhitā*. Now, Pāṇini gives the *prakriyā* as follows:- का + ऊरू = काव् + ऊरु (एचोऽयवायाव:) = का ऊरू (लोप: शाकल्यस्य).

The लोप is according to Śākalya, and Śākalya is the *Padakāra* of the *Ṛgveda*. This naturally suggests a question. Is there any position in the Veda where the व् is not dropped? And we get a reply when we read the पुरुषसूक्त in the *Taittirīya Śākhā*. It reads: कावूरू पादावुच्येते । We are satisfied. So, the *sūtra* लोप: शाकल्यस्य implies that if you belong to *Śākala Śākhā,* you have to say का ऊरू पादा उच्येते. But, if you belong to *Taittirīya Śākhā* you must say कावूरू पादावुच्येते. The *Kāśikā* has brought out this implication clearly. It says वकारयकारयो: पदान्तयो: अवर्णपूर्वयो: लोपो भवति शाकल्यस्याचार्यस्य मतेन ।

So, here the option gets turned into व्यवस्थितविभाषा. The *Vyavasthā* lies in the fact that य् and व् are heard in the *Taittirīya-pāṭha*; it is not heard in the *Śākala-pāṭha* and it is लघुप्रयत्नतर according to Śākaṭāyana (P.8.2.18) which perhaps was according to *Sāmaveda-pāṭha*.

The above three examples will make it clear as to why we have to refer to the Vedic *Saṁhitā* and the *Padapāṭha* to have full appreciation of the Pāṇinian *Sūtras*.

(4) Apart from this the commentators have gone to the extent of saying that some of the Pāṇinian *sūtras* were superfluous and could well have not been written. Thus, Bhaṭṭoji Dīkṣita feels that the *sūtras* P. 8-4-49 to 52 need not have been written at all. ''यरोऽनुनासिक' इति सूत्रात् वा ग्रहणमनुवर्तते इति ''नाज्झलौ'' इति सूत्रे कैयटः । एवं च 'सर्वत्र शाकल्यस्य' इति सूत्रं तत्प्रपञ्चभूतं च पूर्वोत्तरसूत्रद्वयं च नारंभणीयमिति भावः ॥

Thus, he remarks in the *Prauḍha-manoramā* in the context of the द्विर्वचनसन्धि. To grasp his criticism, it is necessary to go into some detail regarding this *sandhi*.

A द्विर्वचनसन्धि is the result of reduplication of a consonant in the *Saṁhitā* form, e.g. the *sandhi* of सुधी + उपास्यः results in सुध्ध्युपास्यः where the consonant ध् in सुधी undergoes reduplication. The *sūtras* pertaining to this topic are given in the *Aṣṭādhyāyī* in the following order:-

1. अचो रहाभ्यां द्वे ।
2. अनचि च ।
3. नादिन्याक्रोशे पुत्रस्य ।
4. शरोऽचि ।
5. त्रिप्रभृति शाकटायनस्य ।
6. सर्वत्र शाकल्यस्य ।
7. दीर्घादाचार्याणाम् । (*Aṣṭ.* 8-4-46-52)

These seven *sūtras* fall into two groups. The first two *sūtras* state the conditions under which reduplication of consonants takes place. The remaining five *sūtras* state where and according to which grammarians it does not take place. Occasions for reduplication given by Pāṇini are as follows:-

(1) (a) There is a reduplication of a consonant in the यर् *Pratyāhāra*, when it follows the letter र् or ह् which is itself following a vowel (अचो रहाभ्यां द्वे). (b) There is a reduplication of the consonant in the यर् *pratyāhāra* when that letter follows a vowel, but, is not followed by a vowel (अनचि च).

(2) These two rules are followed by two prohibitions, which are: (a) there is no reduplication of the letter त् of the word पुत्र when the word आदिनी follows and the sense is that of censure, नादिन्याक्रोशे पुत्रस्य, and (b) *śar* letters are not reduplicated when a vowel follows (शरोऽचि).

(3) These prohibitions are followed by special views of three different grammarians. They are: (a) When there is a conjunct consonant consisting of three letters or more, then there is no reduplication in respect of any letter of the conjunct, according to Śākaṭāyana, (b) Śākalya does not favour any type of reduplication at all, and (c) according to the *Ācāryas*, there is no reduplication when a consonant follows a long vowel.

The rules अचो रहाभ्यां द्वे and अनचि च which ordain reduplication of consonants under certain conditions on the one hand, and the rule सर्वत्र शाकल्यस्य on the other, being contradictory provisions, there results for us an option. This option can be secured in another way also. The rule अचो रहाभ्यां द्वे is preceded by the *sūtra* यरोऽनुनासिकेऽनुनासिको वा (P. 8.4.45). The word यर् from this *sūtra* is carried over (अनुवृत्त) to the next *sūtra*. If along with the word यर् we carry over the word वा also, we can secure the desired option. By such *anuvṛtti,* we can have अचो रहाभ्यां (यरो) द्वे (वा) and (अचो यरो द्वे वा) अनचि.

Bhaṭṭoji in his *Śabda-kaustubha* refers to these two ways of securing this option. He says: अनचि च इति द्वित्वस्यापि वैकल्पिकत्वात् । तत्र द्वित्वस्य वैकल्पिकत्वं 'यरोऽनुनासिकेऽनुनासिको वा' इत्यतः 'वा' इत्यनुवर्तनात्, 'सर्वत्र शाकल्यस्य' इति पाक्षिकनिषेधात् वा ।

Now, out of these two ways of securing option which one should we follow ? The answer is evident. We should get the option by *anuvṛtti* of वा, in the first place, because it is a shorter course (लाघव), and secondly, because when we consider about the first two *sūtras*, the prohibiting *sūtras* are *asiddha*. Kaiyaṭa resorts to the *anuvṛtti* of वा while commenting on the *Bhāṣya* on the *sūtra* नाज्झलौ (P. 1.1.10); he says in the *Pradīpa* द्विर्वचनमपि विभाषा । 'यरोऽनुनासिके अनुनासिको वा' इत्यतो 'वा' इत्यनुवर्तनात् ।

But, this puts us in a difficulty. If the option can be secured by the *anuvṛtti* of वा, then, the three *sūtras* on the option of Śākaṭāyana, Śākalya and *Ācāryas* become superfluous. Their purpose, which according to us is option only, has been already secured by the *anuvṛtti* of वा. Bhaṭṭoji takes this position in the *Manoramā* in the statement which I have quoted at the beginning of this topic.

Thus, the *anuvṛtti* of वा and these three *sūtras* cannot be placed together. We can have either the *anuvṛtti* of वा or these three *sūtras*. In this situation, the author of the *Bālamanoramā* suggests that it would be proper for us not to resort to the *anuvṛtti* of वा in the following *sūtras* rather than to reduce these three *sūtras* to superfluity. He says: एतत्सूत्रत्रयविरोधात् 'अनचि च' इत्यत्र वा ग्रहणं नानुवर्त्यमिति युक्तं प्रतिभाति ।

It should be noted in this context that the *Kāśikā* does not resort to the *anuvṛtti* of वा in P. 8.4.46, though it is carried to P. 8.4.47.

The whole discussion poses a problem for us. If the option could be secured by the *anuvṛtti* of वा (as is done by Kaiyaṭa and followed by Bhaṭṭoji), then why did Pāṇini write these three *sūtra*s at all? Pāṇini, who is so famous for the extreme economy of words in framing his *sūtras*, could have himself realised their superfluity. Moreover, it is not a case of a solitary word or expression or a single *sūtra* even; this superfluity applies to as many as three *sūtras* and that too coming in succession. We cannot say that Pāṇini framed these *sūtras* through inadvertance. Or could there be a purpose other than securing mere option that Pāṇini had by framing these three *sūtra*s?

We do not have any guidance either from Kātyāyana or

Patañjali in this respect. Both of them are silent on these *sūtras*. One thing, however, is certain. Both of them do not regard these *sūtras* superfluous. Had they thought so, they would have certainly said so. Many times Patañjali says:- अयं योग: शक्य: अकर्तुम् । What then is the purpose served by these *sūtras*?

If we study the *sūtras* अचो रहाभ्यां द्वे; अनचि च, and शरोऽचि (P. 8.4.46, 47, 49) together as one unit, we get the following rules of reduplication of letters:-

(i) When a conjunct consonant follows a vowel, the first consonant of the conjunct is doubled (अनचि च);

(ii) When that consonant begins with र् or ह् it is the second letter of the conjunct that is doubled अचो रहाभ्यां द्वे;

(iii) The letter ह् is not doubled, for it is not included in the यर् letters; and

(iv) If a शर् letter follows र् or ह् and is itself followed by a vowel, it is not doubled.

It will be of interest to note here that these rules correspond fully with the rules of *Kramasandhi* of the *Prātiśākhyas* e.g. स्वरानुस्वारोपहितो द्विरुच्यते संयोगादि: (ऋ.प्रा. 6-1), परं रेफात् (6-4), ऊष्मणो वा (6-8), न तूष्मा स्वरोष्मपर: (6-10).

The *Taittirīya* and the *Yajuḥ Prātiśākhyas* also have such rules (For a detailed treatment of this correspondence, see my *Indological Papers*, Vol. I pp. 69-71). The rules of द्विर्वचन of Pāṇini have such a full correspondence with the rules of the *Prātiśākhyas* that in this respect, the *Prātiśākhya* rules appear to serve the basis of Pāṇini.

The rules of द्विर्वचन or वर्णक्रम in the *Prātiśākhya* relate to the recital of the Vedic *Saṁhitā* and therefore we may say that the modes of recital of the Vedic *Saṁhitā* served as the basis of the द्विर्वचन rules of Pāṇini.

Now, the *Prātiśākhya*s themselves refer to more than one mode of *Saṁhitā* recital. For example, the *padas* आ । त्वा। रथम्। were recited in the *Saṁhitā* as आत्त्वारथम् in one school, while according to Śākalya, it would be recited as आत्वा रथम्. He would say अभ्रातेव and not अब्भ्रातेव like others. Where Śākalya recited महत्तदुल्बम् the *Pauṣkarasādi* school of *Taittirīyas* said महत्तदुल्ब्बम्. Thus, the doubling of a consonant while reciting the *Saṁhitā* varied from teacher to teacher and their peculiarities were handed down from student to student in each succeeding generation. Out of these varieties Śaunaka refers to the following:-

(1) संयुक्तं तु व्यञ्जनं शाकलेन (न क्रामति) (6.14). According to Śākalya a conjunct consonant is not to be reduplicated.

(2) दीर्घेण च मेतिवर्जम् (6.13). The letter छ् when preceded by a long vowel as well as a conjunct consonant preceded by a long vowel is not doubled except in the case of मा.

(3) न परक्रमोपधा (6.11). In the case of a conjunct consonant where the second letter is reduplicated, the previous one is not doubled.

(4) परश्च (T. Pr. II.2.23). A consonant followed by a consonant which is already doubled, is not reduplicated. There are many rules of this type. But, these are sufficient for our purpose. Out of these rules of *Prātiśākhya*, given above, the first agrees with the Pāṇinian rule सर्वत्र शाकल्यस्य; (P. 8. 4. 51) the second with दीर्घाद् आचार्याणाम् and आङ्माङोश्च (P. 6-1-74); and the third and the fourth with त्रिप्रभृति शाकटायनस्य respectively. The rule of Śākalya is in complete correspondence with the *Prātiśākhya* rule both in words and in sense, while the other *sūtras* agree in sense though the names of the *Ācāryas* are not mentioned in the *Prātiśākhya*. We may, therefore, say that not only in general rules, but, even the special modes of Vedic recitals on the point of द्विर्वचन as were followed by Śākalya and other *Ācāryas* have corresponding positions in the *sūtras* of Pāṇini.

Now, in so far as the rule of Śākalya as given in the *Prātiśākhya* refers to the Śākala mode of *Saṁhitā* recital, we may, on the basis of correspondence shown above between the *Prātiśākhya* rule and the Pāṇinian *sūtra*, say that the purpose of the *sūtra* सर्वत्र शाकल्यस्य is the same as that of the *Prātiśākhya* rule संयुक्तं तु व्यञ्जनं शाकलेन; that is, it points to the Śākala mode of Vedic recitation. The same may be said about the other two rules, viz, the rules of Śākaṭāyana and *Ācāryas*. We may therefore say that out of the seven *sūtras* given at the beginning, the first two refer to the general rules of द्विर्वचन, the next two refer to its prohibition and the last three refer to the special modes followed by different Vedic *Ācāryas* in the respective Vedic schools. What is all the more interesting, the Pāṇinian method in this respect fully agrees with the *Prātiśākhya* method. The *Prātiśākhyas* also give the general rules of द्विर्वचन first, then the prohibitions and lastly the different modes of the Vedic *Śākhās*. It therefore becomes clear that the purpose of the three *Sūtras* under consideration is not to allow option simpliciter only in respect of द्विर्वचन, but it is to note the different modes of the Vedic recitation which were prevalent and established according to Pāṇini. Though for a grammarian concerned with the *Laukika Bhāṣā* only, they meant only an option, yet, for the reciter of the Vedic *Saṁhitā,* they were not optional in this ordinary sense of option; that is to say, he could not choose any method of recital he liked. If he belonged to the *Śākala Śākhā*, he must follow the rule of *Śākalya*, if he belonged to the *Śākhā* of *Śākaṭāyana*, he must follow that rule. If this is to be termed as विभाषा at all, it is व्यवस्थितविभाषा only. Hence even if we have *anuvṛtti* of वा as suggested by Kaiyaṭa and Bhaṭṭoji, these three rules do not become superfluous, in so far as the general option allowed by वा is restricted by these three *sūtras* according to the *Śākhās* of Vedic recitation.

The intrinsic relation of the Pāṇinian *sūtras* with the *Saṁhitāpāṭha* and the *Padapāṭha* should now be clear to the readers.

The four cases I have discussed above, are taken from the *Laukika* section of the *Siddhānta-kaumudī*. I have shown how, shorn of their Vedic context and referring only to their *Bhāṣika* usage, these *sūtras* cannot be appreciated fully with regard to their import.

Many times again, we are not in a position to understand the peculiar structure of the *Aṣṭādhyāyī* and the order of the *sūtras* therein, if we limit our study to the *Siddhānta-kaumudī* only. For example, we study in the *Kaumudī* all the *Sandhi* rules in one *Prakaraṇa* with its sub-sections as अच्सन्धि, हल्सन्धि etc. Now, in the *Aṣṭādhyāyī* we find these rules at different places, e.g. there is one lot of *Sandhi* rules in the sixth *Adhyāya*, *Pāda* I and another in III. We get one more lot of rules in the eighth *Adhyāya*. These three lots are separated by nearly two chapters dealing with other matters. We wonder why it is so and feel that it would have been better if all the *Sandhi* rules would have been grouped in one lot and placed together at some convenient place in the *Aṣṭādhyāyī*. I have shown in detail elsewhere (see my paper on अष्टाध्यायीतील संहिताधिकारांविषयी थोडेसे published in the *Vidarbha Samshodhan Mandal Varshik*, 1980) how it is not possible to disturb the original placing of the *Sandhi sūtras* without violation of the Pāṇinian technique, and that they are to be kept where they are placed by Pāṇini, if we are to follow the Pāṇinian technique and method. We must remember that Pāṇini had no intention to teach us grammar as we understand it today. His purpose was to describe to us the morphological analysis of the *padas* in the language which was already known to the students; and the *padas* are taken for study as one lot consisting of words that are both *Vaidika* and *Laukika*.

Then again many *sūtras* of pre-Pāṇinian grammarians have been made known to us by Pandit Yudhiṣṭhira Mīmāṁsaka. I have given in the fifth chapter all these *sūtras* together for the benefit of the students. A comparison of the rules of Pāṇini with these *sūtras* will throw some new light on the understanding of Pāṇinian grammar.

Taking into consideration all these points, I feel that there is a need for the fresh study of the *sūtras* of Pāṇini. In the present work, the *sūtras* should be studied in the context of the *Saṁhitāpāṭha* and the *Padapāṭha* of the *Veda* along with the *Bhāṣika* context; they should be compared with the *Prātiśākhya* rules; the *Kṛt* affixes and the *Uṇādi* should be placed against the derivations of the *Nairuktas* and the *sūtras* should be compared with available *sūtras* of the pre-Pāṇinian period. This will give us some idea as to how the efforts of the previous thinkers merged into Pāṇini's *Aṣṭādhyāyī* to make it both a *Vedāṅga* and a *Bhāṣika Vyākaraṇa*.

■■

Bibliography

Abhinavabhāratī: Abhinavagupta
Agniveśya Gṛhyasūtra
Aitareya Brāhmaṇa
Amarakośaṭīkā: Bhānujī Dīkṣita
Āpastambha Dharmasūtra
Āpiśalī Śikṣā
Aṣṭādhyāyī: Pāṇini
Āśvalāyana Gṛhyasūtra
Atharvaveda
Atharvaveda Prātiśākhya: Hemacandra
Bālamanoramā
Baudhāyana Gṛhyasūtra
Bhāṣāvṛtti: Puruṣottamadeva
Bhāṣāvṛtti: Commentary by Sṛṣṭidhara
Bhāṣikā-sūtravyākhyā: Anantadeva
Bhūmikā (a commentary on the Prakriyā-kaumudī)
Bṛhadāraṇyaka Upaniṣad
Bṛhaddevatā
Brahmāṇḍa Purāṇa
Bṛhatśabdenduśekhara: Nāgeśa
Cākravarmaṇa
Candragomin's Vṛtti on Pratyāhāra-sūtras
Caraka-Cikitsā-sthāna (a commentary): Jajjahaṭa
Carakanyāsa: Bhaṭṭāraka Haricandra
Cārāyaṇīya Prātiśākhya
Cārāyaṇīya Śikṣā
Caturadhyāyī
Daśapādī
Devabodha
Dhātupāṭha-ṭīkā: Cannavīra
Dhātuvṛtti
Durga Bhūmikā

Dvādaśārṇava Cakraṭīkā: Mallavādinkṛta
Gaṇaratnamahodadhi: Vardhamāna
Gopatha Brāhmaṇa
Haimabṛhatvṛtticūrṇi
Haimavṛttyavacūrṇi
Haimaśabdānuśāsana
Hiraṇyakeśīya Gṛhyasūtra
Jaiminīya Upaniṣad Brāhmaṇa
Jayamaṅgalā (a commentary) on Bhaṭṭi
Kālāpa Candra Sandhi: Suṣeṇa Vidyābhūṣaṇa
Kāṇva Saṁhitā
Karṇadīpa
Kāśakṛtsna Vyākaraṇa Tathā Unke Upalabdha Sūtra: Mīmāṁsaka Yudhiṣṭhira
Kāśikā
Kātantra-vṛtti: Durga
Kātantra-Vyākaraṇa
Kāṭhaka Saṁhitā: (Kṛṣṇa Yajurveda)
Kavikalpadruma: Bopadeva
Kāvyādarśa: Daṇḍin
Kāvya Mīmāṁsā: Rājaśekhara
Kṛṣṇacarita: (ascribed to) Samudragupta
Laghuśabdenduśekhara
Laugākṣi Gṛhyasūtra: a Gloss by Devapāla
Mādhyandina Saṁhitā and Padapāṭha
Mahābhāṣyadīpikā: Bhartṛhari
Mahimnastotra (a commentary): Madhusūdana Sarasvatī
Māhiṣeya: a commentary on the Taittirīya Prātiśākhya
Maitrāyaṇyāraṇyaka
Maitrāyaṇī Prātiśākhya
Maitrāyaṇī Saṁhitā (Śukla Yajurveda)
Muṇḍakopaniṣad
Nānārthārṇavasaṁkṣepa: Keśava
Nighaṇṭu
Nayacakraṭīkā: Mallavādinkṛta

Nirukta
Nirukta (Commentary): Durga
Niruktabhāṣya: Skandasvāmi
Nyāsa (a commentary on the Kāśikā by Jinendrabuddhi)
Nyāyamañjirī: Jayantabhaṭṭa
Padamañjarī
Pāṇinīya Śikṣā; Pāṇinīya Śikṣā Sūtra
Paribhāṣāsaṅgraha
Paribhāṣāvṛtti: Puruṣottamadeva
Paribhāṣenduśekhara
Phiṭsūtra: Śantanu
Pradīpa: Kaiyaṭa
Prakriyāsarvasva: Nārayaṇa Bhaṭṭa
Prauḍha manoramā: Bhaṭṭoji Dīkṣita
Pūrvamīmāṁsā
Rāvaṇabhāṣya
Ṛgveda bhāṣya: Veṅkaṭamādhava
Ṛgveda Saṁhitā and Padapāṭha
Ṛk- Prātiśākhya
Ṛk-Tantra
Rudrādhyāya: ed. by Kashinath Shastri Lele
Rūpamālā: Vimala Sarasvatī
Śabdakaustubha: Bhaṭṭojī Dīkṣita
Śabdaśaktiprakāśikā: Jagadīśa Tarkālaṁkāra
Sāma Uttara
Sāmaveda Saṁhitā and Padapāṭha
Śāṅkarabhāṣya
Śāṅkhāyana Āraṇyaka
Śāṇkhāyana Gṛhyasūtra
Śatapatha Brāhmaṇa
Siddhānta Kaumudī: Bhaṭṭoji Dīkṣita
Siṁhasūrigaṇi: Mallavādiṅkṛta
Śiśupālavadham: Māgha
Sṛṣṭidhara's Commentary on the Bhāṣyavṛtti
Svarānukramaṇī: Veṅkaṭamādhava

Śvetāśvatara Upaniṣad
Taittirīya Āraṇyaka
Taittirīya Āraṇyaka Bhāṣya: Bhaṭṭa Bhāskara
Taittirīya Prātiśākhya
Taittirīya Saṁhitā and Padapāṭha
Tantravārtika: Kumārila
Taraṅgiṇī: Kṣīrasvāmin
Tattvabodhinī (a commentary on the Siddhānta Kaumudī)
Tribhāṣyaratna
Udyota: (A commentary on the Pātañjala Mahābhāṣya by Nāgeśa)
Uṇādisūtras
Uṇādisūtravṛtti: Ujjvaladatta
Uvaṭa-bhāṣya on the Taittirīya Prātiśākhya
Uvaṭa-bhāṣya on the Yajuḥ Prātiśākhya
Vaidikābharaṇa on the Taittirīya Prātiśākhya
Vājasaneyi Prātiśākhya
Vājasaneyi Saṁhitā and Padapāṭha of Śukla Yajurveda
Vākyapadīya: Bhartṛhari
Vākyapadīya: Commentaries by
a) (Svopajña Ṭīkā): Bhartṛhari
b) Puṇyarāja
c) Vṛṣabhadeva
d) Helārāja
Vālmīki Rāmāyaṇa
Vārtikas: Kātyāyana
Vāyupurāṇa
Vyākaraṇa Mahabhāṣya of Patañjali; F.Kilchorn Ed.: 1977
Yajurveda Saṁhitā and Padapāṭha
Yantrasarvasva: Bhāradvāja

Scheme of Transliteration

	अ	आ	इ	ई	उ	ऊ	ऋ	ॠ
Vowels	a	ā	i	ī	u	ū	ṛ	ṝ
	लृ	ए	ऐ	ओ	औ			
	ḷ	e	ai	o	au			
Anusvāra	.	ṁ						
Visarga	:	ḥ						
Consonants								
	क्	ख्	ग्	घ्	ङ्			
Gutturals	k	kh	g	gh	ṅ			
	च्	छ्	ज्	झ्	ञ्			
Palatals	c	ch	j	jh	ñ			
	ट्	ठ्	ड्	ढ्	ण्			
Cerebrals	ṭ	ṭh	ḍ	ḍh	ṇ			
	त्	थ्	द्	ध्	न्			
Dentals	t	th	d	dh	n			
	प्	फ्	ब्	भ्	म्			
Labials	p	ph	b	bh	m			
Semi-vowels	य्	र्	ल्	व्				
	y	r	l	v				

Sibilants

ś श् Palatal sibilant pronounced like the soft 's' of 'Russian'.

ṣ ष् Cerebral sibilant pronounced like 'sh' in 'shun'.

s स् pronounced as in 'sun'.